Anatomy of Architecture

Anatomy of Architecture

George Mansell

A&W Publishers, Inc.
New York

To JM for being JM

Endpapers: Pompidou Centre, Paris (Chusak)
Title Page: Baalbeck, Lebanon (Hamlyn Group Picture Library –
    George Roger)

Special thanks to Eric Brown and the illustrators at Product
Support (Graphics) Limited: Julian Baker, Gill Ballington,
Shirley Clarry, Graham Corner, Christine Moss, Caroline Plant,
Jonathan Preston, Allan J. Turner, and Derek Woodacre.
Book designed by Glynn Pickerill.

First published in the United States of America in 1979 by
A & W Publishers Inc.,
95 Madison Ave.,
New York, N.Y. 10016
By arrangement with The Hamlyn Publishing Group Limited
Copyright © 1979 by the Hamlyn Publishing Group Limited
London · New York · Sydney · Toronto
Astronaut House, Feltham, Middlesex, England
ISBN: 0-89479-043-9

Library of Congress Catalogue Number 78-71381

Phototypeset by Tradespools, Limited, Frome, Somerset.
Colour separations by Culver Graphics Limited, Lane End,
Buckinghamshire
Printed in Spain

Contents

Introduction

Everybody can recognize a building, but a building is not necessarily architecture. The difference is that a building must have aesthetic appeal to the senses to merit this distinction. Aesthetic appeal is achieved in a number of different ways. For example, it may be the overall shape of the edifice; the arrangement and detailing of the windows; the proportions of doors and windows to solid wall; the rhythm of columns or projections; the line of roof – be it pitched, soaring shell-shaped or domed – against the sky; the massing of glass wall or solid forms in vertical or horizontal lines; the projection of mass into space; colour and texture, carving and decoration; the sequence of rooms and their proportions. All these elements can have their individual appeal, but they do not all have to be present to make architecture. In fact, some styles and movements have relied on very few of them, for example, the decorative form of Late Baroque, known as Rococo. Qualities of painting and sculpture are sometimes present in architecture, but architecture is unique in its quality of enclosing space, and has been referred to as the 'Mother of the Arts'.

Spatial concepts in architecture have developed through structure, and structure has developed through simple column and lintel construction, the arch, vault, dome, and the use of iron, to the amazing feats performed today using steel, glass, plastics, and reinforced concrete. The structural aspect is given prominence in this book because it helps an understanding of the different styles and movements portrayed here. Essentially, therefore, this book is a guide to architecture.

Because the book spans many ages, many civilizations, and many countries, a building chosen to illustrate a point of style or movement will usually be one of a number of possible examples, and there may be other, equally good examples which might have been included, without leading to a better understanding of the subject. Architecture portrays people, and both the structure, and sometimes the immense building operations which went with it, are given space in the book. Tribal or national characteristics, social and political conditions are also mentioned for their influence on the architecture of the time. Obviously, architecture tends to flourish in times of peace, particularly if there is wealth to finance the work; but war brings its influences too. The castle developed because it was prudent to build enclosures which were difficult to invade and easy to defend with relatively few men. The castle and the mediaeval walled city gradually became redundant after the discovery of gunpowder. The Greeks, who had stone and marble ready at hand – superb materials for their style, built their temples in thankfulness to their gods for successes in war. The Romans conquered the Greeks and copied their classical detailing, adding ideas of their own. War and trade were the means by which men learnt and spread fresh ideas, exchanged cultures, and developed new architectural forms. The process still goes on. New building techniques are invented; new problems match them. Manhattan's skyscrapers arose from the need to build upwards rather than outwards in view of the confined space and high land values of twentieth-century New York. But in all ages, in all styles, in all movements, man's spirit of endeavour has reached upwards to produce architecture. Structure, form, and decoration alone cannot produce it.

The material in this book is presented in roughly chronological sequence, so that the reader can follow more easily the development of and changes in style from one period to another. Breaks occur when the story switches from Europe to Central America, India, Japan, and China, all of which developed their own forms of architecture parallel in time to developments in the western world and Asia Minor. The bibliography will assist readers to follow up in greater depth particular aspects of architecture which appeal to them.

The Ancient World

In the western hemisphere, the countries of the ancient world centred around the Aegean Sea and the adjacent mainland. Egypt, Mesopotamia and Persia were graced in the same period with monumental architecture on a scale never attempted by Aegean civilization. The Egyptian pyramids and those of pre-Columbian America of a much later date had certain similarities, but, whereas the Egyptian pyramids were burial grounds, those of pre-Columbian America were platforms for temples, and were only rarely used as tombs.

The ancient Egyptians were ruled by priest-kings, the pharaohs, about whom

we have some knowledge from the valuables, household possessions, wall inscriptions, and carvings buried with them; also from an Egyptian monk by the name of Manetho who wrote a history of Egypt in Greek in the third century B.C. in which he arranged the Egyptian kings into thirty dynasties. It was King Menes of the first dynasty who united upper and lower Egypt and founded Memphis as the captial.

From the very beginning, the Egyptian people regarded their king as a deity, equal to the gods they worshipped, and he was usually identified with one of the gods. As Horus the king was

STEP PYRAMID OF ZOSER, Sakkāra, Egypt. Third millennium B.C.

regarded as the earthly form of the ancient god of the sky, pre-eminent when the two kingdoms of upper and lower Egypt were united. Later, the king was Son of Ra, the sun god; then he took on the personality of Osiris who was supposed to rule over the realm of the dead. In Egyptian mythology, Horus had a number of different identities. There were local gods too who sometimes took the form of animals and retained animal heads when they assumed human form. The religious influence on Egyptian culture cannot be condensed in a few sentences. Some gods were more important than others. According to the Egyptians, the world began when Atum Ra (the sun) created himself and rose from Nun (the ocean). He created Shu (air) and Tefnut (moisture) and these two created Geb (earth) and Nut (sky). Their children were Osiris and his wife Isis, and Seth and his wife Nephthys, Horus being the son of Osiris and Isis.

By the time of King Zoser of the third dynasty (2780–2680 B.C.), united Egypt was so rich and well organized that he was able to commission the great constructions associated with his name. According to Manetho, a senior officer of Zoser's court, Imhotep was responsible for the colossal step pyramid built of limestone at Sakkāra. With its ceremonial and administrative buildings it occupied a huge rectangular space enclosed by stone walls. The pyramid was to be Zoser's tomb, and it became the model for those of his successors, among which the pyramids of Sekhemkhet, Khaba, and Huni have been identified.

The first monarch of the fourth dynasty (2680–2565 B.C.), King Snefru, had the stepped pyramid changed to the four-sided version, the style which those at Gizeh have made world famous. Snefru's architects seem to have been uncertain about the change in style, to judge from the two pyramids built at Dahshūr. One appears to have had a change of slope midway through construction. The other has a less steep incline than usual. It was left to Cheops (or Khufu), successor to Snefru, to build the classic example, made possible by the political and economic circumstances of the time.

The kings of the fourth dynasty were extremely powerful, partly because there had been a period of relative peace and prosperity during the third dynasty, and partly because Snefru, a politically skilful ruler, controlled affairs by appointing to high office family members who supported him. The remains of tombs and funerary inscriptions provide evidence of the King's considerable glory. With the succession of Cheops, the government became even more centralized. He was the embodiment of Horus and, with great resources of men and materials at his command, he was able to have built the Great Pyramid at Gizeh.

Originally, the pyramid was over 228 metres square and 137 metres high and covered 5 hectares or more. The limestone blocks with which it was originally covered had fine joints and weighed 2.5 tonnes each. They were brought in barges by canal and across flooded land from the quarries at Tura or Ma'sara or both. Thousands of peasants provided the labour when floods or other conditions prevented their working on the land. The whole operation must have been a masterpiece of organization and control. A model in the Boston Museum of Science, USA, is a reconstruction of the building process and shows peasants winding their way round the sides of the pyramid in an ascent to the top. The sides of the pyramid faced the cardinal points of the compass, as was the custom and one which was adopted by some other civilizations. Because the plan was changed from time to time during building operations, there are three chambers inside the pyramid. The last one near the centre, the King's chamber, was approached along an upward sloping gallery with corbelled vaulting, and contained the sarcophagus of Cheops. The chamber itself was rectangular in shape, about 10.5 metres long and half as wide. It was 5.8 metres high and roofed with five tiers of massive stone beams separated by air spaces. Near the pyramid to the south-east were smaller pyramids for the King's three queens. There were also graves built for the funerary barges. The huge burial ground at Gizeh has minor tombs, and also contains the smaller pyramids of Chefren and Mycerinos.

The Egyptians had political as well as functional and ceremonial reasons for the great constructions at Gizeh. They wished to focus attention upon the King, to conceal his body and the worldly possessions buried with him for use in his after life. The walls of the tomb were covered with scenes from his everyday life on earth, his achievements and relationship with the gods. Statues of the King were buried with him. In fact, everything was done to recreate for the dead King his life on earth.

The Great Pyramid of Cheops was

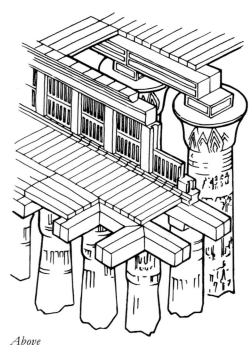

Above
GREAT TEMPLE OF AMMON, Karnak, Egypt. Fourteenth century B.C. Hypostyle hall. Pierced slabs of the clerestory can be seen above the columns.

Opposite
GREAT PYRAMID OF CHEOPS, Gizeh, Egypt. Third millennium B.C. The entrance way.

Below
GREAT PYRAMID OF CHEOPS, Gizeh, Egypt. Third millennium B.C. View from the entrance to the tomb on the north side showing the galleries leading to the Queen's chamber and the King's chamber in the centre of the pyramid.

Opposite
GREAT TEMPLE OF ABU SIMBEL, Nubia. Thirteenth century B.C. The four colossal figures are of Rameses II; the tiny figure is his wife, Nefertari.

built during the period known as the Old Kingdom which finished with the end of the sixth dynasty (c. 2258 B.C.). The next period, the Middle Kingdom, lasted from the seventh dynasty (2258 B.C.) until the end of the seventeenth dynasty (1570 B.C.). The founder of the twelfth dynasty (1991–1786 B.C.), Amenemhat I, established a new capital at Ith-tawe, south of Memphis. Most of the great works of his reign and others of the Middle Kingdom, apart from funerary constructions, were overbuilt during the next period of the New Kingdom, from 1570 to 1085 B.C.

The Great Temple of Ammon, Karnak at Thebes, hailed as the greatest of the Egyptian temples, began as a small shrine during the time of the Middle Kingdom. Thebes had become the capital of Egypt and successive monarchs added to the Karnak temple during the period of the New Kingdom. Thothmes I started the additions; Rameses I, Seti I, and Amenophis III continued the work, as did others later. The Egyptian temple was not a place for congregational worship – ritual was the prerogative of the priests – but the courts and halls added by successive monarchs enhanced the power of the throne and their own deified images in the eyes of the people. Buildings were arranged on strong axial lines. Leading up to them were the great pylons, a typical feature of Egyptian ceremonial architecture. The pylons were pairs of high towers with battered walls, carved and incised, flanking a huge entrance. At Karnak, different monarchs

added their own pylons, building up the emotion of the processional route to the sanctuary, in a similar manner to the entrance portals of the Forbidden City, Peking. From the great court at Karnak the processional way led through six pairs of pylons up to the hypostyle hall, built in the time of Seti I and Rameses II. The hall's stone slab roof was supported by sixteen rows of columns. The two central rows of columns rise higher than those at the sides, reaching a height of nearly 21.5 metres and almost 3.6 metres in diameter each. They divide the central space into three aisles which are dimly lit through stone grilles forming a clerestory supported by the first row of lower columns on each side. The tall columns have bell-shaped papyrus flower capitals and the shorter columns lotus bud capitals. The columns and walls of immense size dwarf the individual, but a sense of scale is restored by the incised figures, which relieve but do not reduce the dominant mass of stonework.

The rock cut temple was another Egyptian form. The Great Temple of Abu Simbel and the smaller temple built by Rameses II in the nineteenth dynasty and inaugurated about the middle of the thirteenth century B.C. illustrates the type. It has a unique history. Abu Simbel was buried in sand for hundreds of years until a Swiss explorer, Johann Ludwig Burckhardt, rediscovered it in 1813. It was nearly lost for ever in the 1960s when the completion of the Aswan High Dam threatened to submerge it 46 metres below the water

of the Nile, raised to form a new lake. A world appeal from UNESCO for assistance in saving the temple resulted in a number of international schemes, of which the one submitted by a Swedish firm of engineers, Valtenbyggnadsbyran, was chosen. An international Joint Venture Abu Simbel was entered into by firms from West Germany, the United Arab Republic, France, Italy, and Sweden, financed through UNESCO by the United Arab Republic and the USA. The temple was cut up into blocks, removed and re-erected on higher ground above the new lake, orientated as originally, but with a concrete vault supporting the overlaying rock. The four colossal seated figures of Rameses II, 20 metres high, carved on the front, originally out of the hill face, are renowned. Over the entrance is a smaller figure of Queen Nefertari. In the main hall are eight statues of Rameses, portrayed as representations of Osiris, about 9 metres high. Carvings and statues, friezes depicting the King's victories, and representations of the gods adorn the interior, and, outside, a famous frieze of Nubian prisoners is incised on the stone wall to the south of the entrance. In the inner sanctuary beyond the main hall are statues of the three gods to whom the temple was dedicated: Ptah, Amon, and Re-Horakti, and a statue of Rameses II himself. The smaller temple, dedicated to Hathor, identified with Queen Nefertari, and rescued at the same time as the larger temple, has six statues on the outside,

9 metres high: two statues of the Queen are flanked by statues of the King. The columns of the hall inside bear the head of Hathor-Nefertari, and the walls are incised with scenes from the King and Queen's reign.

We move on now to Mesopotamia where there was clay in abundance for making bricks, but where stone and wood had to be imported. The temple was the most important complex of the early Mesopotamian cities, and from the temple standing on a mound, the ziggurat or temple tower developed. The remains of the ziggurat of Tchoga-Zanbil (thirteenth century B.C.) in the kingdom of Elam shows that it was four-sided with five stepped terraces. The ground floor tier was shallower than the others, and the first tier terrace was reached by recessed flights of steps in the centre of each side. Thereafter, the steps ascended from one side only, from the south-west side to the second tier, from the south-east side to the third and fourth tiers, and from the north-east to the final ascent.

To the north-east of Elam, the city of Khorsabad, built by Sargon II (722–705 B.C.) contained the most important buildings in Assyria. The city was planned as a square with defensive walls and two circular arched gateways. Sargon's palace sat astride the city walls, at one end, on a vast platform level with the top of the wall. A ramp leading up to the main entrance was arched and set between massive square towers. Inside the gate was the great entrance court with a number of temples to the left-hand side and administrative buildings to the right. Immediately ahead were the private and state apartments with their own large court. The throne room was built around a third court. Walls constructed of mud bricks were usually about 6 metres thick, plastered and decorated with friezes depicting scenes from the King's life. Brilliantly-coloured glazed bricks were a feature of Assyrian art, associated with Khorsabad, and the effigy of a human-headed winged lion was used frequently to guard entrances. This figure was incorporated into the entrance jamb, and was sculpted in such a way as to be complete from either the front or the sides.

The ziggurat itself eventually became a sacred monument, although usually associated with a temple complex. The one at Khorsabad appears linked with the palace, near which it is sited. It is nearly 46 metres square and about the same height. The staircase approach described for Tchoga was abandoned in favour of a ramp along the seven tiers of terraces up to the temple on the summit. The brickwork was plastered and painted in different colours.

Approximately due south of Khorsabad, the city of Babylon on the banks of the river Euphrates was rebuilt by Nebuchudnezzar II (605–563 B.C.). Khorsabad may well have been used as a model. The principal buildings were spread out along the river front with a great processional way behind them, along which the gods were carried to the New Year Festival. The famous Ishtar gate at one end of the processional way had walls finished in blue-glazed bricks decorated with low relief figures of yellow and white bulls and dragons, a masterly piece of craftsmanship. The god of the city was Marduk. Many years earlier, in the second millenium B.C., the idol of Marduk had been stolen by the Hittites, and was only restored to Babylonia by the Kassites a quarter of a century later, by a king named Agum II

Below
PALACE OF SARGON (restored), Khorsabad, Assyria. Eighth century B.C.

Bottom
PALACE OF PERSEPOLIS, Persia. Fifth century B.C. Hall of the Hundred Columns (restored).

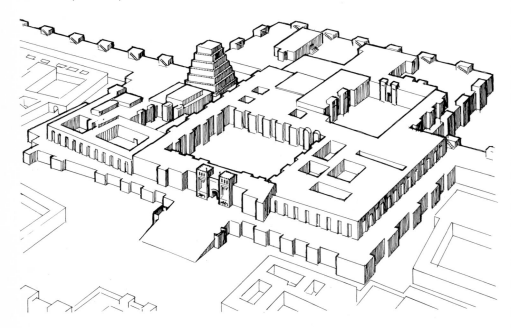

who made Marduk equal to their own god, Shuqamuna. The Elamites overcame the Kassite rule of Babylonia towards the end of the second millenium. Marduk's temple, priests' quarters, and ziggurat occupied a walled enclosure in the northern part of Babylon. The seven-tier ziggurat was the biblical Tower of Babel. Babylon did not possess stone; nonetheless the town walls with closely-spaced towers, projecting inside only, and smooth-faced slanting walls on the outside, presented a formidable defense.

In an easterly direction from Babylon, the palace and city of Persepolis was begun by Darius I (522–486 B.C.), the Archaemenian king who made the city the capital of Persia instead of Pasargadae, the burial place of Cyrus the Great who had conquered Babylon in 539 B.C. The Persians went on to overwhelm northern Egypt in the reign of Cambyces II, who succeeded Darius I. Alexander the Great, who invaded Egypt in 332 B.C., had earlier sacked Persepolis, burning down the palace. The contacts of the Persians, through war, with the Egyptians and the Greeks influenced their architecture, and the later development of Persepolis itself.

Unlike the axial planning of Sargon's palace, the Palace of Persepolis was informal. Darius's apartments and those of Xerxes I (486–465 B.C.) were adjacent to one another. Xerxes began, and his successor Artaxerxes completed, the Hall of the Hundred Columns, a vast throne room over 61 metres square and over 10.5 metres high. The stone columns were fluted, with moulded bases and curious capitals which had Ionic-type volutes, turned on end and topped with a double bull carving. The columns supported the beams of the flat roof. The palace is also noted for the wonderful approach staircase, 6.7 metres wide and shallow enough for a horseman to ride up, and the stonework reliefs at the sides. The endless sculpted figures are arranged in three bands, separated by ribbons of stonework, carved with a regular pattern of rosettes. Similar stone dados line the terrace of the palace's Apadama, the great audience hall of Darius II.

From the mainland, the story of the ancient world shifts to the sea-based power of the Aegean, centred upon the Island of Crete. In the second millenium B.C., the Aegean culture had developed to an extent equalling that of the mainland of Egypt and Mesopotamia. But by 1400 B.C., Cnossos, the capital of Crete, had been destroyed, and the Cretan

civilization collapsed. After that, the mainland centres around the Aegean, constantly at war amongst themselves, gradually gained control of the seas and formed loose alliances with one another. The palace of King Minos at Cnossus, and the smaller palace at Phaestus, are the two important examples on Crete of the dominant building style.

Cnossus was built at the height of Crete's power on a site covering 2.5 hectares or more, with much of the building on two levels. There were halls of state, private apartments for the King and Queen, gardens and terraces and open courts. The only defensive measure was a tower on the north side, with views down the road to the city and port, and another view commanding the entrance approach to the great court of the palace.

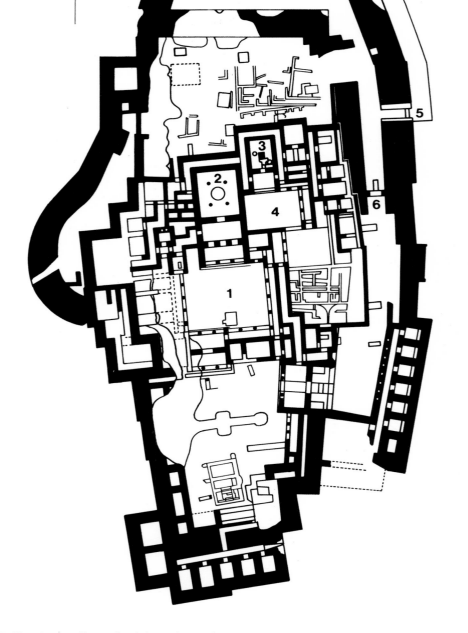

CITADEL OF TIRYNS, Greece. c. 1300 B.C. Plan:
1 court to megaron,
2 megaron,
3 lesser megaron,
4 court to lesser megaron,
5 outer gateway,
6 inner gateway,
7 lower enclosure of citadel.

The royal domestic arrangements were remarkably advanced. The rooms were arranged on two virtually identical storeys and partly on a third storey. A wide stone staircase, with a stone wall on one side and columns opening into a light well on the other, supported the return staircase above, in a similar way to modern buildings. Apartments believed to be for the Queen contained a bathroom, and a water closet with flushing system. The palace had underground drainage with socketed earthenware pipes. The main hall at Cnossus was also interesting. At one end was a court, at the other an anteroom. The anteroom had eleven doors: four opening into the main hall and seven in two sides opening on to an L-shaped courtyard. The doors pivoted back into their jambs – a favourite device in Aegean palaces for important rooms adjacent to open courts, as it enabled the rooms to be opened up in summer. The anteroom at Cnossus made it possible to enlarge the main hall or keep it private. Walls at Cnossus were constructed mainly of gypsum blocks or of stone up to dado height and brick or rubble above the stonework, enclosed by timber framing. Columns throughout the palace tapered downwards. They had large capitals, and were made of cedarwood. The palace of Phaestus was similar to Cnossus, but on a smaller scale.

The collapse of Cnossus and the transfer of power to a more warlike people resulted in a change of function of a palace, as illustrated by the Citadel of Tiryns (*c.* 1300 B.C.) on the mainland. The site was a steep-sided hilltop. The citadel's stone walls, never less than 6 metres thick, were increased to 15 metres thick at points where storage chambers were placed. The entire layout was of a defensive nature. The site was elongated in shape, and the narrow northern half was enclosed with an inner defense wall across the middle. This half was used by peasants and their cattle as a place of refuge at night and against attack. There were, of course, no towns with walls. The higher part of the site was occupied by the palace. From the entrance in the centre of the site, the approach to the palace led through two gateways between ramparts, then through two *propylaea* to the main court in front of the *megaron*, the great hall of the citadel. Both the megaron and propylaea at Tiryns had profound implications for later styles of architecture. The latter foreshadowed the propylaea of classical Greece, for example the propylaea of the Acropolis, Athens.

From the megaron descended the basis of the Greek temple, and the hall of the Roman house, if not the Anglo-Saxon hall in England.

The megaron at Tiryns faced south into a large court. Two wooden columns, tapering downwards and resting on stone bases, divided the entrance into three openings. Inside, four pivot-hung doors led to an anteroom, with access through a centrally-placed doorway into the megaron itself, a large room about 9.5 metres by 12, with four wooden pillars supporting the roof. The floor was of stucco, painted with a checker design. Walls were plastered and painted with a frieze. In the centre of the room was an open hearth and to one side a raised dais, suggesting that the megaron was used as a reception room as well as for domestic purposes.

The palace at Mycenae, built about the same time as Tiryns, was also a citadel. One of its astonishing features is the Lion Gate which still remains. It has an enormous stone lintel, some 5 metres long, spanning the gateway and resting upon massive stone jambs. Above is a triangular opening of corbelled-out stonework filled with a single block of stone. This block is carved with the figures of two lions facing a central column, their forefeet resting on the column's plinth.

Classical Greece

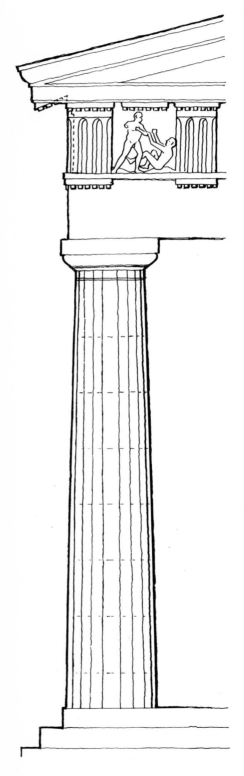

Doric order.

Greek architecture achieved its finest form in the clear statement of the developed temple which had such a profound influence on later western European architecture. Greek enthusiasm for mental and physical culture found expression in the sculptural quality of its architecture. Using entirely different materials and methods of construction, we see a similar striving after form in Oscar Niemeyer's Brazilia Cathedral or the steel and glass towers of Mies van der Rohe in the modern movements of the middle twentieth century.

Political influences were crucial for Greek architecture. After the break-up of the Minoan and Mycenaeum civilizations, the warring tribes gradually settled down over a period of centuries, and, from their intermingling, two very different influences became dominant: those of the Dorian and Ionian races of Greek history. These two races, very different in character, occupied the Greek mainland, Asia Minor, Sicily, and the heel of Italy, and they developed their finest architecture in the cities of the Greek Hellenic period (650–323 B.C.). It was during this time that the Greek cities became united against the Persians whom they defeated at Marathon in 490 B.C., and ten years later at the sea battle of Salamis, and the land battle of Plataea, coinciding with the defeat of the Carthaginians at Himera.

The victorious Greeks were drawn together both on the Greek mainland and in the western lands, and the new spirit of unity combined with the wealth which the victories brought, were responsible for the monumental building which followed, much of it in thankfulness to the gods.

After the death of Alexander the Great in 323 B.C., his empire, which had already shifted its centre from the Greek mainland westward, became split up. There was no great advancement in Greek architecture and in this period of unrest, architectural decadence began to set in. The period was known as the Hellenistic Greek period (323–30 B.C.), and it ended with the Roman occupation of Greek territory. Indeed, the annexation of Greek cities in Italy began in 282 B.C. Sicily was invaded in the first Punic War (264–241 B.C.), and the contact between the Romans and the Greeks brought Greek influence to bear on the development of Roman architecture.

The Aegeans discussed in the last chapter had no noteworthy religious architecture, and it may seem strange therefore that the Greeks were inspired quite differently. But the Greeks were a religious people, and were consciously thankful for their successes in war. They were conscious too of the permanence of spirit life in nature, dedicating shrines and holy places to their many gods. The most important gods were the twelve Olympians of Greek fable: Zeus, the ruler of earth and heaven; Hera, his wife; Apollo, the sun god; Athena, queen of the air; Poseidon, the sea god; Dionysus, patron of wine and drama; Demeter, the goddess of agriculture; Artemis, goddess of the chase; Hermes, messenger of the gods; Aphrodite, goddess of love and beauty; Hephaestus, god of fire; Ares, god of war.

Most Greek temples were dedicated to a god, and each god was supposed to have his or her favourite dwelling place. Thus, Zeus dwelt at Olympus; his wife, Hera, at Samos and Argos; Athena at Athens; Apollo at Delos and Delphi. The temples were not places in which to congregate, as with western religions; congregations worshipped outside the building. Architecturally, therefore, the Greek temple was intended to create an impact when viewed from outside, as it emphatically did.

The developed Greek temple was the result of the Greeks' aspiration to their ideal of a house for a god. It is not surprising, therefore, that the earliest form of temple should have developed from the *megaron* of the Aegean period, discussed in the last chapter. A dedicated temple usually had a statue of the god inside, and it faced eastwards towards the main entrance, through which an outdoor congregation might catch glimpses of their god. The statue stood in the temple's main enclosure or sanctuary, called a *cella* or *naos*. A porch, called a *pro-naos* was built in front of the cella on the east side, and usually another porch, called an *opisthodomus* was placed at the rear on the west side, sometimes fitted with bronze grilles and used by the priests as a treasury. To this basic form the Greeks contributed a colonnaded portico round the temple, known as a *peristyle* – hence the term 'peripteral temple'. An altar was placed outside, in front of the temple, and only a small table for offerings stood in front of the statue.

As in other periods of architecture – for example Romanesque or Gothic – the desire to erect larger or more impressive structures led to changes in style, or the exploitation of new structural materials (such as reinforced concrete in modern times). The early Greek temples had stucco-covered sun-dried brick walls with lengths of timber inserted horizontally to bind the bricks together. The walls were set on a stone base up to 1 metre or 1.3 metres high. The sturdy peristyle or colonnade sustained any outward thrust from the rafters of the shallow-pitched roof, because the roof truss which counteracts the spread of rafters had not been developed in those days. Sometimes, interior columns were used when the span between walls was too great.

Remains of an early Dorian temple to Apollo, at Thermum in Aetolia, indicated that the cella walls were of unburnt brick and that there were columns down the centre to support the roof. The peristyle columns were of wood, as was the network of beams above the columns, but all the columns had stone footings. Even in later temples built in stone or marble, columns were never far apart because of the danger of the lintels cracking. The Greeks were fortunate in having an abundance of stone and marble available for building.

The fully developed Greek temple followed two different styles, adopted respectively by the Dorian Greeks and the Ionian Greeks. These two styles formed the first two Greek orders of architecture, so defined in classical times. An order consisted of the *column* or upright support, the *capital* at the top, the *base* at the bottom and the area of horizontal masonry supported by the

Left
Ionic order.

Below
Corinthian order.

columns, known as the *entablature*. The entablature was divided into three parts: the *architrave* at the bottom, the *frieze* in the middle, and the *cornice* at the top. The proportions of columns, entablature, mouldings, and ornament varied in the two orders, and there was considerable variation in the detail used for different temples.

The Doric and Ionic orders were contemporary, although the Doric is usually placed first. A third order, the Corinthian, came at a later stage when the Ionic order started to become more decorative in its decline. The Doric style developed mainly in southern Italy, Sicily, Cyrenaica in north Africa, and the Greek mainland, while the Ionic spread from Asia Minor. The best examples of both are sited on the Greek mainland.

A people's character as well as their tribal customs may be portrayed in their architecture and art. The Dorian Greeks were sturdy, severe, and self-sufficient, and the simplicity and directness of the Doric style was characteristic of them. The Ionian Greeks were semi-Asiatic, more emotional in character than the Dorians, and the less formal characteristics of the Ionic style might be expected.

The stone and marble details of the Greek styles were derived from the parts of earlier wooden temples. Columns were previously tapered tree trunks. The capital, with its upper portion (*abacus*) square, and lower portion (*echinus*) rounded, was the easiest way of transmitting a rectangular-shaped wall on to a circular column. In the Doric order the abacus was plain, in the Ionic and Corinthian it was moulded. The Doric echinus was plain rounded, the Ionic was decorated, with a moulding (egg and tongue) appearing between the curved scrolls or *volutes*, the most striking feature of the Ionic order. The volutes were derived from the Egyptian Lotus design. In very early forms the volutes were painted or scratched on the wooden surface. An early wooden form of capital, with a *palmette* between the volutes, survives from Neandria in Cyprus. The Greek Corinthian capital was deeper than the Ionic and the sides of the abacus curved outwards to points at the corners. At its best, the capital, with inverted bell-shaped sides, had two tiers of eight acanthus leaves with small volutes, curving outwards to support the corners of the abacus, and inwards to meet under small ornaments. The origin of the style may have been the Egyptian bell cap.

The Greek column also varied according to the three orders. The Doric column was sturdy, had no base and stood directly on a platform, usually with three steps, and called a *crepidoma*. The column normally had twenty *flutes* meeting in sharp *arrises*, and in the Hellenic period its height with capital was about four to six times the diameter of the base. The Ionic column was more slender, measuring about seven times the diameter of the base, had about twenty-four flutes separated by *fillets* and not arrises, and the height including the capital and base was about nine times the diameter of the lower part of the column. The Corinthian column resembled the Ionic but became taller and slimmer as it developed.

TEMPLE OF APHAIA, Aegina. *c.* 490 B.C.
Plan:
1 ramp to entrance.
2 pronaos,
3 cella or naos,
4 opisthodomus.

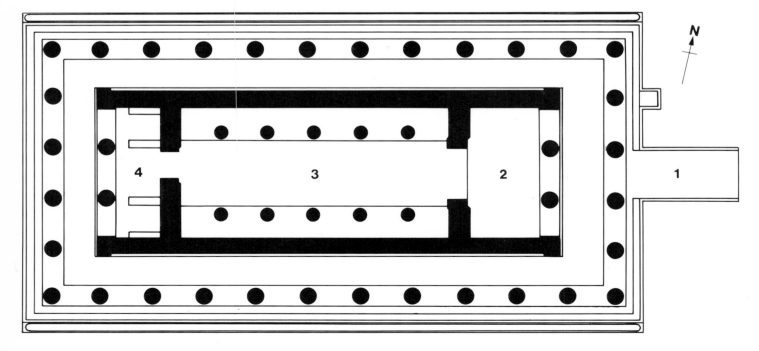

The Greek entablature is clearly identifiable with a wooden structure. The architrave was derived from wooden beams spanning the spaces between the columns. In the Doric frieze, the ends of wooden crossbeams were indicated by the *triglyphs* over each column and over the space between each column; *metopes* represented the spaces between wooden beams. In wooden temples the crossbeams supported the trussless roof rafters, and these would have been fixed to a plate at right angles to the ends of the crossbeams. The wooden plate was represented in stone architecture by the lowest part of the cornice. The *mutules* represented the ends of rafters and the *guttae* the wooden pins holding the rafters to the plate. The Ionic stone entablature started in Asia Minor with an architrave representing two or three

beams and a cornice. Later, influenced by the Doric style on the Greek mainland, the Ionic entablature included a frieze in some cases. The Corinthian entablature was virtually the same as the Ionic in Greek architecture, no doubt because in the Hellenic period the Corinthian order was usually used in Ionic or Doric temples.

In their attention to detail the Greeks introduced refinements to counteract certain optical illusions. For example, the Doric columns of the Parthenon and other temples had a curvature (*entasis*) as well as tapering towards the top, thus increasing the appearance of strength. Also the cornice, architrave, and stylobate of the Parthenon had an upward tilt in the centre, to counteract the appearance of sagging in their long horizontal lines.

TEMPLE OF APHAIA, Aegina. *c.* 490 B.C. The pro-naos, in front, is approached by ramp to the stylobate. The interior of the naos had two rows of columns. The columns, capitals, and the entablature proclaim the temple's Doric origins. The column and beam structure was used universally by the Greeks. Timber roof structures were without trusses.

Greek Doric temples varied in size as the style developed, but the plan changed little in its basic form. The early temple at Thermium had five columns facing front and rear and fifteen at the sides. Later examples were shorter in proportion. The temple of Aphaia, on Aegina, an island near Athens (*c.* 490 B.C.), is considered to be virtually the most perfect Greek temple. Aphaia had six columns facing the front and rear and only twelve columns facing the sides. The interior had two rows of two-tier columns separated by a simple architrave. Most of the external columns were monolithic, but some were built up in drums, a common form of construction. The building materials were largely limestone coated with marble stucco. The entablature was brilliantly coloured and the pediments – the triangular-shaped gable ends to the roof at

Below
PARTHENON, Athens. Begun 477 B.C.

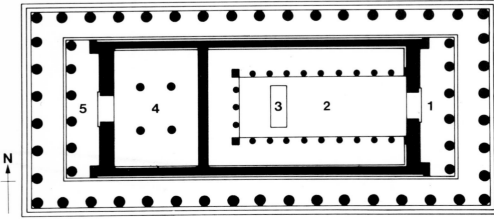

Left
PARTHENON, Athens. Begun 447 B.C.
Plan:
1 pronaos,
2 cella or naos,
3 statue of Athena Parthenos,
4 Parthenon or Virgin's Chamber,
5 opisthodomus.

Opposite
CHORAGIC MONUMENT OF LYSICRATES, Athens. *c.* 334 B.C.

front and rear – were filled with marble sculpture. The Doric temple of Poseidon, Paestum (*c.* 460 B.C.), slightly earlier than Aphaia, is one of the best preserved of Greek temple remains. The temple of Zeus, Olympia (*c.* 460 B.C.), and the Theseion, Athens (449–444 B.C.) were other examples of the Doric style at its best. The Theseion was converted into a church by the Byzantine Greeks, and an apse was added to the end. But the most famous of the Doric temples was the Parthenon, by the architects Ictinus and Callicrates.

Built between 447 and 432 B.C., the Parthenon was dedicated to Athena Parthenos, the virgin Athena. It was a vast structure, with eight columns in the front and to the rear, and seventeen columns facing the sides. The external columns were 10.4 metres high. The cella had a columned ambulatory on three sides. The statue of Athena Parthenos carved in wood by the great Greek sculptor, Pheidias, was embellished with gold, ivory, and precious stones. The entablature was quite remarkable. Bronze shields ornamented the architrave, and the friezes inside and outside the building were beautifully sculptured, showing evidence of Ionic influence. The frieze along the top of the cella was the famous Panathenaic scene of Greek knights, cavalry, chariots, men, and youths which every fourth year ascended the Acropolis to present the 'Peplos'–a kind of shawl–to the goddess Athena. Portions of the frieze carved in low relief marble can be seen in the British Museum, in the Louvre, and in the Athens Museum. The fate of the Parthenon has been as remarkable as the building itself. It became a Byzantine Christian church in the fifth-sixth centuries, a Latin church under the Frankish dukes of Athens in the thirteenth century, and a Turkish mosque in the fifteenth century. It was much damaged by explosion when the powder magazine stored there by the Turks blew up in the seventeenth century, and further damage occurred through an earthquake in the nineteenth century.

The equivalent of the Parthenon in Ionic architecture was to be found at Ephesus, Asia Minor. Ephesus was one of the earliest Ionic settlements and became the leader of the Greek cities in the Ionian Federation. The Ionic temple of Artemis, Ephesus, was rebuilt five times. The fifth temple, known as the Later Temple (*c.* 350 B.C.), and the fourth temple, known as the Archaic Temple (*c.* 560 B.C.), were considered to be one of the seven wonders of the ancient

ERECHTHEION, Athens. *c.* 421–05 B.C.

world in their time. Unlike Doric temples, the Ionic temple of Artemis had double columns to the peristyle. Exceptionally, the temple had eight columns with sculptured lower drums facing the front and spaced at decreasing intervals from the centre outwards. Of the columns, which numbered 117 according to some authorities, 36 were sculptured at the base, and much of the detail varied. In its time, the Later Temple of Artemis was the centre of the Ionian festival in Asia Minor, as the Parthenon was the centre of the Panathenaic festival on the mainland. Another famous example of the Ionic style with a double-columned peristyle was the temple of Didyma, near Miletus. Begun in about 330 B.C. just before the end of the Hellenic period, building went on during the Hellenistic period, but the temple was never completed.

Most well known of the Ionic temples is the Erechtheion, on the Acropolis at Athens, by the architect Mnesicles (421–405 B.C.). Externally, the temple has been much restored, but nothing is left of the interior. The plan is unusual in its irregular form and its standing on different levels connected by steps. A much photographed feature is the Caryatid Porch on the south side. Instead of columns, six draped female figures (Caryatids) carved in marble and standing 2.3 metres high on a solid marble wall, support the flat marble roof. The figures lean outwards slightly,

three to the east and three to the west, thus giving the impression of carrying a heavy load. The Erechtheion was built in Pentelic marble. Like the Parthenon it suffered changes. These began with alterations in Roman times, and its subsequent conversion into a church and then a Pasha's residence.

The temple of Apollo Epicurius, Bassae (*c.* 450–425 B.C.), designed by Ictinus, used all three Greek orders. Doric columns were used externally, Ionic and Corinthian columns internally. Built of limestone, with marble for sculptures and other important details, the temple faced north instead of east. The Corinthian columns at Bassae were the earliest examples of the Greek Corinthian order on record.

An important example of temple architecture in Hellenistic Greece was the Corinthian temple of Zeus Olympius, to the south-east of the Acropolis, Athens, designed by a Roman architect Cossutius and begun in 174 B.C. The temple had double rows of columns to the peristyle and three rows to the front and rear. The building was never completed and some of the columns were taken to Rome at a later date for use in a temple on the Capitol. The Olympieion, as the temple was called, was mainly Greek and influenced the development of the Roman Corinthian style.

This guide has concentrated attention on the Greek temple because that was the dominant building type and the one the Greeks sited on the best vantage points. Nonetheless, during the Hellenistic period, the Greeks developed a civic style of architecture. Important settlements in Ephesus, Delos, Corinth, and elsewhere showed regular planning systems with streets at right angles to one another. The centre of the social and business life of the city was the *agora* or town square, with monuments, shrines, colonnaded porticoes, places of entertainment, and the *stoa*. The stoa was usually a long colonnaded building, serving many different purposes. It was used for shelter near shrines and other places and included small shops. Stadia and theatres were open-air structures and in the early days other kinds of meetings were held in the open air too. As beam and column construction advanced, public buildings for assembly became possible and usually had special names, such as the Thersilion and Megalopolis (*c.* 370 B.C.). Tombs, like the Ionic Nereid Monument, Xanthos (*c.* 400 B.C.) or the Mausoleum, Helicarnassus (355–350 B.C.), also testified to the genius of the Greeks. Helicarnassus was erected to King Mausolus, and the term mausoleum is derived from his tomb.

Houses seemed to have received scant architectural attention until the Hellenistic period. The early houses are assumed to have been single storey with walls of unburnt brick on a stone base. There were no windows and the houses opened on to narrow streets. The usual arrangement was a principal room on the north side, looking towards the winter sun and facing a small court, with other rooms round the court from which they gained light. The megaron from the Aegean age still survived as the main apartment in many houses. Later houses, as at Delos in Asia Minor, included a peristyle, often with beautiful marble columns, very similar to the Roman *atrium*. Plans of such houses were normally irregular and the number of rooms varied. An example of a house at Delos with a fully colonnaded court is the 'Maison de la Colline'. The plan is regular and there are upstairs rooms. The court had a water cistern placed centrally below it.

Residences of a grander nature were developed by the Greeks, but never reached the artistic achievement of their public buildings. The further development of the classical styles was left to the Romans whose architecture is discussed in the next chapter.

THEATRE, Delphi. *c.* 150 B.C.

Roman Development

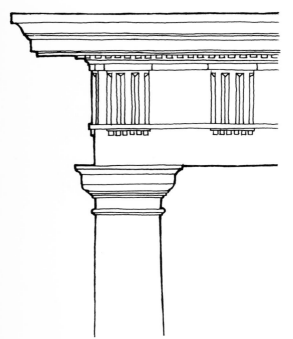

Doric order.

In the mythical story of Rome's foundation, the twin sons of the Vestal Virgin, Rhea, by Mars, the Roman God of War, were left to drown on the banks of the river Tiber. The river subsided, leaving the forsaken twins on dry ground to be found by a she-wolf who mothered them. The adult Romulus slew his twin brother, Remus, founded Rome by the Tiber, and returned to heaven to become the Roman god, Quirinus. The early records give the year 753 B.C. as the date when Romulus carved the furrow which marked the early city of Rome. From that moment until her glory diminished, Rome never looked back.

In the centuries that followed, Rome's story, until almost the first century B.C., is one of constantly recurring wars. Originally, the city was ruled by the Etruscans, who dominated South Etruria. As Etruscan power waned, Rome became increasingly powerful among her sister cities, and began to gain their support. The Roman character of seriousness, dedication to law and order, stoicism in adversity, and ability to organize pushed the citizens ahead. From a small town, Rome became a city, a city state, and, through war and conquest, a great empire. The first people to come into conflict with Rome outside Italy were the Carthaginians. After the first Punic War (261–241 B.C.), Sicily was annexed to Rome. A setback occurred when Hannibal defeated the Romans in the second Punic War (218–201 B.C.), and the Carthaginians were overlords of Rome until Carthage was finally defeated in the third Punic War (149–146 B.C.) and became, with all its lands in Africa, a Roman province. Macedonia and Greece became provinces of Rome in the same century and Greek influence began increasingly to affect Roman architecture. By the last century B.C. Spain and Syria were overrun and the foundations of the Roman Empire were secured.

Colonial expansion did not help the regime at home. A city republican state was not organized to cope with social disorder, which led to the need for a firm hand. The rivalry between the leading personalities of the Republic ended in Civil War between Pompey and Julius Caesar, the successful conqueror of central Europe. Caesar prevailed and became a virtual dictator, but his success was short-lived; he was assassinated in the Senate in 44 B.C. There followed a struggle for power between Marcus Antonius (Mark Antony), Caius Octavius, a relative of Julius Caesar, and Lepidus, whom the Senate had appointed as Triumvirs to settle the constitution. Lepidus faded out. Antony (as history relates) married Cleopatra of Egypt and they were defeated by Octavius at the sea battle of Actium. Antony and Cleopatra committed suicide and Octavius returned to Rome to become the first Emperor with the title of Augustus. During Augustus' long reign from 27 B.C. to A.D. 14, Rome became the leading city of the known world, and the period, rich in architecture and the development of civic amenities, set the pattern for later years. It was indeed the 'Golden Age' of Roman culture. Many temples, including those of Mars Ultor, and Castor and Pollux in Rome (the latter was dedicated in 483 B.C., after the Tarquinians had been defeated), and the Maison Carrée, Nîmes, were built in his reign. The theatre of Marcellus and part of the Forum Romanum, started by Julius Caesar, were also completed.

The Mausoleum of Augustus, a much restored ruin in Rome, bears some resemblance to its original glory. The famous Altar of Augustan Peace, dedicated in the second decade B.C. after the Emperor's return from a successful campaign in Spain and Gaul, was lost until pieces of it found their way into the Medici family's hands in Florence in the fifteenth century. The frieze shows in sculpture figures of Augustus, his wife Livia, his son-in-law Agrippa and his stepson Drusius with members of Augustus's court. Fragments collected from museums and excavations have been reassembled in the twentieth century.

The rule of Augustus was followed by that of Tiberius (A.D. 14–37), Caligula (37–41), Claudius (41–54) and Nero (54–68). Tiberius, in whose reign Christ was crucified, was a soldier and a fair administrator; Caligula was a despot of the worst kind; Claudius enlarged the empire and furthered the reorganization of the administration; Nero's excesses brought rebellion at the end of his reign, and he committed suicide. This ended the Julio-Claudian dynasty and there was unrest until the Senate, under considerable pressure, made a soldier, Vespasianus, the commander in Judaea, emperor. He ruled as Vespasian (69–79), founded the Flavian dynasty and was succeeded by his sons Titus (79–81), and Domitian (81–96). During the period of the Flavian emperors, the Colosseum, Rome was started and completed. The Flavians were followed by the Antonines, during whose rule there was

Below Left
Corinthian order.

Below Centre
Ionic order.

Bottom Centre
Composite order.

Below Right
Tuscan order.

perhaps a closer rapport between the emperors and the civil service. The five Antonine Emperors were: Nerva (96–98), Trajan (98–117), Hadrian (117–138), Antonius Pius (138–161), Marcus Aurelius (161–180) and his son Commodus (180–192).

Trajan can be singled out as a good emperor, responsible also for many great constructions, for example his large Forum and Basilica, his triumphal arches at Ancona and Beneventum, and the Column in Rome raised in his honour. Commodus, the last of the Antonines, was as incompetent as other young emperors before him. His assassination in 192 led to a struggle for supreme power among rival candidates. Septimus Severus, after a number of campaigns, became master of the Roman world. He died in 211 and was succeeded by Caracalla (211–217), his eldest son. There followed a period of unrest and short-lived emperors, Macrinus, Elagabulus, Severus Alexander and Maximus. After the death of Severus Alexander, barbarian attacks on the empire increased and the problem of holding the empire together was only partially resolved by Diocletian's reforms. He became emperor in 284 and appointed four persons, including himself, to share power through the empire. Further troubles grew from the new system of government and were not resolved until Constantine became emperor on Diocletian's death in 316. The conversion of Constantine to Christianity and the subsequent effect on architecture is referred to in later chapters.

This short account and chronological story of dynasties underlines the turbulent and forthright nature of the Romans, their ruthlessness in obtaining their goals, and, perhaps, their obsession that the law should be seen to support their ambitions. Roman architecture is characteristic of this complicated nature.

The Romans were essentially practical builders and borrowed without scruple from the earlier Etruscan cultures, and later from the Greeks, adapting ideas to their own considerable skill as engineers. They used the three Greek orders – Doric, Ionic and Corinthian but made changes to them. The Roman Doric was slimmer in proportion than the Greek Doric, was given a base, and the upper portion of the capital (abacus) was moulded. The Tomans added two further orders: the Tuscan order which was similar to the Roman Doric but the column was without flutes, and the Composite order in which Ionic volutes and the Corinthian Acanthus leaf motif were combined in the capital. The Tuscan order came from the Etruscans who used the column and beam construction familiar in Greek architecture. The Romans also used column and beam construction, but as the empire expanded and Rome became richer, the demand for more elaborate building stimulated Roman inventiveness. The arch and the vault attempted by the Etruscans and developed by the Romans, and the Roman invention of concrete, made their wonderful buildings possible.

Roman concrete was made of small pieces of broken brick, travertine or tufa (a kind of volcanic rock) laid on thick beds of mortar composed of lime and local sand called *pozzolana* which came from the volcanic parts of Italy. Walls and the solid bases for buildings were usually built of concrete and faced with regularly cut pieces of stone, often laid diagonally. Some walls were of stone laid dry and held with cramps. Brick was sometimes used as a facing to the concrete core. Stone for vaulting had to be cut to the required shape but the Roman concrete simply needed rough form work. The Romans used the *barrel vault* (also known as a *tunnel vault*) supported on solid walls below the circular arch of the vault (see p. 149). They also used the *groin vault* which was the intersection of two barrel vaults of equal span over a square space (see p. 87). The load was

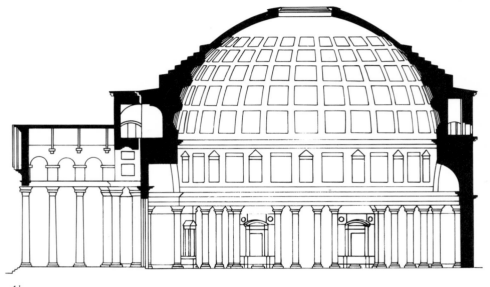

Above
PANTHEON, Rome. 120–24. Plan.

Below
PANTHEON, Rome. 120–24. Section.

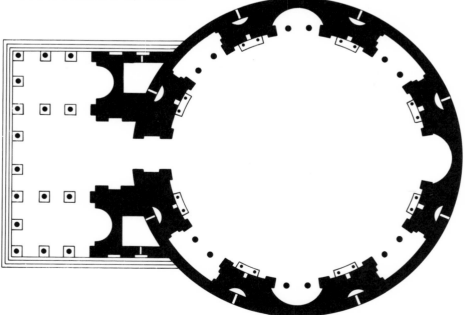

Opposite
PANTHEON, Rome. 120–24. The coffered dome and part of the interior.

taken on piers at the four corners of the square and the groins were the intersections of the two barrels. The Romans buttressed their vaults by using extra thick walls, by balancing one vault against another, or by using *semi-vaults*.

The Roman town typified the Roman desire for order and was laid out with military precision based on a square. Streets were placed at right angles to one another, and as far as possible slopes were eliminated by excavating vast flat areas linked by steps. Large towns were called colonies and the same types of principal building were to be found in most, but there was no pre-set order or arrangement, the most suitable site for a particular building type being the one usually adopted. The Roman forum occupied a central position because it was the principal meeting place in the town; with it was usually the basilica, the halls of justice, prominently sited. The basilica was normally a long hall with arcaded corridors on each long side, where legal discussions and arguments took place. In Rome, the Tribunal of the Hundred Councillors took place in the main hall of the Basilica Julia, in the forum. The markets were an important adjunct of the forum. Trajan's great markets in Rome were carved out of the hillside at different levels and had covered ways in front of the shops. Usually, the public areas of town centres were arcaded on both sides, as a refuge from sun or rain. The amphitheatre, thermae (baths), and theatre were usually placed further out from the centre; temples were sited where required, commonly near the forum.

Temples were not the greatest of Roman structures as in the case of the Greeks, but they were among the more important buildings. One of the better-known and well-preserved temples is the Maison Carrée. It has free-standing columns, six seen from the front and three from the side view. Columns, bases and capitals are Roman Corinthian, which was already a fully developed order. Indeed, the Maison Carrée has all the basic elements of a Greek temple, Romanized, and the principal of interpreting the building from outside is typically Greek.

The Pantheon, Rome, built in the second decade of the second century A.D. for the emperor Hadrian, is one of the best-preserved of Roman remains and a marvel of engineering. Apart from the portico, the interest centres on the circular interior of the temple, the opposite of the rectangular plan of the Maison Carrée. The walls rise in a vast drum carrying the coffered dome, which has a circular opening to the sky at its apex. There are eight niches within the thickness of the walls, six with pairs of free-standing columns. The eighth niche is the entrance from the vast portico in front. The diameter of the circular interior of the temple is more than 43 metres, and the dome above is a remarkable structure built of Roman concrete. The five rows of coffering and the varying thickness of the dome's shell help to reduce its weight. From its widest at the walls, it reduces in six steps, visible on the outside, to the final curved shell of about 1.2 metres in thickness. The dome was originally lined with bronze plates which were later replaced by lead. The lower part of the walls outside was faced with white Pentelec marble to match the Corinthian capitals of the portico columns which are of smooth Egyptian granite. Although stripped of so much of its original marble interior and of the gold which used to adorn the ancient bronze doors, the Pantheon remains a wonderful tribute to Roman architecture because of its splendid proportions. In the seventh century the temple was dedicated to S. Maria ad Martyres, after the bones of Christian martyrs were brought there from the catacombs. It is commonly known as S. Maria Rotonda today.

The majority of Roman houses, even those of the wealthy, contained no bathing facilities, and therefore the public baths or thermae built by successive emperors were focal points of social life in even the smallest town. The

Below
MAISON CARRÉE, Nimes, France. *c.* 16 B.C.

Opposite
HADRIAN'S VILLA, Tivoli. *c.* 124. A portion of the island villa colonnade.

largest thermae were in Rome, and their size and magnificence may be judged by the Baths of Diocletian, which were set in a 12 hectare park and could accommodate 3000 bathers. The layout of Diocletian's thermae, and those of Caracalla, was rectangular, with the halls, vestibules, and courtyards arranged symmetrically about cross-axes. In the centre was the central hall or *cella media*. Leading from it on the short cross-axis was the *tepidarium* or medium temperature bath. The *caldarium* or hot bath projected out from the long side of the building. In the opposite direction to the calidarium, leading from the cella media, was the open-air cold pool, the *frigidarium*, largest of all the pools and obviously popular in hot weather. On either side of the frigidarium were anterooms for changing. The changing rooms were also entered from vestibules leading from the two entrance halls to

the baths. On the far side of each of the changing rooms were colonnaded courtyards leading to gymnasia (*ephebea*), equipped with all manner of devices for games and exercises. Thermae were usually raised on a podium, beneath which were the boiler rooms and services for the baths. The park in which the thermae stood was enclosed by a wall with a variety of pavilions and halls used for libraries, rest-rooms and studies, built against it.

The magnificence of imperial Rome was implicit in the grandeur of the thermae. To the highest and the lowest in the land they served as reminders of the emperor's power and of the benefits he could bestow, in the same way as the circuses and gladiatorial combats. The interiors of thermae were rich with different coloured marbles, heavily ornamented columns, capitals and entablatures, and with statuary and carvings.

Each emperor strove for popularity through the luxuriance of the baths. The first thermae of Rome were those of Agrippa, built in the last quarter of the first century B.C. Those of Titus were built in the first century A.D., Trajan in the second century, Caracalla and Diocletian in the third. At Timgad in North Africa there are remains of at least seven thermae. Thermae have also been found in Germany, and in other parts of the Roman Empire. The splendour of Diocletian's thermae has been preserved in the part which Michelangelo converted into the Church of S. Maria degli Angeli in 1563, retaining much of the structure and original decoration.

The Roman theatre was earlier than the thermae, and to some extent its form was a copy of the Greek theatre, but the seats were arranged in a semicircle, instead of in a horseshoe shape, and the semicircular area at ground level in

Below
COLOSSEUM, Rome. 72–80.

Opposite
COLOSSEUM, Rome. 72–80. Four colonnades on the facade have the Doric order at the bottom, Ionic and Corinthian above. Part of the cutaway portion reveals walls underneath which enclose cells and passageways and support arches and vaults below the sloping tiers of seats. A canvas awning (velarium) manned by soldiers was strung across the stadium to make a sunshield.

front of the stage was used by important members of the audience. In the Greek theatre this space was circular and used by the orchestra. Early Roman theatres were sometimes carved out of the hillside, in the manner of the Greeks. The theatre of Marcellus, begun by Julius Caesar (*c.* 25 B.C.), and completed by Augustus, is free-standing, and part of the ruins can be seen in Rome today.

The Colosseum, at one end of the via Sacra in Rome, is structurally similar to the theatre of Marcellus, but immense in size. It measured over 183 metres by 156 by 46 high. The designers of the building were required to accommodate 50,000 spectators, with space above and below ground for all kinds of games, contests, and other events. The result

was an engineering achievement made possible by the use of concrete. The whole structure was a honeycomb of solid walls with vaults above them enclosing cells and small chambers and supporting the tiers of seats, the arena, and the various communicating corridors. The concrete used for the structure has been found to vary in order to produce less weight where required. Thus, brick and tufa were used for the supporting walls and pumice stone for the vaults. The exterior walls were faced with travertine blocks fixed with metal clamps and laid dry. Originally there were four storeys to the arched facade which have attached columns ascending in Ionic, Doric and Corinthian orders, with Corinthian pilasters at the top. Only

part of the facade remains today. The building, begun by Vespasian (c. A.D. 70) and completed by Domitian, his son, twelve years later, was called the Amphitheatrum Flavium until the eighth century. The events at the Colosseum's inauguration are said to have lasted 100 days, in which nearly 5000 animals and as many gladiators were slain. In the third century A.D., the Colosseum was struck by lightning and was restored by Severus Alexander. The first millenium of Rome's foundation was celebrated there with magnificent games, including a spectacle in which 2000 gladiators fought in pairs. The building fell into disuse after Honorius abolished gladiatorial contests in A.D. 404. In later centuries much of the travertine was

removed and carted away for newer buildings until Pope Benedict XIV declared the monument sacred because Christians had been martyred there.

From the Colosseum the people of Rome either walked, were carried in a litter or drove in chariots back to their homes, which were as varied as their means of transport.

The palaces of the Roman emperors were on the same grand scale as their public buildings. The great Palatine Hill overlooking the city of Rome was the obvious choice of site, and the ruins of palaces from Augustus in the first century B.C. to those of the third century A.D. have been uncovered there. The arrangement of halls and open spaces was axially planned, and the very varied

accommodation included temples, a banqueting hall, private apartments, schools, libraries, a walled garden, barracks and staterooms.

Nothing remains of Nero's incredible Golden House on the slopes of the Palatine Hill, but there are remains of Hadrian's villa at Tivoli built in the second century A.D., and of Diocletian's palace at Spalato (Split). Hadrian's villa occupied a park nearly 18 kilometres square. There were halls and apartments, colonnaded courtyards linked together, theatres and thermae, as well as the other buildings normal to a palace, and formal gardens, foundations, and statuary. Diocletian's Palace stands on the Adriatic Sea coast and it formed the greater part of the town of Spalato. In

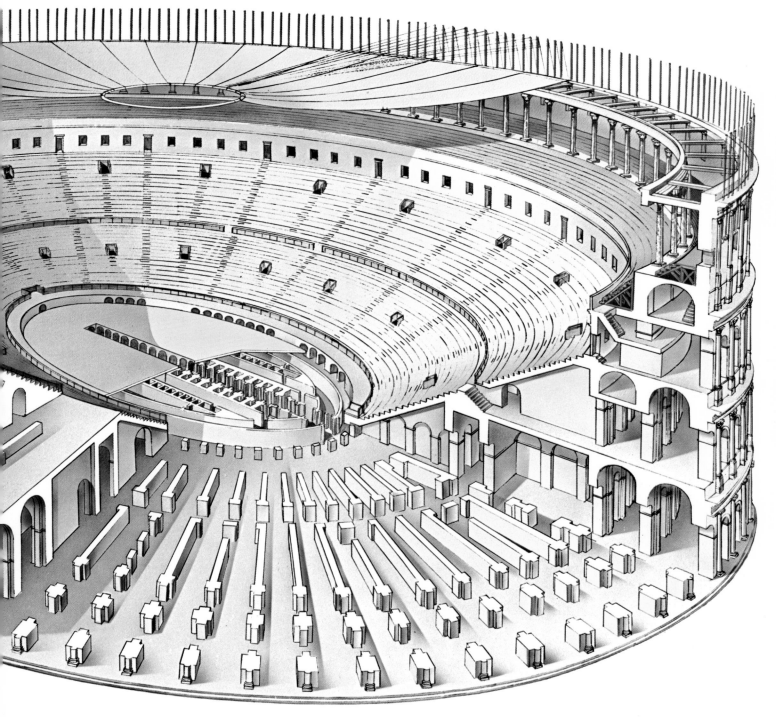

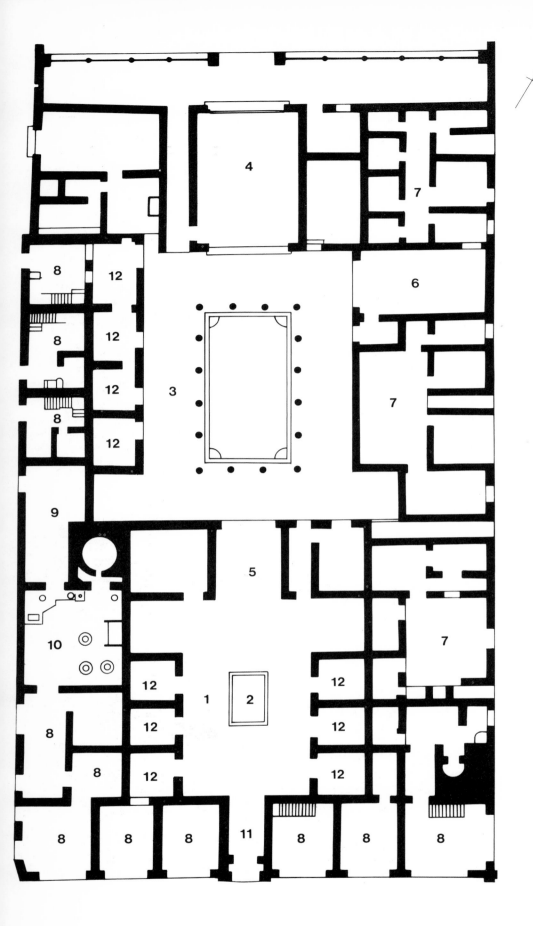

character, it was different to the earlier palaces and royal villas. It was a fortress-style palace, rectangular in plan, enclosed with high walls and covered an area of about 3 hectares. At the four corners of the rectangle were square projecting towers. The front faced the sea to the south with a long gallery behind the wall. Flanking the gallery were the royal apartments, the Temple of Jupiter and Diocletian's mausoleum. These occupied half the site. In the centre of the remaining three sides were gateways flanked by octagonal towers. The east and west gateways were linked by a broad colonnade bisected in the middle by another colonnade leading to the north gateway. The two halves of the northern part of the site were occupied by quarters, for officials on one side, and probably for women on the other. Arcades lined the walls of the northern half and six small square projecting towers were placed between the four corners and the three gateways.

At the other end of the housing scale were flats at Ostia, the port of Rome: blocks of several storeys, built of brick-faced concrete for dock workers. In Rome itself space was scarce and houses often adjoined shops, or apartments were built in storeys, as might be expected in a congested city. The house which has influenced the form of present-day houses in the western world was the typical Roman mansion. The fourth-century House of the Surgeon, Pompeii, is an early example, and the House of Pansa, Pompeii, the fully developed dwelling. The central feature of both was the *atrium*, a covered court with a small opening to the sky beneath which was

Left
HOUSE OF PANSA, Pompeii. Plan:
1 atrium,
2 impluvium,
3 peristyle,
4 reception room,
5 tablinum,
6 dining room,
7 another house,
8 shop,
9 office,
10 bake house,
11 entrance,
12 bedrooms.
Below
HOUSE OF PANSA, Pompeii. Section.

a tank (*impluvium*) to catch water from the sloping tiled roofs of adjoining apartments. The principal rooms of the House of the Surgeon faced on to the atrium. In the later House of Pansa, only the rooms used for receiving guests and for formal occasions faced the atrium, which was linked to a Greek-style peristyle court through an open-ended living room called a *tablinum*. The peristyle court became a common feature of mansions in the second century A.D. Family rooms faced inwards on to the peristyle court, and the court was laid out with flowerbeds, statuary, and sometimes a fountain. Walls of mansions were profusely decorated with fresco paintings. Floors were usually of patterned mosaics, or marble of different colours. Statuary, vases, lamps, and sometimes fountains were used as decoration in most rooms, and reclining couches were used for dining. The light robes used by the Romans made them very conscious of the climate, and in order to take advantage of winter sunshine and gain protection from the summer heat, the rooms leading off the peristyle court were changed to suit the season.

The enormous number of fountains in Rome, and the need for water to serve the thermae, made the Romans conscious of water supplies. They well understood that water in whatever carrier will tend to rise to its own level. Since labour was relatively plentiful, they were able to build huge aquaducts from the water sources serving their cities. Eleven aquaducts served Rome. Perhaps the best-preserved of the aquaducts is part of the one which serves Nîmes, known as the Pont du Gard. It has three tiers of arches spanning the river Gard. The top channel laid to a slight fall carries the water. The span of the top arches measures almost 4.5 metres which gives an indication of the aquaduct's size. The top tier has mortar between the joints of the stonework. The remainder of the structure was laid dry without mortar.

Monuments and memorials to commemorate victories are a familiar sight in most countries. The Romans seem to have preferred triumphal arches or victory columns. Many of Rome's triumphal arches have been destroyed, but the Arch of Titus (A.D. 82) at one end of the via Sacra and the Arch of Septimus

HOUSE OF THE VETTII, Pompeii. 1st century. A typical Roman peristyle.

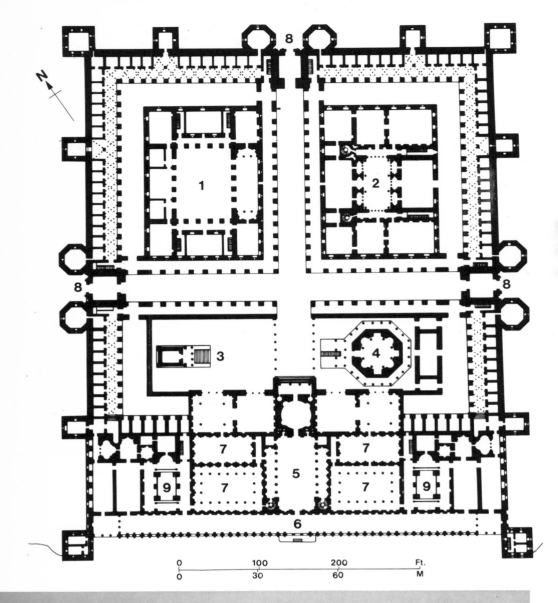

Above
PALACE OF DIOCLETIAN, Spalato
(Split), Yugoslavia. *c.* 300. Plan:
1 womens' apartments,
2 officials' apartments,
3 Temple of Jupiter,
4 Diocletian's mausoleum,
5 atrium,
6 grand gallery,
7 reception hall,
8 gateway,
9 bath.

Left
PONT DU GARD, Nîmes. *c.* 14.

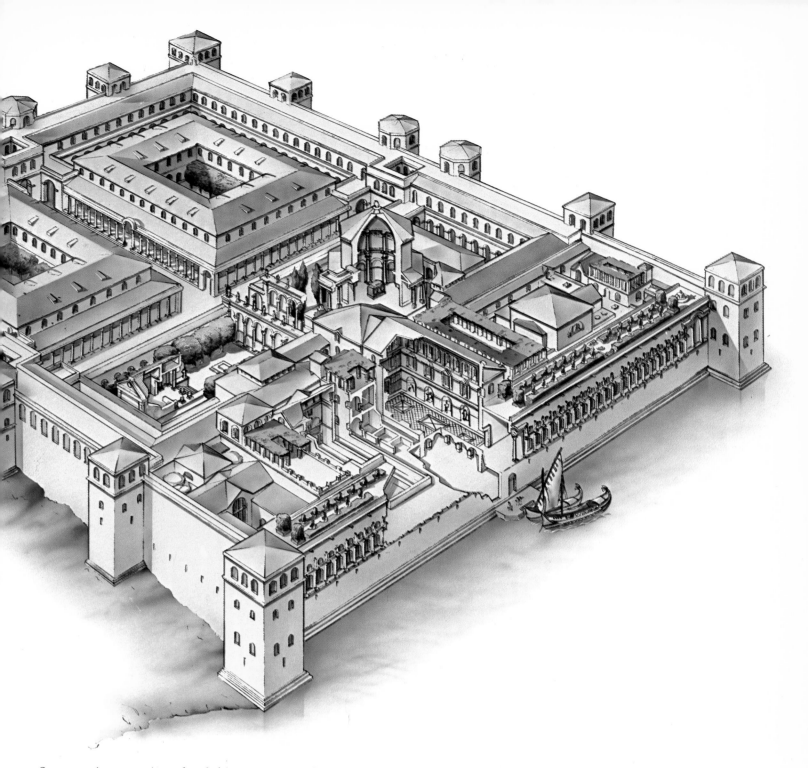

Severus (A.D. 203) and of his sons Caracalla and Geta at the other, still stand. The Arch of Titus, adorned with suitable sculpture and inscriptions, has a single opening and was erected by Domitian in honour of his brother Titus's capture of Jerusalem in A.D. 70 The Arch of Severus is of white marble, has three openings and commemorates his victorious campaign against the Parthians in Mesopotamia. The most impressive of the victory columns is Trajan's Column (A.D. 113) in Rome. Built of Parian marble, it has a continuous spiral band of carving proclaiming Trajan's military successes against the Dacians in two memorable campaigns. The column stands over 30.5 metres high on a pedestal carved with trophies. The hollow shaft contains a

spiral staircase with small openings in the shaft to light it. Originally the plinth at the top of the column supported a statue of Trajan, but this was replaced in 1587 by a statue of St Peter.

The story of Roman architecture would not be complete without mention of the circus for horse and chariot racing. The form was borrowed from the Greek circus. The greatest was the Circus Maximus, situated between the hills of Rome and dating as far back as Julius Caesar. None of it remains, and there are only remnants of the much later Circus of Maxentius (A.D. 311). The Circus of Maxentius had the typical layout: a long arena with circular ends, and tiers of marble seats above sloping vaults and supporting walls in the manner of the Colosseum.

PALACE OF DIOCLETIAN, Spalato (Split), Yugoslavia. c. 300. The enormous extent of the palace/fortress (restored) is its most striking feature. The cutaway portion reveals part of the grand gallery running alongside the waterfront: the atrium; Temple of Jupiter, and Diocletian's mausoleum. Beyond, in the northern sector of the palace, are the officials' quarters to the right and the women's quarters to the left.

Early Christian Churches

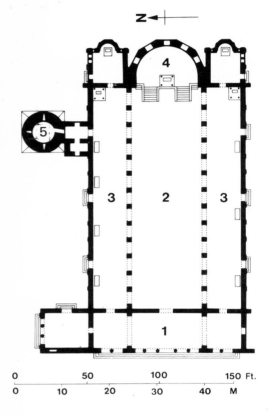

S. Apollinare in Classe, Ravenna.
Plan:
1 narthex,
2 nave,
3 aisle,
4 apse,
5 *campanile*.

Rome was the centre of the world in the period which dates from about 300 to 800, and naturally the early missionaries of Christianity, St Paul and St Peter among them, came to Rome on their travels. Converts were made and Christianity grew until it was recognized as the equal of other religions by the Edict of Milan in 313, and proclaimed the official religion of Rome by Constantine in 326. There was, however, little progress in Christian architecture until the invasion of Europe by German tribes was halted by the defeat of Attila, their king, at the battle of Châlons in 451. There were further troubles for Rome when the Lombards, who in later years made such impact on Romanesque architecture, invaded Italy and held the northern part for the next two hundred years. The empire was rejoined with northern Italy again in 800 when Charlemagne was crowned by the Pope in Rome, and the title of the empire was changed to that of Holy Roman Empire, as a result of the adoption of Christianity. Historically, the style did not change after Charlemagne, but buildings continued to follow the form, at least in Rome, up to the Renaissance.

The basilican church, as the earliest church was called, had a narrow central hall with aisles on either side and an apse at the east end. Its form was based on the 'Basilica', the Roman hall of justice, or possibly on the Roman villa. Opinions differ on the exact origins. The entrance from the west was usually, but not always, through an *atrium*, a colonnaded open court, leading to the *narthex*, a narrow covered vestibule running the full width of the church. The central hall was entered from the narthex and the side aisles were separated from it by columns. Sometimes there were double side aisles, as for example in the old basilican Church of St Peter's, Rome (*c.* 450), built by Constantine and pulled down to allow the present St Peter's to be erected. Old St Peter's also had a *bema*, a rectangular space before the apse

which was perhaps the beginning of the transepts in later churches. Another variation from the simple basilican plan, for example at S. Apollinare in Classe, Ravenna (*c.* 530–540), was rooms on either side of the apse. S. Apollinare in Classe also possessed a tower, or *campanile*, on its north side. When there was a gallery over the aisles, as at S. Agnes, Rome, it was used by women in preference to the aisle opposite that occupied by the men of the congregation.

One of the puzzles of these Early Christian churches was the absence of domes. Roofs were always pitched, yet the Romans had knowledge of the dome. One explanation is that the early Christians may not have wished to identify themselves with the ruling aristocracy of Rome and her sophisticated cities, or, that since Christianity was not at first a state religion, external ostentation was discouraged, as in the case of the Byzantine churches in Bulgaria during the Ottoman oppression. Opinions differ on the point.

The external features of these churches were the gable-ended, double-pitched roof over the nave, single-pitched over the aisles, covered with Roman tiles; and rough stone walls with regularly spaced circular-headed windows, placed at low level to light the aisles and at high level to light the nave. Sometimes the apse, roofed with a half vault, had windows. For all its simplicity, it was from the basilican church that the great Romanesque and Gothic cathedrals developed.

Constantine and his successor Justinian were responsible for many Early Christian churches. The few that remain have been altered or added to by later generations. One of the earliest, the Church of the Nativity, Bethlehem, which supposedly marks the birthplace of Christ, was first built in 330 and rebuilt two hundred years later. The nave, approached through the atrium and the narthex, has double aisles on both sides, and the east end has three

Above
S. Apollinare in Classe, Ravenna.
Mid-sixth century.

Right
S. Apollinare in Classe, Ravenna.
Section showing apse (left) and semi-dome
beneath the pitched roof.

apses (*triapsial*). Massive Corinthian
columns separate nave from aisles and
support an entablature. The Church of
the Holy Sepulchre, Jerusalem, originally built by Constantine over the site
of Christ's tomb, bears little resemblance
to the typical Early Christian form.
Persians and Muslims damaged it,
Crusaders restored it, and much has
been added.

   The fourth-century Church of S.
Paolo fuori le Mura (St Paul's without
the walls), Rome, was one of the largest
basilican churches. It was destroyed, and
then rebuilt in the nineteenth century in
its original form, and possesses an unusually wide bema divided into two by
a colonnade. There were variations in
the early basilican churches, but a constant feature was the long uninterrupted

0   10   20   30   40   50   60   70 Ft.

0   5   10   15   M

S. Stefano Rotondo, Rome. *c.* 468–83.

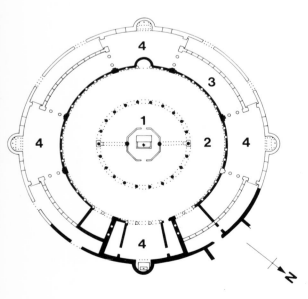

S. Stefano Rotondo, Rome. Plan:
1 central area,
2 inner ambulatory,
3 outer ambulatory,
4 chapel.

progression from entrance to apse and high altar: the even rhythm of clerestory windows at high level, and rows of columns on either side of the nave. This majestic procession is illustrated vividly by the two mature Early Christian churches in Ravenna, S. Apollinare Nuovo and S. Apollinare in Classe, both completed in the early part of the sixth century and erected by the Roman emperors Theodoric the Great and Justinian respectively. Both churches have typical plans: single aisles separated from the nave by columns; a nave higher than its width; a row of high clerestory windows; and a semicircular apse, polygonal on the outside. The aisle columns have circular arches which replaced the classical form of column and entablature of earlier churches.

S. Apollinare Nuovo is famous for its Byzantine columns and capitals, and the long procession of rather rigid figures in glass mosaic above the colonnades. On the north wall are female saints led by the Magi. On the south wall leading from Theodoric's Palace are male martyrs. Between the clerestory windows

are more saintly figures depicted in glass mosaics. Byzantine influence is apparent also in S. Apollinare in Classe: in the columns and capitals separating nave and aisles, and in their richly decorated circular arches. Bands above the arches are decorated with rows of medallions, 1.5 metres in diameter, depicting portraits of the bishops of Ravenna.

A different form of church was used at this time for baptism, which took place at Easter, Pentecost and Epiphany, with large numbers of people requiring total immersion. In the early days, Roman temples and tombs were sometimes used to provide the large space required. Later, circular or octagonal-shaped baptisteries were built with a central area encircling a bath, and sometimes with an ambulatory, or double ambulatory as in S. Stefano Rotondo, Rome. On the outside, roofs were pitched and tile covered. S. Stefano Rotondo has flat ceilings inside, but the Baptistry Nocera has a double row of ancient columns supporting a dome over the central space, and barrel vaults over the surrounding ambulatory.

Byzantine Style

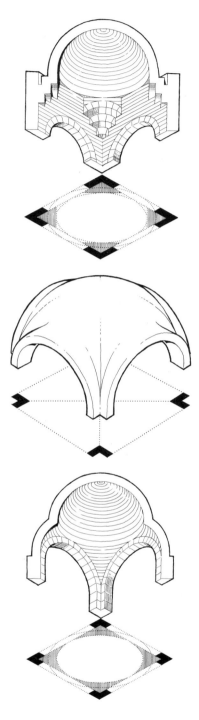

Historians ascribe the beginning of the pure Byzantine style to the fifth century and it has influenced architects right up to the present day. Its development was uneven. The circular dome covering a square plan – the principal characteristic of the Byzantine church – was to be found in Italy at the same time as the basilican plan of the Early Christian churches. Eventually, the Byzantine style dominated in the eastern part of the Roman empire, taking its name from the capital city, Byzantium, later called Constantinople, and today Istanbul.

The emperor Constantine moved the Roman empire's capital from Rome to Byzantium in 330, in order to have greater control over the more valuable eastern section. The problem of the empire's control had been appreciated by his predecessor, Diocletian, who had recognized that Rome was too far west, so he built his own palace at Spalato (Split) and created two other centres of government besides Rome. Constantine ruled strongly until 337 but was followed by weak emperors, and this brought about the division of the empire in 364 into two parts, east and west, each with its own emperor.

In the east, the new religion – Christianity – was gathering momentum, and, not surprisingly, churches became the most important type of building in the new style. But the church plan was changed. Now it was shaped like a Greek cross (a cross with arms of equal length) or an inscribed Greek cross (a Greek cross within a square) and a central dome was placed over the square area formed where the cross arms met. The adoption of this centralized plan, so different from the western style church plan, continued after Early Christian, through Romanesque and Gothic architecture up to the present day, surviving with little change for a thousand years. Its form was peculiarly suitable for the liturgical and processional procedures of the eastern Christian churches, in which the clergy dominate the proceedings from the centre of the church under the great dome.

The Byzantine dome and the one used in Islamic architecture were constructed differently from the Roman dome. The

Top
Squinch: the shaded areas on the plan indicate the squinch at each corner.

Centre
Domed groin vault.

Above
Pendentive: the shaded areas on the plan indicate the pendentive at each corner.

Right
S. Vitale, Ravenna. *c*, 547.

Romans placed their dome over a solid circle of walling; the Pantheon, Rome, is an example (p. 26). A dome could be raised higher by building a circlet of walling to make a drum before the dome started its curve. Windows could be placed in the drum, as for example at S. Vitale, Ravenna. Another form of domical roof used by the Romans was an extension of the groin vault into a *domed groin vault* by eliminating the

Opposite
S. VITALE, Ravenna. *c*. 547. Central octagon with chancel to the right.
Below
S. VITALE, Ravenna. *c*. 547. Plan.
1 central octagon,
2 outer octagon,
3 chancel with apse,
4 atrium destroyed,
5 narthex.

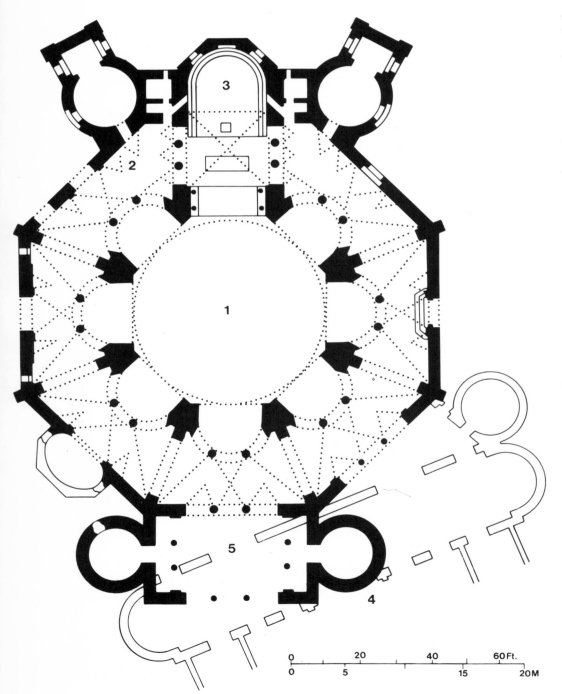

groins. The limitation of the domed groin vault was the low height dictated by the arches over the short sides of the square. Nonetheless, the domed groin vault gave greater height than a vault with groins, and it opened up to the Byzantine builders the idea of striving to vault larger square areas with domes. Two methods were attempted successfully. The first was to erect small arches called *squinches* across the four corners of the square and to spring the dome from above them. As squinches abutted on to the arches, they were required to take part of the dome's thrust before it was transmitted to the four corner piers. The second method used predominantly in Byzantine churches was to use triangular shaped sections, called *pendentives*, over the four corners of a square

to transform the square into a circle. Thus, the full thrust of the dome was transmitted through the arches and pendentives on to the corner piers. Additional buttressing of the central structure of Byzantine churches was provided by the smaller domes, semi-domes, and vaults which usually crowned the remaining areas of the building.

Byzantine domes and vaults were constructed of brickwork which was allowed to settle before the interior surface was finished in slabs of marble or rich mosaics. Bricks were usually thin, almost 4 centimetres thick, laid on thick beds of mortar composed of lime, sand, crushed brick, stone or pottery. Exterior walls were of brick with mortar joints, sometimes nearly 8 centimetres thick. Plain brickwork was relieved by laying the bricks in patterns – herringbone, chevron, and similar designs – and by the rich texture of brick and mortar. Stone was also used to form bands in the brickwork of arches and other distinctive features, giving variety and interest to the building.

In contrast with the simplicity of their brick exteriors – Byzantine churches are noted for their clear outlines and surface textures – the interiors were often rich in decoration, in a manner still followed today. Byzantine capitals were usually robust but intricately carved, starting with a square shape at the top and converting to a circle at the meeting with the column below. Columns were often of marble. To strengthen them, bands of bronze were used below the capital and above the base. Coloured marbles and opaque glass mosaics were used more extensively and richly than ever before to cover walls, domes, apses, vaults, and arches with a continuous pattern of decoration in abstract and natural forms, portraits and pictures. A design often used was to fill the central dome with the face and torso of Christ, with the figure of a saint or angel on each pendentive. The Madonna and child often occupied the apse wall at the altar end. Saints and scenes from the gospel story decorated other parts of the church in vivid picture stories, which were both impressive and understandable to peasant folk who could neither read nor write. In later churches, and in many of those restored today, painting on wall surfaces (fresco painting) often replaced mosaics. Two of the great churches in the Byzantine style were S. Vitale in Ravenna, the chief Byzantine town in Italy, and St Sophia in Constantinople, the capital of the Byzantine Empire.

S. Vitale, Ravenna, begun *c.* 527 has the typical centralized plan of the Byzantine style but its shape is octagonal. Eight massive piers with arches over them enclose the central octogan and support the dome and drum by means of eight pendentives. Seven of the eight arched bays of the central octagon have pairs of columns arranged in a semi-circle, with further pairs of columns above them, forming a kind of colonnade to the gallery over the aisle surrounding the inner octagon. The eighth bay of the central octagon opens into a chancel and apse beyond it. The church entrance, through the bay opposite the chancel is approached from a narthex. Dim light for the central area comes from eight circular arched windows in the drum. The construction of the dome is very unusual. The builders wanted it to be light, and there was no problem with the weather because of the tile-covered pitched roof over it. Instead of bricks, earthenware pots were laid side by side,

fitting into one another. Assisted by the extreme tightness of the 'pot' construction and with the help of the drum walls throwing the weight downwards, the builders were able to support the structure solely by means of the heavy piers, without the aid of buttresses (as at St Sophia).

The church was constructed in Justinian's time, and the event is recorded on the sanctuary walls. The emperor Justinian, his wife Theodora, and the court, wearing costume of the time, are depicted in rich mosaic. Justinian's court vied with its Arab contemporaries in oriental splendour. Ceremony, both religious and secular was elaborate, with vestments and chants to match. An endless succession of festivals, processions and special occasions marked the calendar. Byzantine art and architecture followed the elaborate fashion of Justinian's court, and the richly carved capitals to the columns, the mosaics, and other details of S.

Above
St Sophia (Hagia Sophia), Constantinople (Istanbul), Turkey. *c.* 532–37.

Left
S. Vitale, Ravenna. *c.* 547. Detail of the capitals and arches in the upper tier of the chancel.

Vitale, reveal something of its sumptuousness today.

Ravenna's importance grew, particularly after the resistance to the Lombard invasion of northern Italy in the last quarter of the sixth century. But Constantinople remained the capital. After its founding as the centre of the Christian Roman Empire, many of the old pagan temples in Constantinople were destroyed. A great number of Christian churches were built and the monastic establishments grew. In Constantinople, Justinian commissioned St Sophia, his greatest church, also SS. Sergius and Bacchus, begun just before S. Vitale and similar to it in many respects.

St Sophia or Hagia Sofia, Church of the Holy Wisdom, was built between 532 and 537. The first architect was Anthemios of Tralles, the second architect, Isidorus of Miletus. The plan shape is basically an inscribed Greek cross. The entrance from the west leads pro-gressively through a large atrium, now destroyed, a triple entrance way, and an outer and an inner narthex running the full width of the building, before entering a roughly oval-shaped hall with an apse and an altar at the east end. The hall has the typical Byzantine church centre: four piers at the corners of the square rising in circular arches to support a central dome by means of four pendentives. At Hagia Sophia, two semi-domes on the east-west axis and either side of the central dome, supported by piers and circular arches, complete the roof over the hall. There are four *exedrae* between the piers. On the north and south sides of the church are aisles with galleries over them linked to a gallery over the narthex. The galleries were used by the women, and were reached by steps inside the building and by ramps outside.

Much of Hagia Sophia's appeal comes from its size. The inside is dominated by the central dome, over 30.5 metres in diameter. The thrust from the dome is taken partly by the semi-domes on the east and west axis, but mainly by the massive buttresses to the north and south, built into the outer walls of the aisles and linked by arches to the four central piers. The dome was built of bricks roughly 60 centimetres or more square and 5 centimetres thick, with mortar joints nearly as thick. The domes and semi-domes, visible on the outside, were covered with thin lead on wooden battens. The early dome was too weak and collapsed after about twenty years. Its successor was built slightly higher. Various coloured marbles – white, green, blue and black – fixed with metal clips to the walls and piers, and marble slabs on the floor, were used to decorate St Sophia's interior. The Turks added plasterwork to the interior, also the four minarets, after the defeat of the Byzantines and the fall of Constantinople in

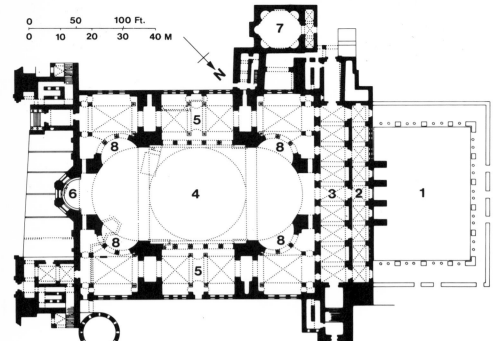

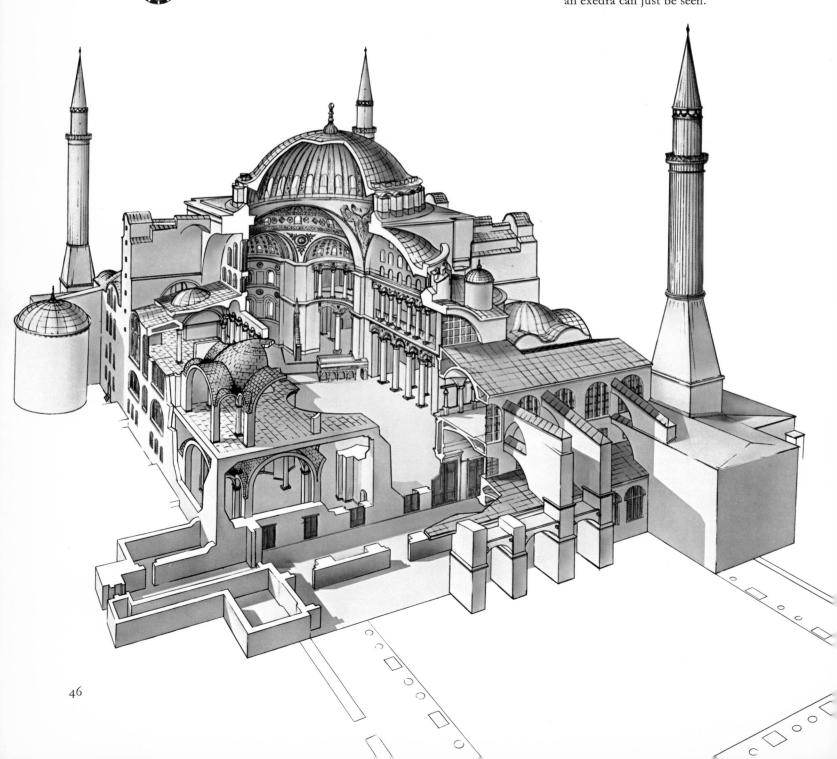

Left
St Sophia (Hagia Sophia),
Constantinople. *c.* 532–37. Plan:
1 atrium destroyed,
2 outer narthex,
3 inner narthex,
4 oval shaped central area,
5 aisle with gallery over,
6 apse
7 bapsistry
8 exedra.

Below
St Sophia (Hagia Sophia),
Constantinople (Istanbul), Turkey.
c. 532–37. Part of the huge central dome
and one of the two giant semi-domes have
been cut away to show the interior. In the
left foreground, one of the minarets and
part of the outer and inner narthex have
been cut away to show more of the
anatomy. The outline of the destroyed
atrium in front of the entrance is indicated
on the ground. At the east end of the oval
hall, part of the apse (with windows) and
an exedra can just be seen.

St Basil, Moscow. *c.* 1554.

1458. For some time Hagia Sophia was used as a mosque; today it is a museum.

St Mark's, Venice, built between 1063 and 1085, although much later than the classic examples of the style, illustrates fine Byzantine art. The first view of the church shows the work of other periods. Millions of visitors to Venice have gazed at the four bronze horses from Nero's triumphal arch, stolen from Constantinople and now perched on St Mark's roof, or watch the striking of the hour by the figures of Gog and Magog. The church's unique golden domes, framed and constructed of wood over the original brick Byzantine domes, were added in the thirteenth century; mosaics were added to the exterior during the Renaissance; and the pinnacles and canopies above the five entrances in the west front are fifteenth century Gothic additions. The plan, without the later work, is shaped like a Greek cross. The dome over the central square is more than 12 metres in diameter, and its four piers, measuring about 8.5 metres by 6, have pierced arched openings at ground and gallery levels. The interior is remarkable for all surfaces are covered with brilliant mosaic and marble, illustrating bible scenes such as the Creation, Christ's miracles, and events from the lives of the Saints.

The traditions of Byzantine church architecture, particularly the covering of interior wall surfaces with fresco paintings of biblical scenes, has continued into the twentieth century. More common are the simple brick churches with a centralized plan and pitched roofs which can be seen in many parts of the Aegean and the Balkan countries.

Islamic Forms

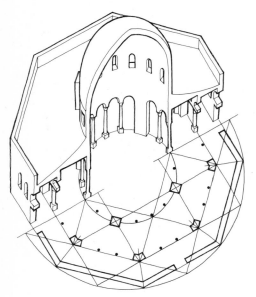

Above
DOME OF THE ROCK, Jerusalem.
Begun 688. Section.

Opposite
DOME OF THE ROCK, Jerusalem.
Begun 688

The architecture of Islam dates roughly from the seventh century and in its early years ran parallel with early Christian and Byzantine architecture from which it borrowed ideas, particularly the use of the dome. The style, like Byzantine, has continued to the present day, and the modern mosques now beginning to grace the western world make an interesting, if unusual, contribution to western architecture.

The spread of the Muslim faith and its subsequent influence on architecture emanated from Mecca, across to Africa, north of the Sahara, and to Egypt. From there it spread southwards and eastwards in Africa, and to southern Spain from the ninth and tenth centuries onwards, later reaching Russia, Mongolia, Afghanistan, Pakistan, and India during the ensuing five hundred years.

In the early centuries of Muslim influence, military conquest was the driving force. In the cities they conquered and in the new cities they created in devastated areas, the Muslims built their own mosques and palaces. As in some other cultures the Muslim faith influenced the style of architecture. The prophet Muhammad founded the faith at Mecca. He moved to Medina in 622, the year which marks the start of the Muslim calendar. The faith is regarded as the first revelation of God through his prophet Muhammad. The principles of the faith were established by Muhammad after he moved to Medina. They govern all religious and secular matters, people's behaviour, and their buildings. The principles are set out in: the *Koran*, the revelation of God through Muhammad; the *Hadith*, a collection of sayings; and the *Law* which is based on Muhammad's instructions. What was important for architecture was that the Law preached tolerance of the other two religions – Jewish and Christian – thus preventing the entire destruction of their religious buildings. There were other effects; for example, at Valecho Turnova, the ancient capital of the second Bulgarian empire, there are churches with Byzantine interiors and huge barn-like roofs, built during the Turkish occupation. The religion was tolerated, but the outside of the church was required to be unassuming.

Under the rules of Islam, as the faith is called, members were bound to make a pilgrimage to the prophet's birthplace, Mecca. As Islam spread, a constant stream of pilgrims from different countries visited Mecca and took architectural ideas back to their own countries where they were combined with local building styles. Islamic architecture was centred upon God. The rules demanded that the plan be symmetrical and a formal landscape was often included as part of the overall design. There were a number of architectural features commonly used. These included arcades, halls with domes, courts, and imposing entrance ways. The most familiar characteristics were the horseshoe, pointed arches and two-centred pointed arches, round and pointed top domes, and 'stalactite vaulting' known as *muquarnas*.

The mosque was the centre of Islamic culture, a place of congregation, meditation and prayer. But it was also used for official meetings, as a market place, and travellers could find shelter there. The first mosque is said to have been the courtyard of the prophet's own house, and this must have influenced ideas of a mosque's use in the future.

The first purpose built mosque was in Kufa, constructed in about 638. In true Islamic tradition, the corners of the boundaries were determined by firing arrows into the air and marking where they fell. In the fully developed mosque the place of assembly was a large hall for prayers. The Imam, who led the congregation in prayer, occupied a niche called a *mihrab* at the end of the prayer hall on the axis pointing towards Mecca. The Imam had to be visible to the lines of worshippers for the ritual movements which included prostration. Announcements were usually made from the

Right
DOME OF THE ROCK, Jerusalem.
Begun 688.

Opposite
GREAT MOSQUE, Córdoba. Begun
c. 786.

Below
GREAT MOSQUE, Córdoba. Begun
c. 786. Vaulting.

nimbar, a raised platform approached by steps and sometimes canopied. The minaret – a slim tower with a single or sometimes two or three balconies – was used by the *muezzin* for the call to prayer four times a day – at daybreak, noon, mid-afternoon, and sunset. Minarets were introduced fairly early on and their numbers vary: a single minaret for a small mosque, four and sometimes more for a larger one.

The courtyard was an important element in Islamic architecture, not confined to the mosque. It usually contained sculpture, trees, and shrubs. Arched porches, gateways, and halls for various purposes are other typical characteristics.

The Dome of the Rock, Jerusalem, built at the end of the seventh century on Mount Moriah, the mountain from which the prophet Muhammad is said to have ridden at night to heaven, is one of the early Muslim buildings. Another extant mosque is the Great Mosque, Damascus, converted from a temple by the Caliph Al-Walid after the city fell to the Arabs early in the eighth century. The Caliph was the title of the spiritual and military ruler of Islam in succession to the prophet Muhammad. It was Caliph Abd-ar-Rahman I and his successors who were responsible for the Great Mosque, Córdoba, begun in the late eighth century. The mosque has a number of arcades placed in lines parallel to the main axis of the prayer hall. A variety of classical columns, used for the arcades, were too short. Therefore columns were placed on top of one another to gain height, and the arches of the lower columns acted as stiffeners. The visual affect of interlacing arches at different levels is remarkable. The same device was used for the Great Mosque, Damascus, which has an entablature between the lower and upper rows of columns. The first arches at Córdoba were circular, but cusped and horseshoe arches and ornate forms of vaulting were added later. A most striking feature is the striped pattern of brick and stone used alternately for the *voussoirs*, the wedge-shaped pieces forming an arch. The Great Mosque, Córdoba, is now a cathedral.

The Muslim hold on southern Spain was already weakened when the Alhambra was built at Granada as a fortified palace in the late fourteenth century. The magnificent design, one of the tourist attractions of the Costa del Sol today, is set in a large garden which ranges from a formal layout to informal, natural planting. A series of courts and pavilions lead off one another in a series of superbly arranged spaces. The whole complex stands, for defense purposes, on a hill, and at various points in the layout there are splendid views over the tiled roofs of Granada. The Court of the Lions, formally used for public events of an official kind, is typical of the sensitive detailing. The court has arcades on four sides. The entrance is at one end of the long axis and the Hall of Justice at the other. There are less important halls opening off the arcade on the cross axis. The slender columns of the arcading build up into tall blocks of masonry, known as *dosserets*, from which the pointed arches ascend. The whole of the upper structure is elaborately carved with miniature columns and filigree plaster work. Such work is still carried out today in the Arab countries of the Middle East, in the private residences of the wealthy. The Court of Myrtles at the Alhambra Palace was reserved for the use of the ruler. At the end of it is the Comares Tower, containing the Hall of Ambassadors, topped by a dome.

The greatest architect of the Turkish mosque was Sinan. He regarded the Selimiye Mosque at Edirne, a Turkish town near the Bulgarian and Greek border, as his greatest work. The mosque, with two colleges, makes a single symmetrical design. There are four minarets, each with three balconies. The central dome, larger than St Sophia, measuring more than 30.5 metres in diameter, is supported by eight enormous piers arranged octagonally, and clearly visible on the outside.

Less than one hundred years later, in the seventeenth century, the Taj Mahal was built in Agra in India. The architecture is Islamic, but the tomb is in the Mughal tradition, surrounded by walls and standing in formal gardens. This famous and much photographed building was commissioned by the Emperor Shah Jehan, a great patron of architecture, as a memorial to Mumtaz-i-Mahal, his most favoured wife. The dominant visual element is the large outer pointed dome over the centre of the square-planned mausoleum. The outer dome is supported at the four corners of the plan by a massive system of lesser domes and walls with pierced arched openings. Four imposing entrance ways are placed in the centre of the four symmetrical sides of the tomb, and slim circular minarets mark the four corners of the walled enclosure. The outer shell of the central dome is nearly 61 metres high and the inner dome nearly 24.5 metres high by 18.3 metres in diameter. The magic quality of the Taj Mahal comes from the white marble of the exterior, its intricate carving and the wonderful reflections from the pools in the formal garden. The interior is also intricately carved, particularly the elaborate marble screen enclosing the tomb of the Shah and his wife.

In addition to the mosques and palaces of Islamic culture, the collection of courts, markets, and narrow streets, huddled together to form small towns or villages, have produced some remarkable architectural forms. Well-known examples include the 'Beehive' village near Aleppo, the great trading centre in Greek, Roman and later times, and the city of Shibam in southern Arabia.

The palaces and forts of Egypt and north Africa, in addition to the Mosques, developed their own forms of architecture influenced by the spread of Islam through its conquering forces. The distinguishing features were the same: the pointed dome, the pointed arch, bands of brick and stone used alternately on walls and arches, crenellated parapets, and pierced stone grilles. In India, the great tombs of the Sultans, built between the fourteenth and sixteenth centuries, were among the greatest Islamic forms.

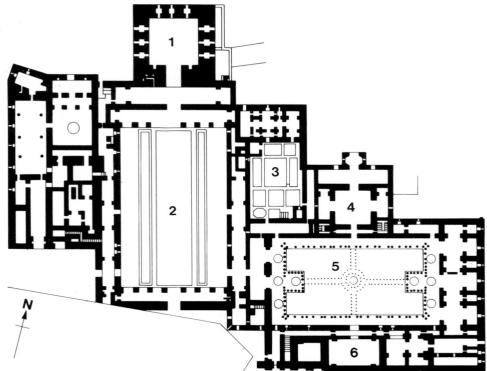

Above
ALHAMBRA PALACE, Granada.
c. 1338–90. Court of the Lions. There are
muqarnas arches and vaults in the
foreground.

Left
ALHAMBRA PALACE, Granada.
c. 1338–90. Plan:
1 Hall of Ambassadors,
2 Court of Alberea,
3 baths,
4 Hall of Two Sisters,
5 Court of the Lions,
6 Hall of Abencerrages.

Opposite
SELIMIYE MOSQUE, Edirne, Turkey.
c. 1570–75.

TAJ MAHAL, Agra, India. *c.* 1630–53. A feature is the great thickness of the dome's masonry and its supports. These are buttressed by the heavily built shapes at the four corners of the buildings topped by smaller domes. The minarets at the corners of the site are built slightly outwards to ensure that they fell that way in the event of a collapse.

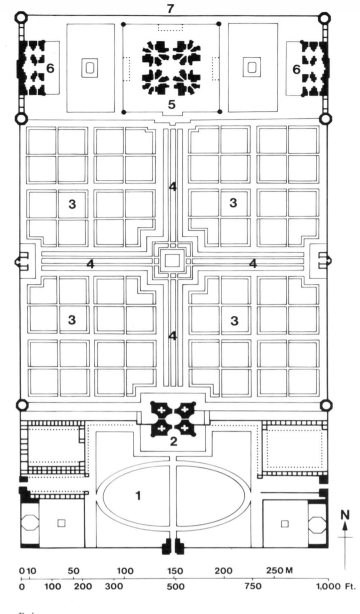

Right
TAJ MAHAL, Agra, India. *c.* 1630–53.
Plan:
1 entrance court,
2 great gateway,
3 garden courts,
4 canal
5 mausoleum,
6 mosque,
7 River Jumna.

N ▲

0 10	50	100	150	200	250 M
0	100	200	300	500	750	1,000 Ft.

Below
BEEHIVE VILLAGE at Bunessmir, Aleppo,
Syria.

Pre-Columbian America

Long before the Spaniards under Cortés invaded Mexico in the first quarter of the sixteenth century, even before the Indian tribes, the Mexicas or Aztecs, dominated the central area, there were mysterious civilizations with magnificent pyramids, temples and citadels, the remains of which may be seen throughout Mexico and other parts of meso-America. The indications are that the civilizations had large populations of a deeply religious people. Who they were, what they used their ceremonial buildings for, where they came from, and where they disappeared to, is not known. Certainly there are sculptured figures and wall carvings to give indications, but no records such as would be expected if the peoples had been conquered by invaders. The Indian tribes who followed after them used the buildings and in some centuries copied them, adding their own innovations. But the Indians seemed unaware of the origins of the buildings, and, until the coming of the Spaniards, they were unknown to the outside world.

Meso-America covers a large area of Mexico and the countries of Central America, and many different cultures prevailed there. The middle of America about the tenth millenium B.C. consisted mainly of lakes. The tribes lived there by hunting and fishing. Those early American Indians are now believed to have been descended from peoples migrating from Asia. The first glimmerings of a culture began with the Olmecs who, by the first century B.C., had developed artistically in pottery and figurines. Their distinctive art forms were the jaguar, stylized figures of the jaguar god, and enormous human heads with heavy features. Similar heads are often seen in modern buildings in Mexico. Olmec was the culture from which sprang the Teotihuacán civilization, Maya and Zapotec. All these later civilizations used platforms with sloping sides, topped with small temples. Their vast cities usually contained a ball court, with two long parallel sides. There the ball game, with its religious overtones, invented by the Olmecs was played sometimes with lives at stake. The game was played with a solid rubber ball about 12.5 centimetres in diameter. Players wore pads on hips, elbows, and knees,

TEOTIHUACÁN, Mexico. 600 B.C.–A.D. 300. Plan:
1 Pyramid of the Moon,
2 Pyramid of the Sun,
3 Street of the Dead,
4 citadel,
5 Southern Pyramid and Temple of Quetzalcoatl.

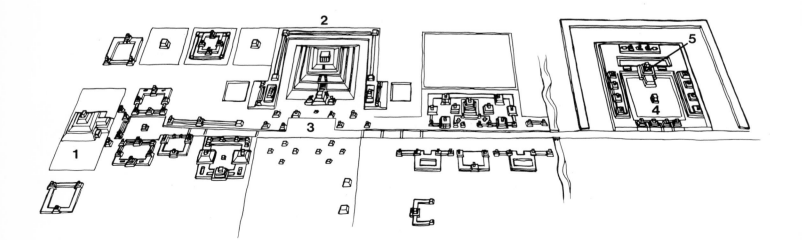

as shown in mural paintings, and it is believed the ball had only to be touched by such parts of the body.

The greatest city of these early civilizations is Teotihuacán, north-east of Mexico City. Its origins are obscure. The name Teotihuacán meaning 'the place of the dead' or 'the place where those who die become gods', (which may have related to early human sacrifice) was given to the city by the Toltecs, a warlike people who invaded the valley of Mexico in the tenth century A.D. and dominated the other tribes. Teotihuacán, like the cities of other cultures, developed over centuries. Its time scale has been divided into four chronological periods: preclassic or formative (about 600–300 B.C.), early classic (about 300 B.C.–A.D. 300), late classic (about 300–600), and the decadent period (about 600–900). In the preclassic period Teotihuacán was laid out in a grid pattern. At the height of its development the city extended 18 square kilometres, taking in the local centres of Atetelco, Tepantítla, and others. No defensive walls existed. Some time in the classic period a central axis (later called 'the street of the dead' by the Aztecs) was carved through the middle, from the so-called citadel (*ciudadela*) and temple of Quetzalcoatle to the Pyramid of the Moon at the north end of the street, a distance of over three kilometres.

The Pyramid of the Sun, the largest structure at Teotihuacán, standing over 61 metres high, lies to the east midway along the street of the dead. The pyramid rises in four stages. A broad flight of steps ascends from the west, facing the street of the dead, and axially on a line with the setting sun on the day of the summer solstice. The rise of each step is greater than the tread, making direct ascent difficult. The basic material of the pyramid is sun-dried bricks, over which was laid a layer of stone and stucco. Unfortunately the stone was removed in error in the first decade of the twentieth century. At the top of the pyramid there used to be the usual small temple-like structure. In front of the sun pyramid is an open plaza, and beyond groups of cell-like dwellings, arranged one on each side of small rectangular sunken courts. The dwellings had portico-type entrances, approached from the court, and divided into three openings by pairs of columns.

The street of the dead was lined with palaces and temples. Today the small platforms or pyramids with three or four tiers, their staircases fronting the street, line it on both sides. The street widens into a plaza at the north end in front of the Pyramid of the Moon, the second largest structure at Teotihuacán. Like the Sun Pyramid, the Moon Pyramid rises in stages but is much smaller. At

PYRAMID OF THE SUN, Teotihuacán, Mexico. 600 B.C.–A.D. 300.

Above
TEOTIHUACÁN, Mexico. 600 B.C.–A.D. 300. Street of the Dead. The Pyramid of the Sun is on the left.

Right
PALACE OF THE GOVERNORS, Uxmal, Yucatán, Mexico. Eighth/ninth century. The Puuc style of the Maya.

Opposite
TEMPLE OF QUETZALCOATL (Feathered Serpent), Southern Pyramid of the Citadel, Teotihuacán, Mexico. 600 B.C.–A.D. 300. The exposed feathered-serpent-headed frieze.

PALACE OF THE GOVERNORS, Uxmal, Yucatán, Mexico. Eighth/ninth century. An arched entrance way.

the citadel, is an earlier temple of the feathered serpent god, Quetzalcoatl. This has been partly uncovered to show a magnificent carved talud tablero, with sculptures of sea shells, serpents, marks of Tlaloc, the rain god, and projecting heads of Quetzalcoatl. The Sun and Moon pyramids were completed over a long period from about 300 B.C. to A.D. 300 or later. The citadel was begun much later and was probably completed before A.D. 600. At that time, the style was changed, and lower platforms were built.

The citadel, named by the Aztecs many years after it was built, is today a flat grassed court about 1 kilometre square, fenced on three sides by long two-tiered platforms. Each platform is topped by four two-tiered pyramids. In the centre of the court is a single platform. The construction is stone rubble set in clay, originally faced with 10 to 12 centimetres of brilliantly painted stucco. None of the stucco remains except for small patches on the stone-work close to the ground. Teotihuacán still has many buildings unexcavated and over the whole site are numerous mounds indicating their presence. There are even older remains at Monté Alban which was started before Teotihuacán.

At Monté Alban (white mountain), Oaxaca, the temple complex went through a number of building phases, the earliest in the eighth century B.C. Like Teotihuacán, it was ruled by a religious hierarchy which dominated the peasant and farming communities of Oaxaca. The peasants and farmers would visit the sacred centre for religious rites connected with fertility, growth, rain, and sun which so affected their daily life. The priests at Monté Alban, as at Teotihuacán, became more powerful and numerous, gradually increasing their occupancy of the centre. In later years building at Monté Alban was influenced by Teotihuacán, but Monté Alban's distinguishing features were its wide staircases and broad balustrades never matched at Teotihuacán.

Another great culture, the Maya, existed in Yucatán, El Salvador, and Honduras. Yucatán in the south-east of Mexico has some of the most interesting remains, rescued from dense jungle growth, still encroaching in many parts, and hiding unknown archaeological treasures. The climate of Yucatán is very hot and the soil poor but there is an abundance of stone for building. The Mayan civilization was technically ahead of its contemporaries in meso-America. The Mayans invented a calendar, were

its base a broad staircase ascends through five stepped terraces in front of the pyramid. The terraces are of a style called *talud tablero*. The *tablero* is a frieze within a bold frame, and it overhangs the *talud*, a band of masonry set on a slant between friezes. The talud tablero terraces of the Moon Pyramid are of a late form which was stucco-covered and brightly coloured or painted with figures. The same style was used for the stepped terraces of the citadel. But under the Southern Pyramid, which forms part of

advanced in mathematics and astronomy, and used a method of vaulting with an arch built out by corbelling (that is building out the stonework in steps). On the facade an arch often had the appearance of a triangle. The classic period of Mayan architecture was between the first and third centuries and the tenth century. The work of this period has been uncovered at Palenque in the jungle of Chiapas. Uxmal and Chichén Itzá came later, and their development (about 1300) was influenced by the Toltecs and the work at Teotihuacán. Some time after the classic Mayan period came to an end in the tenth century, Chichén Itzá became the capital of the Toltecs in Yucatán, and the style of building at both Uxmal and Chichén Itzá after that period became known as *Toltec-Maya*.

The temple layouts, pyramids, and ball court at Palenque are classic, but the most interesting find was made in 1952 in the Temple of Inscriptions. Here the rare discovery was made of the tomb of a Mayan priest-king, his sarcophagus covered by an 8 tonne sculp-

tured tombstone slab. His skeleton with a green jade funeral mask, bracelets, necklaces, and other adornments was revealed. A replica of the tomb and its remains, together with the jewels, are to be seen in the Mayan section of the modern Anthropological Museum building, by Pedro Ramirez Vasquez, in Chapultepec Park, Mexico City.

The Palace of the Governors at Uxmal, dating from the eighth/ninth centuries, illustrates the *Puuc* style of the Maya, notable for its clean proportions and restraint. Decorative carving was reserved for the heavily sculptured frieze above a plain stone-walled ground floor, enlivened by doorways along the front. The design is symmetrical, even to the arrangement of the decorations on the frieze, but there is no evenness. Decoration is balanced, and the doorway spacing converges at the centre. It is a remarkably sensitive piece of design. Triangular arched entrances separate wings of a later date from the central block. The palace measures more than 91 metres in length, is some 12 metres deep and

PALACE OF THE GOVERNORS, Uxmal, Yucatán, Mexico. Eighth/ninth century. Detail of the frieze showing key pattern.

Above
CASTILLO, Chichén Itzá, Yucatán,
Mexico. Eleventh/twelfth century. A
four-sided pyramid topped by a temple
with two chambers. There were two
constructions, both of the Toltec-Mayan
period. The cut away portion shows part
of the earlier pyramid, which had only one
staircase, nine stages, and a temple on top.

Left
CHICHÉN ITZÁ. Yucatán, Mexico.
Tenth to thirteenth centuries. Plan:
1 Well of Sacrifice,
2 Ball Court,
3 Temple of the Jaguars,
4 Temple of the Warriors,
5 castillo,
6 High Priest's grave,
7 nunnery.

Opposite
TEMPLE OF THE WARRIORS, Chichén
Itzá, Yucatán, Mexico. Tenth to thirteenth
centuries (built during the Toltec-Mayan
period). Detail of the Kukulcan columns.

N

0   150 M

0   450 Ft.

stands about 9 metres high. A great platform along the front is approached up a broad stone staircase. In the centre of the forecourt is a piece of sculpture representing a two-headed jaguar. From the front, doorways lead to vaulted chambers. The whole temple has been magnificently restored. The so-called Nunnery, the Ball Court (between the Nunnery and the Governor's Palace), and the Pyramid of the Sorcerer are among other buildings of Uxmal, not all of them fully restored. The Pyramid of the Sorceror has been enlarged five times, beginning with the Puuc style and showing Toltec influences in the latest exterior, on which there are carvings of Quetzalcoatl whom the Mayas called Kukulcan.

Chichén Itzá's development began in the classic Mayan period about the eighth/ninth centuries A.D. and continued into the later Toltec–Mayan period between the tenth and thirteenth centuries. The Toltecs were a warrior tribe worshipping gods who demanded war and human sacrifice, unknown in the classic Mayan period. The Toltecs were also great builders. Chichén Itzá orig-inally covered an area of about 3.2 kilometres by 2.5. Many of the principal buildings have been restored. One of them, the Castillo, is a pyramid 24 metres high; it has four sloping sides with wide staircases to the top, orien-tated to face the four cardinal points of the compass. Each staircase has 91 steps and four times 91 plus the platform on which the Castillo rests equals 365, the number of days in the solar year: factors which are believed to have had some religious significance. The temple on the summit has two chambers: one guarded by a stone *chac-mool*, a sacred figure half reclining on a plinth with head sideways and knees drawn up. Human hearts were placed in a recess in its centre. The guardian of the other chamber was a red stone jaguar with jade eyes.

In other parts of the city were great constructions: the Platform of the Eagles and Tigers, with four stairways, notable for the feathered serpent motifs of Toltec origin; the Ball Court, more than 122 metres long and more than 36.5 metres wide with flanking walls 6 metres high on the long sides; the Temple of the Jaguars; and the sacred well in which human sacrifices were made by drowning. Assemblies of fighting men, never required in classic Mayan times, had their special building: the Temple of the Warriors and Hall of 1000 Columns, the columns decorated with eagles and tigers, the Toltec military orders. The temple stood at the top of a three-tier pyramid with typical Toltec talud tablero panel elements on the sloping sides. The temple at the top was larger than usual with two square columns, representing Kukulcan – the serpent god, with feathered heads at the base and rattles at the top – dividing the entrance into three. Square columns inside supported the roof beams. Puuc Mayan style was certainly intended for the temple walls, plain stone for the lower part and upper panel richly carved in-cluding masks of Chac, the Mayan rain-god figure.

Mayan architecture came to an end suddenly because, it is widely believed, there was a revolt against the religious hierarchy which had probably made the peasants' lives miserable. They slew the priests and returned to their villages of

thatch and pisé, still found in the jungle communities today. But the buildings continued to be used for ceremonial purposes.

The Mexicas or Aztecs, after much wandering in the twelfth to fourteenth centuries, settled in central Mexico with their headquarters at Tenochtítlan. They became mercenaries of a dominant tribe called the Tepanecs and were thus experts at war. Eventually the Aztecs became all-powerful themselves and founded an empire (c. 1376), extending as far as Veracruz and Oaxaca. They were a fierce and cruel people and, although they worshipped Toltec gods – Tezcatlipoca, god of the sky, Tlaloc, the rain god, and Quetzalcoatl, the feathered serpent – their pincipal deity was Huitzilopochtli, god of the sun and war. To him they sacrificed their prisoners in thousands, cutting out their hearts. The vast structures at Teotihuacán and in the Yucatán were used in the ceremonies, but the greatest structural achievements of the Aztecs lay in the planning and building of Tenochtítlan – later Mexico City. It was

the Aztec monarch Montezuma II who reigned at Tenochtítlan when the Spaniard Cortés arrived there. Owing to inferior weapons and partly because of an old legend that Quetzalcoatl would one day return to earth, Montezuma, uncertain whether or not Cortés was the returning god, ultimately surrendered to him in 1521. The Aztec Empire gradually succumbed, and the Spanish colony, New Mexico, was founded.

South America was dominated by the Inca civilization. Cuzco was the name of the great Inca city of the fifteenth century and the Inca empire of that time was the largest in pre-Columbian America. The remains of the great fortress of Sacsayhuamán, guarding the city of Cuzco on the north side, show that it consisted of three terraces of stone walls defending an inner citadel. The citadel had stone buildings for storing water and for housing the garrison. The terrace walls were angled, to facilitate cross-fire against attackers. Cuzco remained the centre of the Inca empire until the Spanish invasion of Peru in 1533.

SACSAYHUAMÁN, Cuzco, Peru. *c.* 1400. Inca masonry fortifications.

64

Indian Architecture

The earliest known civilization in India came from the Indus Valley some time in the third millenium B.C. The discovery was made in the 1920s when the remains of two major cities were found: Harappā in the Punjab, and Mahenjo-Daro on the river Indus. The cities are interesting because their layout and characteristics were more advanced than the periods which followed. Uncertainty surrounds the people who founded them, but it is thought they came overland from Mesopotamia, since many of the items found are similar to those of about the same period in that country. Mahenjo-Daro was laid out as a symmetrical city with main avenues orientated north-south and minor streets at right angles to them orientated roughly east-west, similar to early cities in China. In addition to dwellings there were markets and warehouses built of kiln-dried bricks. This is remarkable because the area which is today mainly desert must have possessed an abundance of trees in those early days. Wood remains of lintels also show that trees were plentiful and there may have been upper floors in wood, but none remain. The Indus civilization seems to have disappeared after about a thousand years, probably as a result of invasion which has successively made its impact on India and left its mark on architecture from the Aryans to the present day.

Aryan tribes invaded India during the second millenium B.C., but by 500 B.C. were largely absorbed into the indigenous Dravidian population. The Aryans brought with them their thirty-three Vedic gods. They were mainly associated with elements such as sun, fire, water, and wind. The greatest god was Indra, God of the Atmosphere and Thunder. The Dravidians believed in incarnation through their cult of *bhakti* and therefore followed image worship.

India has more than eight hundred different dialects, and broadly speaking they are divided into Dravidian and Aryan languages. The Dravidian influ-ence is strongest in southern India where the Dravidian languages predominate and the people are short and dark-skinned. The tall, fair-skinned and long-nosed Aryan people are mainly found in northern areas. From these two cultures the Hindu religion was born, narrowing the gods down to three: Brahma, Siva, and Vishnu. Brahma was the God of the Universe. Siva was the God of Destruction, but as a means to recreation. Vishnu was mild and benevolent, and, in Hindu art, is shown in many different manifestations. His followers reach salvation through personal service and devotion. The differences in outlook between the conquering Aryans, the ancient customs of the Dravidians, and the aborigines were reconciled by the Hindu caste system, which still exists strongly in India today. The caste system divides people into social groups: *Brahmins*, who were priests and policy makers; *Kshatriyas*, rulers and warriors; *Vaishyas* the merchants and farmers; and *Shudras*, labourers and unskilled workers. The Brahmins dominated the system.

The influence of the Brahmins, which had produced a rigid form of life under the caste system, was challenged in the sixteenth century B.C. by Jainism founded by Mahāvira (599-527 B.C.), of Brahmin caste, and by Buddhism, founded by Siddhārtha Gautama of high-born family in the Kshatriyas caste. Like Hinduism, both Jainism and Buddhism, born in India, became world religions. In Jainism, salvation was reached through progressive reincarnation. Atonement for sin was made through rebirth (*karma*) as an animal or slave. Ascetism and meticulous care in not harming any living creatures was part of Jain philosophy. In Buddhism, the goal was freedom from karma, by right thought and right action.

These three religions, Hinduism, Buddhism, and Jainism all affected Indian religious architecture. Jain temples are similar to Hindu temples but the ornamentation is usually richer. Buddhist temples and shrines are usually intended for a multitude of worshippers. Architecture was also influenced by the cultures of later invaders, culminating in the French and English incursions of the mid-eighteenth century onwards. The Muslims first invaded India successfully in 711. They had conquered a large part of northern India by the thirteenth century and introduced Islamic architectural forms. Much earlier, the Greeks, under Alexander the Great, had invaded India and reached the river Indus. Alexander was forced to with-

GREAT STUPA, Sāñchī. Mid-first century B.C. The mound represented the heavens; the mast with umbrellas, the world's axis.

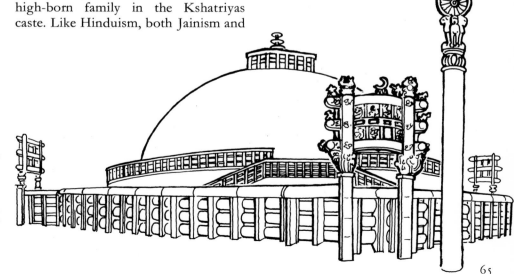

draw and died at Babylon in 328 B.C., but India was opened up to Hellenistic art and Greek columns found their way into Indian temples. The first Indian empire was created by the Emperor Maurya about this time, and during the Mauryan Period (322–185 B.C.) the Emperor's Great Palace of sunbaked brick and wood at Pātaliputra, long since disappeared, was reputed to have rivalled the great palaces of Persia.

The Sunga Period (185–72 B.C.) was notable for the development of the Buddhist form of shrine, known as the *stupa*. Originally the stupa was simply a burial mound for noblemen or holy men. The famous Emperor Asoka of the Mauryan dynasty ordered stupas to be built in every important town to contain relics of the Buddha. The same emperor ordered rock-cut caves for Jain ascetics, which were copies of huts in wood and thatch. Although in later examples the stupa itself became a symbol of worship, usually containing a seated figure of the Buddha, early stupas had no other function than to contain Buddha relics. Outwardly they were simple shapes, rounded to represent the heavens. The central mast (*yasti*) on the top represented the axis of the world, and the succession of umbrellas (*chatras*) symbolized heavens ascending to the Brahma heaven at the top. The Great Stupa, Sāñchī, dating from the Āndhra Period (72–25 B.C.) is typical of the early form. The gateways with their triple crossbeams (*torana*) are reminders of the Japanese *torii* (p. 79).

The Buddhist religion spread to Burma and Ceylon, and ultimately across the world. The stupa grew in importance, and the greatest example in which the Buddhist ritual of circumambulation plays a paramount part, was built at Barabudur, Java, in the eighth or ninth century. The complex stands on a small hill in the plains of Java, and the design has a spiritual symbolism, found in the Temple and Altar of Heaven in Peking, China (p. 77). The plan of Barabudur is square. The first circumbulatory ascent is through five receding terraces, which amount to corridors of stone, with the enclosing stone walls elaborately carved with scenes from the life of Buddha. These terraces represent life on earth. In the centre of each terrace at the four points of the compass are elaborate stone portals opening up vistas of the central stupa at the top of the monument. Thus, the pilgrim is constantly reminded of his goal as he ascends the five terraces. The next stage consists of three circular receding terraces, winding to the main stupa at the top. These terraces are open, and outlined by seventy-two small stupas each with a seated statue of Buddha facing outwards. The terraces represent heaven, and the Buddhas, facing all directions, the omnipotence of the deity. This very difficult concept has been successfully mastered in a truly wonderful and elaborate piece of architecture.

The second important Buddhist religious building was the temple. Early Buddhist temples were probably made

STUPA OF BARABUDUR, Java. Eighth/ninth century. The lower five receding terraces represent life on earth; the upper three open circular terraces 'heaven'. The enormous scale of the monument may be judged by the steps going up to the top in the centre of each side. As the pilgrim makes a circumambulatory ascent, the final stupa is seen from each quarter looking along the steps, gradually coming nearer and nearer. Each of the seventy-two smaller stupas contains a seated figure of the Buddha facing outwards.

Above
STUPA OF BARABUDUR, Java. Eighth/
ninth century. Stupas in the three tiers
below the top form part of 'heaven'.

Right
GREAT STUPA, Sāñchĭ. Mid-first century.
Torana, East gateway.

of wood, and the next stage was to cut temples from the living rock, of which an early example is the second century B.C. Chaitya Hall at Bhājā. The hall is oblong in shape with an apse at one end. Rows of columns down both sides of the hall and around the apse marked off a narrow continuous aisle, used for circumambulation. The apse contained a stupa cut from the rock.

The largest of the Buddhist rock-cut temples is the Chaitya Hall at Kărli, dating from the first century B.C. The temple is almost 38 metres long and over 13.5 metres wide. The vault of corbelled stonework, barrel-shaped, rises almost 14 metres to the crown. The construction of so large a building hewn from the rock was ingenious. First, the front stonework was smoothed over on the cliff face, and the entrance and front features carved out. Then the vault was broken into from above and the whole of the inside columns and stupa hewn from the solid rock. Debris of rock and earth was taken through the cave entrance.

In early rock-cut temples, wooden beams were fixed across the vault to resemble the framed roof structure of a free-standing building. Sometimes, when the cave face was open, the front was built of wood. During the Gupta Period (320–600), when unified rule in India was restored, the chaitya hall became a free-standing temple. An example in brick existing at Chezarla is now a Hindu temple dedicated to Siva.

Hinduism gradually gained greater strength over other cultures in India. From 765 until the nineteenth century, when the influence of European architecture began to be felt, Hindu dynasties were in power and Hindu religious architecture reached its peak. In Hindu architecture, there were handbooks of instructions about the choice of site, the method of construction, details of how the outside walls of temples should be treated, and layouts to suit different gods. The building manuals, called *sastras*, also described rituals and gave dimensions suitable for their observance in religious buildings. This degree of

consideration for careful ritual planning and progressive decoration was never reached in Christian architecture of the Middle Ages. In India, the elaboration of ritual architecture seems to be a vain attempt to excel in what had gone before. To some extent this may reflect the fact that, in spite of an older civilization, India did not achieve the breakthrough into the age of science and discovery achieved in the West.

The most important element of the Hindu temple was the *garbha-griha*, a small shrine with a conical structure towering above it called the *sikhara*. Sikhara means mountain peak, and refers to the mountain peak of the world, sacred to the Hindu god Siva. The Hindu temple, like its Greek counterpart, was a dwelling place of the gods, and was not intended for congregational use like the Buddhist temples and shrines. The top of the sikhara was called the *kalasa*, and was often shaped like a stupa. Leading up to the sikhara and its garbha-griha was a series of porches known as *mandapas*, and used for re-

Opposite
CHAITYA HALL, Bhājā. *c.* second century
B.C. Rock-cut temple.

Above
LIṄGARÀJA TEMPLE, Bhubaneswar,
Orissa. *c.* 1000.

Right
LIṄGARÀJA TEMPLE, Bhubaneswar,
c. 1000. Plan and section:
1 hall leading to
2 shrine.

GREAT TEMPLE, Madurai, southern India. Enlarged in the seventeenth century.

ligious dances, ceremonies, and music.

In the Liṅgarāja temple at Bhubaneswar in Orissa, southern India (*c.* 1000), the sikhara has the typical beehive shape. The vaulting of the sikhara is constructed of corbelled out masonry, ending in a stupa-like cap. The mandapas were used for festivals and assemblies of worshippers. The exteriors of the walls are richly carved. The significant feature of Liṅgarāja and similar Hindu temples is the colossal weight of masonry used in proportion to the space enclosed.

The final development of the Hindu temple in Dravidian southern India was to provide additional accommodation for certain processions, when the gods were removed from their shrines and displayed to the masses of people who had come to see them. The Great Temple, Madurai, was enlarged for this purpose in the seventeenth century, almost to the size of a small city. The temple site was roughly rectangular and surrounded by high walls. At the main

points of the compass in the walls are huge entrances called *gopurams*, their high battered walls, elaborately carved, towering above the remainder of the temple and the lowly homes of the inhabitants. Inside the walls there is a complicated maze of colonnades and courtyards linking up pavilions and halls around the central shrine. Processions, bazaars, law sittings, ritual dancing, and religious instruction take place in the centre, and there is a bathing pool for purification, surrounded by columned cloisters. There are over two thousand columns in the halls at Madurai. The halls replaced the mandapas of earlier Hindu temples.

Madurai was the capital of the later Pandyan Nayak dynasty, in the seventeenth and eighteenth centuries, and the last of the five Hindu states which dominated India from the sixth century. Innovation in Hindu architecture virtually ceased after Madurai and the coming of western influences to India.

Chinese Architecture

China is larger than the whole of Europe. Its legendary civilization is more than three thousand years old, but meaningful architectural records date back to a few centuries B.C. Following the period of the Warring States (fifth–third centuries B.C.), Ch'in Shih-Huang-ti, or the First Emperor, united the empire in 221 B.C. Ch'in's rule was oppressive and ended in civil war from which Liu Bang emerged victorious to found the Han dynasty (206 B.C.–A.D. 220). During his time Ch'in pieced together the sections of wall built previously to protect the north against raiders, and forced thousands of men to create the Great Wall. At that time the wall was built mainly of earth and rubble with stone used only to reinforce it. During the Han regime the principles of Chinese town planning based on the square and the central axis were established, and also the Chinese *tou-kung* bracket system. Both are referred to later. The failure of the Han was followed by several centuries of war and general disturbance – a period known as 'The Three Kingdoms and Six Dynasties'. The empire was not restored again until the Sue dynasty (589–618), which was followed by the T'ang dynasty (618–907). In both periods there was increasing interest in architecture. The three great spiritual influences were Taoism, Confucianism and Buddhism.

Taoism, founded by Lao-tzu in the sixth century B.C., was a philosophy in which the spiritual goal was harmony with the Great Order (*Tao*). It applied to groups of persons as well as individuals. The artist's interpretation of it, whatever the medium used, was to portray the spiritual essence of the subject. The concept of Tao was present in Confucianism, dating from the fifth/ sixth centuries B.C. In the Confucian philosophy there were moral laws governing the world and the universe. Man had to develop all his talents to reach his set goal – Tao or the Mandate of Heaven, which was heaven itself. The

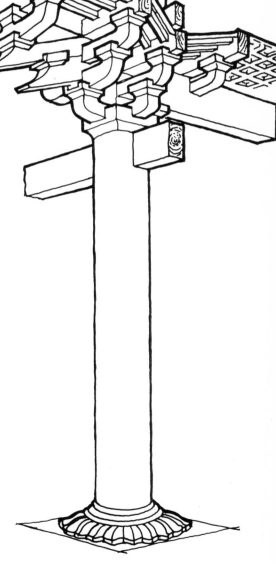

TOU-KUNG bracket system.

established order was important, especially the concept of the family coming between the individual and the state. Obligations rather than rewards were regarded as man's lot. Broadly, in western terms, Taoism is more mystical and less rational than Confucianism which represents a more conservative attitude to living.

Buddhism came to China under the Han dynasty when small groups of Buddhist monks settled in the country. By the middle of the sixth century the religion was well established and there were about 35,000 monasteries or more. One of the effects this had on architecture was the introduction of the Buddhist practice, following Indian precedent, of building pagodas in stone and brick, rather than wood in the typical Chinese manner.

During the seventh and eighth centuries China was master of central Asia and Korea. Trade flourished and so did literature and art. But invasion from Tibet and Mongolia split the country into two during the Five Dynasties Period (907–960), and during the Song Period (960–1279), until Genghis Kahn and his Mongols swept the country. Genghis Kahn established his capital at Peking in 1260. Under Kublai Khan, the grandson of Genghis Khan, Peking became the centre of the Mongolian empire's trade. Yuan (1279–1368) was the name of Kublai's dynasty. His Peking court was famous and was visited by travellers from all over the world, including the Venetian explorer, Marco Polo, who lived in Peking for about twenty years. Unrest towards the end of the dynasty brought fresh rebellion. The Mongols were driven back behind the Great Wall and a new dynasty was founded called the Ming Dynasty (1368–1644). After 1644 the rulers of China came from a tribe who invaded the country from Manchuria. The Manchus' dynastic name was Ching, and they ruled until 1911, retaining Peking as their capital.

Throughout this period of Chinese history the Great Wall was in constant use, sometimes as a defensive rampart but always as a means of communication. In the sixth and seventh centuries rebuilding and repairs had been carried out on a gigantic scale, with conscripted and convict labour reaching a million men in one year. For a time, until the Ming ousted the Mongols, the wall was less important for defense purposes, but to guard against further Mongol invasion, the wall was moved southward in the centre. It now extended roughly 2750–2900 kilometres and, although its condition and quality varied, the best

sections restored by the Ming equalled the high standard of the town walls. In certain respects the Great Wall is similar to Hadrian's Wall which runs between England and Scotland. It follows the natural contour of the countryside, with watch towers, gates, and ramped approaches placed at intervals along it, but its stonework side walls are battered and rise 6–7.5 metres. The road is about 6 metres across at the top and the surface is of brickwork. The parapet wall, crenellated on one side only, is 1.5 metres high.

In their study of the universe the ancient Chinese regarded the earth as a square. Bearing in mind the philosophy of Taoism, the concept of a city, palace, mansion, or house planned as a square is perhaps understandable. Cities were planned almost square with streets at right angles to one another orientated south–north, west–east. Walled enclosures filled the spaces between the streets, creating courtyards of different sizes, according to the social order of palace, mansion, or house. There were two ways of planning within the courtyard: buildings were either placed in line with

the gateway on a south–north axis, the entrance being on the south side; or buildings were placed to the sides of the court with the principal building in the centre of the north side on an axial line with the gate in the south wall. The entrance and principal building always faced south, which was associated with summer warmth and goodness, while north signified cold, winter, and evil. The social standing of dwellings was easily recognizable by size, magnificence, and colour used in decoration, a carefully considered ingredient of Chinese architecture. The advantages of the Chinese system of planning was the ease with which further squares or rectangles could be added, and the system of courtyard or axial planning could be adopted or combined at will.

One of the earliest cities planned on these principles was the new city near Hang Ta-hsing laid out towards the end of the sixth century by the ruling Sue. The palace was set against the north wall on the central south–north axis, with the administrative city spread out below. There were elven broad south–north avenues, the central one leading from

the city gate to the palace, and fourteen west–east streets. Even the planting was symmetrical – with one exception. There is a story that the architect for the city used to watch it being built from beneath a tree. The tree was out of line, but the Emperor was so pleased with the results of the architect's work that the tree was allowed to remain. The same kind of planning was adopted in Nara, Japan, in 710 and in Kyoto in 794 (pp. 79 to 81). Both Japanese cities were smaller by nearly half than Hang Ta-hsing which was slightly more than 78 kilometres square.

The method of constructing buildings of wood, used in China and subsequently adopted in Japan, dates from before the period of the Warring States. At that time all major buildings were constructed on a platform of compressed earth faced with brick or stone. This was essential in order to help preserve the wooden superstructure by good drainage beneath. Embedded in the platform were pillars, usually of wood, supporting a complex roof structure. In many cases the pillars were slanted inwards slightly, giving the impression of strength, which the Greeks also achieved in their columned temples by means of *entasis* (p. 19).

The basis of the roof structure was a square bay with pillars at the corners. Beams spanned the pillars transversally and longitudinally. Above the beams were brackets supporting short vertical struts and more crossbeams holding *purlins* in place. (Purlins are the long roof beams at right angles to and supporting the rafters). The system repeated itself with the crossbeams becoming shorter as the roof became higher. The key to the system was the special bracketing, which at times reached a cluster of supports. The system of bracketing known as *tou-kung* underwent many changes in its long use over many centuries and fifty or more forms are known, but the basic system shown in the illustrations remained the same. The cluster bracket was particularly complicated at the eaves where the object was to carry the roof outwards as far as possible beyond the pillars. The Chinese beam frame had its problems. As the roof structure was built up, brackets and purlins and the loads they carried rested on the beams below. This build-up of weight from the roof covering, and the added weight of snow, demanded very deep beams or very short spans across the bays. Finding trees large enough to provide the size of beam required must have been a

deciding factor in the length of span. But the Chinese system allowed the builders to slope the roof in either a convex or concave direction. Curves could be designed precisely by shortening or lengthening crossbeams. So important was the arrangement of the roof structure that in China the roof was completed first. Pillars were then positioned exactly at the right points.

In China, roofs were usually covered in tiles laid in rows from ridge to eaves. The tiles were semicircular and rows were laid convex-concave-convex, to form a gutter between each row of convex tiles. Underneath was a thin layer of clay or wood shingles, laid on battens as in the west. Tiles were glazed

Opposite
GREAT WALL OF CHINA. Begun in the third century B.C. Rebuilt extensively in the sixth/seventh centuries.

Below
FO KUNG TEMPLE, Ying-hsien, Shansi. *c*. 1056. Pagoda. Section.

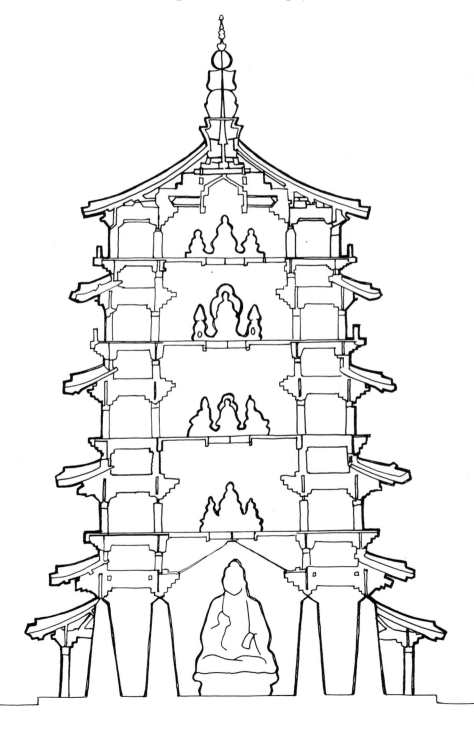

Below
TU LO TEMPLE, Chi-hsien, Hopei. *c.* 984.
Hall of Kuan Yin. The two galleries form
part of the circumambulation of the
gigantic idol of Kuan-yin.

Top
Fo Kung Temple, Ying-hsien, Shansi.
c. 1056. Pagoda.

Above
Imperial Palace, Peking. Late sixteenth
early seventeenth century. Gate of
Supreme Harmony (Taihe Dian). The gate
leads to the main courtyard in front of the
official buildings.

blue, yellow, or green, and for ordinary work a grey-brown colour.

Among the best of Chinese architecture were the religious buildings. A fine example is the Hall of Kuan Yin, part of the Tu Lo Temple, Chi-hsien, Hopei, built c. 984, the second oldest building in China. The roof is typical and shaped to enclose the 15 metres high statue of Kuan Yin. The statue fills an enclosure the full height of the hall with galleries on two levels surrounding it. The ridge is 21 metres from the floor. The hall measures approximately 20 metres by 15, with 20 bays: five bays running lengthways and four crossways. The eaves at ground level project 4.5 metres. The heaviness of the projection of the eaves at ground floor and upper roof level is cunningly softened by the balcony which juts out at first floor level.

The Pagoda of the Fo Kung temple, Ying-hsien, Shansi, c. 1056 is another typical example of Chinese beam frame construction. The building rises five storeys and the plan is octagonal.

For sheer grandeur the Imperial Palace at Peking, dating from the fifth century and restored in the sixteenth and nineteenth centuries, must take first

place. Although it is now a museum, the impressive layout and style is probably very much as it was in the days of Kublai Khan. The palace, the 'Forbidden City', which so impressed Marco Polo, was in fact a city within cities. Outside the walls was the Imperial City surrounded by walls and moated. Beyond the Imperial City was the Inner City, the north part of Peking, surrounded by walls. To the south of the Inner City was the Outer City, also surrounded by walls. The palace is a walled enclosure about one kilometre long south to north and three-quarters wide west to east, surrounded by a moat, sited centrally on the south–north axis of the Old Imperial City which no longer exists. The impressive parts of the palace are: the arrangement of the official halls; and the long avenues marking the ceremonial approach to them, which originally extended beyond the south entrance of the palace to the entrance of the Imperial City. Each stage of the ceremonial approach is heralded by a splendid gateway followed by an enclosed courtyard.

The first gateway, T'ien-an Men (Gate of Heavenly Peace), approached over five bridges across the narrow moat, heralds the entrance to the old Imperial

City. Across a short courtyard is the second gateway, the Duan Men, leading to a longer courtyard. At the end of this courtyard is the third gateway, the Wu Men, built in 1420, rebuilt in 1647, and restored in 1801. The Wu Men, the most elaborate of the processional gateways, is 122 metres long with wings extending southwards down both sides of the approach court, topped with twin towers on each side. Beyond the Wu Men is a vast paved court, crossed from east to west with a curving stream, the River of Golden Water. The stream is crossed by five marble bridges, the centre one reserved for the Emperor's use. A fourth gateway, the Taihe Men (Gateway of Supreme Harmony), beyond the paved court leads to the main courtyard in front of the three official buildings which are positioned in line on a three-tiered terrace.

Built in the seventeenth and restored in the eighteenth century, the three buildings, once used for official ceremonies, are called Taihe Dian (Hall of Supreme Harmony), Zhonghe Dian (Hall of Middle Harmony) and Borohe Dian (Hall of Protecting Harmony). The terrace is enclosed by a wall which has storage buildings placed against it and minor entrances leading out of the court. The Taihe Dian and the Borohe Dian are both pillared halls with double-hipped roofs. The former was used for the more important ceremonies including the Emperor's coronation. The Zhonge Dian, smaller than the other two, was used mainly as a rest-room for the Emperor. All the tiled roofs of the palace were glazed yellow, the special prerogative of the Emperor.

In contrast with the palace, the grid of ordinary Peking streets presented an appearance of grey-painted windowless walls, relieved by the doorways leading into courtyards, and the colourful crowds of people. The planning of the courtyards has already been described. In addition there were the gardens, usually with a pool, ornamental trees, shrubs, paving, flowers in pots, and so on. In a house with two courts, the southern court with an entrance to the street would usually be reserved for receiving visitors, while the inner court behind would contain the family accommodation.

The Temple and Altar of Heaven is another magnificent complex in Peking, showing Chinese axial planning at its best. On the south–north axis is a brick-paved raised causeway over 30.5 metres wide extending the length of the entire scheme. Both the temple and altar were begun in the fourteenth/fifteenth century and restored in later centuries. The open-air Altar of Heaven consists of three stepped circular terraces with marble balustrades and stairways at the four points of the compass. The top tier is a flat circle. The stairways are approached through a circular compound entered at the four points of the compass through triple entrance ways. Beyond the Altar of Heaven is a small pavilion and two smaller buildings in a circular compound. Beyond the compound is a gable-roofed gateway leading to a long expanse of causeway through parkland bordered with trees. A second gable-roofed gateway at the end of the parkland leads to the circular Temple of Heaven. The temple stands on a three-tiered platform with marble balustrades and steps. Its roof is three-tiered, covered with blue glazed tiles, used on other tiled roofs in the complex. The temple structure is brightly painted in red, blue, and gold. The parkland was used for grazing the cattle offered in sacrifices which usually took place in spring and summer, in exchange for rain and a good harvest, or when a special situation arose such as a drought.

Opposite
IMPERIAL PALACE, Peking Late sixteenth early seventeenth century. Hall of Middle Harmony (Zhonghe Dian).

Below
TEMPLE OF HEAVEN (Tian Tan) Peking. Begun in the fourteenth century. Hall of Prayer for Good Harvests (Qui Nian Dian).

Japanese Architecture

Japan was virtually isolated from the western world until the second half of the nineteenth century. Outside influence before that time came mainly from India and China, via Korea. In early architecture the driving force was religion, a story repeated in many periods of building. By the fourth century the Shinto religion had emerged, in which everything natural was related to and associated with divinity, even man himself. Possibly the natural features of Japan gave strength to the early beliefs: the wild mountainous terrain, rocks and water in plenty, an enormous variety of trees and shrubs, and the ever-present threat of earthquakes. In Shinto, the divine is expressed by the word *kami*. Divinity was not omnipotent, although it might be high, swift, beautiful, or fearful, in a superhuman fashion. Thus, certain animals, plants and trees, water and mountains, thunder, birth, growth, and ageing are all *kami*, as well as human beings. Some Shinto gods had *mitama* (souls) which in a shrine took the form of a sacred object (*shintai* or 'god-body'). This might be a mirror, a sword, or even a smooth round stone.

In the fourth century, the imperial family came to be recognized as the ruling authority throughout Japan. The first emperor of Japan was Jinmu Tennŏ. According to legend he was the grandson of the Sun Goddess Amaterasu Ō-mikami, who gave him the mirror, sword, and jewel, the most sacred symbols of the imperial throne.

In the early days, Shinto worship may have influenced the use of 'living' building materials, mainly wood, which has persisted through the centuries. No doubt too, wood was the most suitable building material, if earth tremors were to be encountered. Even today, some of the massive reinforced concrete structures in modern Japan bear some resemblance to the heavy wood construction of the past.

The holiest Shinto shrines in Japan are those at Ise, occupying fenced enclosures in the heart of a forest of cryptomeria trees. There are two shrines built between the third and fifth centuries. The Naiku (inner shrine) is dedicated to the Sun Goddess. The Gekū (outer shrine) is dedicated to Toye-uke-bime-no-kami, the Goddess of Food. The shrines are replaced with replicas of the old shrines every twenty years. The wood used for the framework of posts, beams, and rafters is *hinoki*, a white Japanese cyprus, which is stripped of bark and planed smooth, but otherwise left in its natural state. The roofs are thatched. An important detail at Ise

HŌRYŪJI TEMPLE, Nara. Seventh century. Plan:
1 southern gate,
2 pagoda,
3 Kondō (main hall),
4 cloistered walk,
5 middle gate.

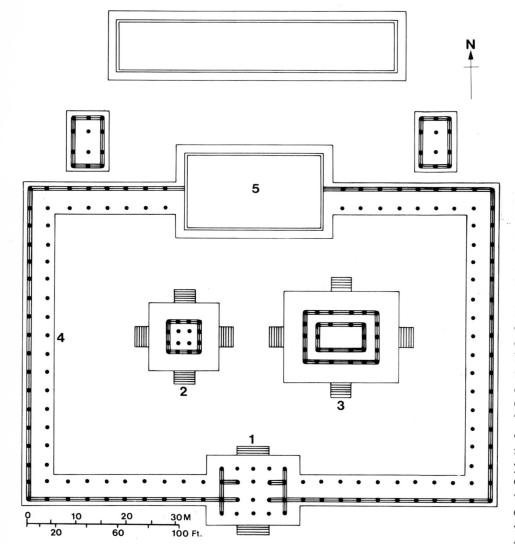

is the type of gateway used – the *torii* which is peculiar to Shinto. The gateway has plain wooden rounded posts either side, a widely projecting deep beam over the top, chamfered to a slope on the upper side to throw off rainwater, and a smaller beam between the posts below.

Buddhism came to Japan in the Asuka Period (538–645) when, in the middle of the sixth century, a statue of Buddha and other Buddhist material were presented to the Japanese emperor. The new religion was not widely accepted until Buddhist monks gradually infiltrated the country, and Prince Shotoku Taishi (572–621), nephew of the Empress and her Regent, became an enthusiast. By the end of the seventh century there were well over five hundred Buddhist temples in Japan.

Early Buddhist temples usually followed the strictly symmetrical form of the Chinese Buddhist complex. A rectangular colonnade with an imposing portal in the centre of the south side formed a complete enclosure, in which

the Buddha hall, pagoda and lecture hall were lined up on the south–north axis with other buildings to the north of them. Later, the Japanese broke with this tradition and disposed the buildings differently. For example, at Hōryūji, one of Prince Shotoku's temples near Nara, the Buddha hall (*kondō*) and pagoda (*gojunoto*) are placed either side of the central axis. The original buildings were replaced in the seventh century after a fire. The Hōryūji kondo is claimed to be the oldest wooden building in the world. Images of Buddha were placed in the kondo of a Buddhist temple, while the pagoda usually held relics. In later Japanese Buddhist temples, the kondo became the central building of the enclosure.

During the Nara period (645–793), Buddhism became the official state religion of Japan. Its adoption was marked by the building of the Tōdai-ji Monastery, Nara, founded *c.* 745, one of the largest and most important in the country. The enclosure was about 3.2 kilometres square. The kondo in the

HŌRYŪJI TEMPLE, Nara. Seventh century. Main hall (Kondō). Claimed to be the oldest wooden building in the world, but reconstructed after a fire in 1949.

centre, known as the Daibutsuden Hall or Hall of the Great Buddha, is nearly 61 metres long by 52 metres deep and over 45.5 metres high. It is the largest wooden building under a single roof in the world. The hall was dedicated about the middle of the eighth century by the Emperor Shomu to the Nairocana Buddha, whose huge bronze seated statue, over 15 metres high, occupies the place of honour in the hall.

The Tōdai-ji Monastery suffered from natural disasters destroying its pagodas and gates, but the Daibutsuden Hall survived them, only to be burnt down in the twelfth century and replaced with a true copy except for certain structural alterations and fewer bays. The original system of pillars, beams, and brackets used for the construction was the Chinese beam-frame and bracket system (*tou-kung*) previously described. The tou-kung system continued to be used in later periods with modifications introduced by the Japanese.

The *shosoin*, the imperial treasure house, is within the Tōdai-ji enclosure. Artistic, ceremonial, and other objects belonging to the Emperor Shomu have been stored there since the middle of the eighth century. The building, resembling a log cabin, is raised off the ground on forty wooden pillars. It has three sections, no windows, and a door in the centre of each section. The *hinoki* logs used for the walls were laid dry, one upon another, and crossed at the

corners. Shrinkage of the logs in dry weather and swelling in wet give a measure of air-conditioning within the building, creating an atmosphere suitable for grain stores which were similarly built.

At the end of the Nara period the capital was changed to Kyoto. The new capital, like Nara before it, was laid out in the Chinese manner in a symmetrical pattern of streets and enclosures at right angles to one another, measuring almost a square – about 4.8 kilometres by 5.6. The royal enclosure dominated Heian-kyo, as it was called then, at the north end in the centre. Temples and the houses of nobles and the poor were spread out below. The principal buildings with white plastered walls, red painted woodwork and blue glazed tiled roofs must have made a splendid sight. The two most important buildings of the imperial compound were the Emperor's front hall of audience (*shishinden*) and his dwelling (*seiryoden*), used later for ceremonies and connected to the shishinden by a corridor. The buildings were reconstructed in the middle of the nineteenth century, so we have some idea of their interiors: polished wood *hinoki* floors, heavy wood pillars, white plastered upper walls, open wooden roofs, paper-covered partitions on light timber frames. The entire roof structure is supported on the columns, and the partitions on all sides of the building are hung to swing upwards into a hori-

zontal position, to expose the audience hall with its dais at one end. Following Chinese traditions, the shishinden is placed on an axial line with the main gate, with an open court between the gate and the building.

The move to Kyoto marked the beginning of the Heian period (794–1185) and the founding of a permanent capital for Japan. Before that time the Emperor chose where he wished to live, and that became the capital with all the court and officials around him.

In the Heian period different Buddhist sects developed, and architectural characteristics of Buddhist temples began to appear in Shinto shrines. The Japanese pagoda developed its own characteristics. Both the Japanese and Chinese pagodas were based on the form of the Indian *stupa*. Japanese pagodas were erected, like the stupa, on a stone base, and were usually five or seven storeys high. Each storey, with its beautifully carved roof, was smaller as it progressed upwards until it was finally capped by a ringed mast similar to a stupa mast. An unusual structural device in Japan was a huge post centrally placed on stones, or hung from roof beams, which acted as a stabilizer and allowed the pagoda to rock in an earthquake.

Members of the Imperial Court were given rectangular plots of land around the Emperor's enclosure at Kyoto, and their mansions were lesser versions of

the royal apartments. The *shinden* style of dwelling, as it was called, used the paper-covered partitions. The enclosure was arranged symmetrically in the Chinese manner. The main dwelling, the shinden, faced south across an open court, with less important halls to the east and west. In larger mansions, these halls were extended to the south with covered colonnades ending in partitions, making a U-shaped enclosure of buildings around the court. Any additional buildings were placed north of the shinden.

Japan entered a time of civil war and rebellion during the Kamakura period (1185–1336) when the great clans wrestled for power. Finally, the Minamoto prevailed and set up a military style government of the samurai warrior class at Kamakura, while the Emperor remained at Kyoto, the official capital of Japan. Zen Buddhism began to penetrate Japan at this time. Its rules for military and social behaviour, based on meditation and self-discipline, found sympathetic accord with the samurai. In the fourteenth century the Emperor became involved in the civil wars. The outcome was victory for Ashikaga Takauji of the Minamoto, who became *shogun* (military leader) of a new government at Muromachi, a district of Kyoto. Military feudalism under the shogunate administrations lasted throughout the Muromachi period (1336–1573), the Momoyama period (1573–1638) and

the Edo period (1615–1867), until the impact of European culture on Japan.

The Ashikaga shoguns ruled throughout the Muromachi period, but their authority was weakened by the Onim Civil War (1467–77). The result was that the *daimyo*, local feudal lords, became more powerful, and a spate of castle-building took place in the late sixteenth century.

Castles were usually situated on mountain tops, plentiful in Japan. The outer rampart, sometimes surrounded by a moat, was a battered stone wall, like the *glacis* of western castles. But the other reason for the stone-walled base was the difficulty of building on a mountain top

Opposite
TŌDAI-JI MONASTERY, Nara.
Daibutsuden (hall of the Great Buddha).
c. 752. Reconstructed in the twelfth
century and again in 1709. The largest
wooden building under one roof in the
world. The construction shows the
Chinese beam-frame and bracket system
adopted by the Japanese. The huge
15-metre-high bronze statue of the
Nairocana Buddha occupies the centre of
the hall.

Right
YAKUSHIJI TEMPLE, Nara. Eastern
Pagoda. Eighth century. The cutaway
portions reveal the system of framing and
bracketing which is traditional in Japan
and makes possible considerable variation
in the roof shapes.

without a massive foundation. A *donjon*, the highest tower of the complex, was the final defensive stronghold of the daimyo. If a castle fell, the donjon was rarely assaulted before the daimyo had committed honourable suicide, signifying his defeat. In early times, battles with swords and bows and arrows were fought in the open, as in the west. When guns were introduced, castle design became more complicated, and as the threat of war receded the donjon became more lavish in its domestic arrangements. It retained its visually dominant appearance as a symbol of authority.

The main donjon at Matsumato Castle (1597) survives as an example of the fully developed style. It was supported in defence by a smaller donjon, connected by a corridor at low level, which was also the entrance to both donjons. The warrior who built it was one of the daimyos of the Ogasawara family in the Nagano Prefecture. The hipped roofs were designed with different pitches to throw off the heavy snows. The outer walls are white plastered with hinged black panels, through which to hurl missiles, no doubt influenced by western ideas. The whole edifice of white and black walls, and curved roofs towering above the other buildings, must have been an impressive display to the people of the time.

Dwellings in Japan gradually became formalized in their structure, materials, and layout in the style known as *shoin*. This was the Japanese style of house normally adopted from the end of the sixteenth century onwards. The term shoin has had many meanings in Japanese architecture: the Buddhist monk's private study in early periods; the warrior classes' private room for study and meditation in the middle ages; a house with a reception room; and finally the wider use of the term.

The shoin house was usually rectangular, built of framed timbers supporting the traditionally curved roof with a wide overhang to the eaves. The floor was raised some 60 centimetres above ground on stout pillars and resting on stones to give good drainage. The proportions of the rooms were based on the *tatami*, the rush mats laid upon the floor, usually 2 metres by 1. The proportions of the screen walls dividing the room spaces were also based on the size of the tatami, thus achieving a modular proportion throughout the house. The external screens (*shoji*) were light wood frames covered on one side with translucent paper. The indoor

screens (*fusuma*) were similar but covered on both sides with opaque paper. The shoji were made up of sections, which could be slid and folded noiselessly one upon another. The fusuma were similar, and the overhang of the roof protected them against driving rain and summer sunshine, but allowed the winter sun to penetrate the house.

Many such traditional dwellings and Japanese hotels exist today. The floor is still a most important element in the Japanese way of life, whether house or hotel, as mats are placed on it for sitting and eating, and quilts for sleeping. The placing of ornaments or pictures is meticulous, to suit the chosen wall space from the viewpoint of a person seated on the floor. Cloth slippers are worn indoors and outdoor shoes discarded before entering the house. The garden is another important element of the Japanese house, consisting of rocks, pools, plants, and trees carefully trained and shaped to suit an overall landscape design of balance and composition, however unpretentious.

KAGAWA PREFECTURE BUILDING, Takamatsu. 1958. Architect: Kenzo Tange. The reinforced-concrete design echoes in a remarkable way the forms of traditional Japanese wood construction.

Romanesque Style

The early international Romanesque style is believed to have originated from Lombardy at the beginning of the ninth century. The ideas spread to Dalmatia, southern France, Catalonia, Burgundy, and the Rhineland. Following the traditions of Rome, vaulting characterized Romanesque architecture at its peak, and the semicircular arch was the common element to be found among the expressions of the style and the varied combination of forms which appeared in different countries. The growing power of the church, and its unique position as a source of culture and spiritual uplift, were largely responsible for influencing the development of features which brought Romanesque to maturity in the eleventh and twelfth centuries.

Charlemagne's Frankish empire covered what we now call France, Germany, Belgium, Luxemburg, most of Italy, and Spain. With this vast domain, Charlemagne fostered Christianity, sometimes using force. He also forged political and ecclesiastical ties with Rome. He died in 814, after ruling for fourteen years and, as a result of weak successors, thirty years later France and Germany were divided, with important repercussions for architecture. Invasion of the Empire followed: Turks invaded from the south, Vikings from the north-west. The Vikings (Danes) attacked England and settled in northern France (Normans). With the breakdown of the Empire's city life, the ensuing chaos and conquest produced a state of restlessness in Europe which led to feudalism. Lord and peasant became closely linked with recognized bonds of service and dependence; the church occupied itself with the spiritual well-being of both.

Neither serf nor baron was literate. What culture and ordered life there was came from the monasteries. The various religious orders with their vows of chastity, obedience, and poverty provided establishments which were havens of rest and relative security in a chaotic and dangerous world. The monasteries often started in a humble way: a villa or hunting lodge might be bequeathed as an offering of thanks, and life would go on there much as usual, similar to a farmstead in central Europe today, without resort to modern farm implements.

Monasteries grew in importance, and, as early as the tenth century, many had gained freedom from lay or religious meddling in their affairs, and sometimes the right of 'sanctuary' observed by the code of chivalry. Cluny, a monastery in Burgundy, some 96 kilometres north-west of Lyons, was the main source of changes in church design. Under successive abbots of great inventiveness and vision, Cluny began to draw the other monasteries under its wing to form the Congregation and Order of Cluny. At the height of its power under Hugh, Abbot 1049–1109, Cluny controlled 1450 or more houses, and Cluniacs were as famous for their liturgy and chants as they were for their inventiveness in architecture.

The long straight churches of the early Christians no longer met the needs of a religion which was now a thousand years old. More clergy, mass said everyday, visiting pilgrims, relics of saints to be placed on view – all these changes required more altars and spaces to enclose them. The Cluniac answer to these requirements began with the second church (Cluny II) which had apses at the east ends of the aisles, on a level with the central apse. Cluny III, which heralded High Romanesque, had an ambulatory with apses at the east end of the church, and two transepts with pairs of apses on the east side of each arm.

In central Europe, the change from early Christian church design was marked by St Michael, Hildesheim, built between 1001 and 1033. Hildesheim had two transepts with an apsidal chapel on the east side of each arm. Small staircase towers were placed at the four

BORGUND CHURCH, Sogne Fiord, Norway. *c*. 1150. Typical Norwegian stave church of the period. Stave churches were built entirely of wood with shingle roof covering.

transept ends and major towers over the crossings. Between the crossings the nave was divided into three almost square bays, with aisles to north and south. The north aisle contained the two entrance ways used by monks in preference to an entrance from the west – an unusual arrangement, but one used in monastery churches. We know that Berward, Bishop of Hildesheim, was responsible for St Michael's and perhaps we should be grateful to him for the famous bronze doors, showing in fine detail the Creation, Fall, and Redemption, dedicated in 1015, and now installed in Hildesheim Cathedral.

Enlarged church plans had to be accompanied by technical innovation on the part of craftsmen and builders. The art of vaulting, so well understood by the Romans, and exploited by the Byzantines, was taken a stage further. Up to the end of the tenth century, aisles of churches were usually barrel or groin vaulted, but the nave had a flat ceiling under a pitched roof. Apses were vaulted. Fire was a frequent occurrence and builders were anxious to extend their vaulting to the nave.

The first innovation was the division of the tunnel-like barrel vault into bays. This was done by building circular arches at regular intervals below the surface line of the finished vault, and erecting the vault in sections instead of in a long line. Visually, the transverse arches broke the nave up into compartments. A similar method was employed for the groin vault, with semi-circular arches below the vault surface at the boundaries of bays. The groin vault was the result of two short barrel vaults of equal span intersecting at right angles. The intersections of the vault shell formed the groins. Vaults were constructed by forming mounds of earth pressed into the shape of the finished vault, and also by means of form work. By building vaults in compartments, form work could be removed more easily and re-used more frequently.

Although groin vaults could be used for the square compartments of side aisles with few difficulties, the problem of vaulting an oblong compartment presented the Romanesque builders with a number of problems. The transverse arch of the rectangular bay was shorter than the diagonal across the corners, so the apexes of the arches were at different heights. This was overcome to some extent by springing the arch at a higher point, a system known as *stilting*, but the result was unsatisfactory. There was also the risk of collapse from sagging. At S. Michele, Pavia, a twelfth century church in Italy, the problem was avoided altogether by making the nave bay almost square and equal to two aisle bays, and constructing nave and aisle vaults at different heights. Eventually the problem was overcome by building groin vaults, with ribs at the groins projecting below the vault. This, coupled with the pointed arch, introduced the Gothic style described in a later chapter. The origin of the ribbed vault and the pointed arch at the end of the Romanesque period is obscure. The Islamic forms of the East, coupled with improvements in vaulting techniques in the West, may have produced the initial idea. Their appearance in a number of Romanesque churches during the early part of the twelfth century in Europe leads to the conclusion that there was no single point of origin for the great Gothic cathedrals. Certainly the Normans exploited the ribbed vault and built their finest example at Durham.

Although a Romanesque cathedral, Durham's nave and chancel (*c.* 1130) are roofed with pointed rib vaults instead of the hitherto customary flat ceiling. The roof of the nave is typically Norman. Columns made up of shafts in clusters alternate with enormous round columns decorated with zigzags and lozenge shapes. Similar abstract carvings decorate the recessed circular arches. Abstract forms used by the Normans contrast with the animal and foliage forms common in southern France and Italy, but the latter may be found on capitals in the crypt of Canterbury Cathedral. Such

Above
ST MICHAEL'S CHURCH, Hildesheim, Germany. *c.* 1001–1033. Nave.

Opposite
DURHAM CATHEDRAL, England. *c.* 1093. Nave.

Below
THIRD ABBEY CHURCH, Cluny, Bourgogne (Burgundy). 1080–1121. Plan:
1 entrance (thirteenth century),
2 tower (thirteenth century),
3 minor nave,
4 major nave,
5 west transept with chapels on the east side,
6 choir,
7 east transept with chapels on the east side,
8 ambulatory with five radiating chapels.

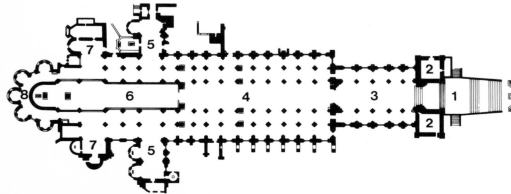

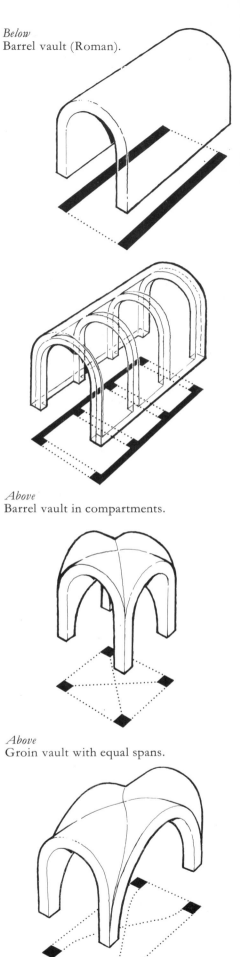

Below
Barrel vault (Roman).

Above
Barrel vault in compartments.

Above
Groin vault with equal spans.

Above
Groin vault over a rectangular space.

work was often copied from transcripts and paintings by stonemasons.

In northern France Romanesque architecture developed with similar characteristics to those of Norman England, the political dominance being the same. Even before the defeat of King Harold of England by Duke William of Normandy in 1066, Harold's predecessor, Edward I, had introduced Normans to important posts in England. Robert

of Jumièges, for example, was made Primate of England by Edward. The direct result of such strong ecclesiastical ties was the similarity of the churches commissioned by William the Conqueror on both sides of the English Channel.

St Étienne, Caen, begun by William about 1068, has a long nave in eight compartments, entered from the west through three portals. The nave leads to transepts, and originally there was

an apse at the east end, until it was extended a hundred years later into a semicircular-shaped ambulatory with altars in alcoves on the east side. The semicircular arrangement known as a *chevet* was particularly suitable for the practical job of displaying holy relics. St Étienne's nave has shafts running up the faces of piers from floor to vault ribs. They alternate with slightly more slender shafts which rise to support the centres of the arches – an early example of sexpartite vaulting (p. 89). Long shafts in the nave, foreshadowing Gothic developments, were used in many other Romanesque churches: St Trinité, Caen and St Étienne at Nevers in France, and in England at Ely Cathedral and Durham.

Romanesque architecture is considered to have developed farthest towards Gothic in England and northern France. But other countries in Europe, following local traditions and blessed with wonderful building materials, used planning ideas and details in different ways, resulting in a variety of regional styles.

In central Italy, Pisa Cathedral, begun in 1063, with its campanile, the famous leaning tower, and baptistry, makes one of the most renowned architectural

groupings in the world. The Campo Santo is the fourth building in the complex. The cathedral's plan is an extension of the basilican church form. A long nave has double aisles on either side, and the transepts have single aisles with an apse at the end of each, forming small attached basilicas. The nave aisles are extended beyond the east side of the crossing up to the apse. All the aisles have galleries above them, making a continuous upper floor except over the entrance and the east end. Galleries have single-pitched roofs, the nave a double-pitched roof. Aisles are groin vaulted and the crossing is domed. The columns of the nave are of classical Roman origin, and striped (zebra) work in different coloured marbles used higher up resembles Byzantine and Islamic decoration. The apse mosaics also betray Byzantine origins. The west front is a striking feature of the church. Four tiers of arcades rise above the red and white striped marble entrance in spectacular fashion. The west front was not completed until the thirteenth century. The transepts and dome over the crossing are also later than the nave.

The circular leaning tower, more than 15 metres in diameter, has six tiers of arcading in decorated marble. There

were other circular towers in central Italy, but subsidence at the time of building the Pisa tower caused the building gradually to lean over to a difference of more than 3.5 metres from the vertical between top and bottom. More modern foundations have been placed to arrest the movement. The baptistry at Pisa has the typical central circular space (about 18 metres in diameter), surrounded by an aisle with a gallery above it. It was begun in the middle of the twelfth century, the campanile some twenty years later. Both were completed, with the additions to the cathedral, by about the third quarter of the thirteenth century. Considering the span of time taken in building the complex, the three designs have an astonishing unity.

The early international Romanesque style created in Lombardy spread to Spain through the Catalan monasteries. One of the finest early examples was S. Maria, Ripoll (*c.* 1020–1032), a monastery in Catalonia in the north-east corner of Spain. The church has a nave and double aisles ending in transepts, with three apses on the east side of each arm and a main apse facing down the nave. The material was rough stone which suited the heavy piers supporting the

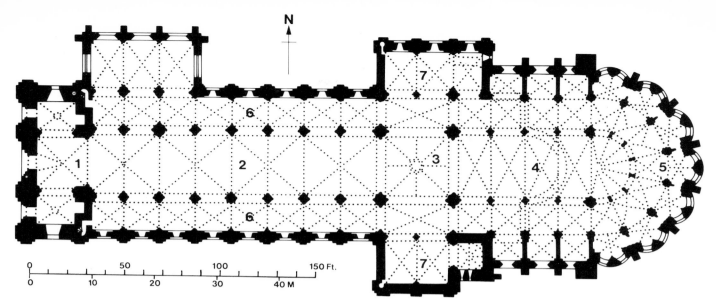

0   50   100   150 Ft.

0   10   20   30   40 M

Opposite
CANTERBURY CATHEDRAL. *c.* 1073. The crypt under the choir. The crypt column heads are decorated with foliage and animal forms, unlike most Norman work in England.

Above
ST ETIENNE CHURCH, Caen. *c* 1068–1115. Plan:
1 entrance vestibule,
2 nave with sexpartite vaulting,
3 crossing,
4 position of original apse,
5 chevet (added in the twelfth century),
6 aisles with galleries overhead,
7 transept.

Left
ST ETIENNE CHURCH, Caen. *c* 1068–1115.

Below
ST ETIENNE CHURCH, Caen. *c* 1068–1115. Nave.

89

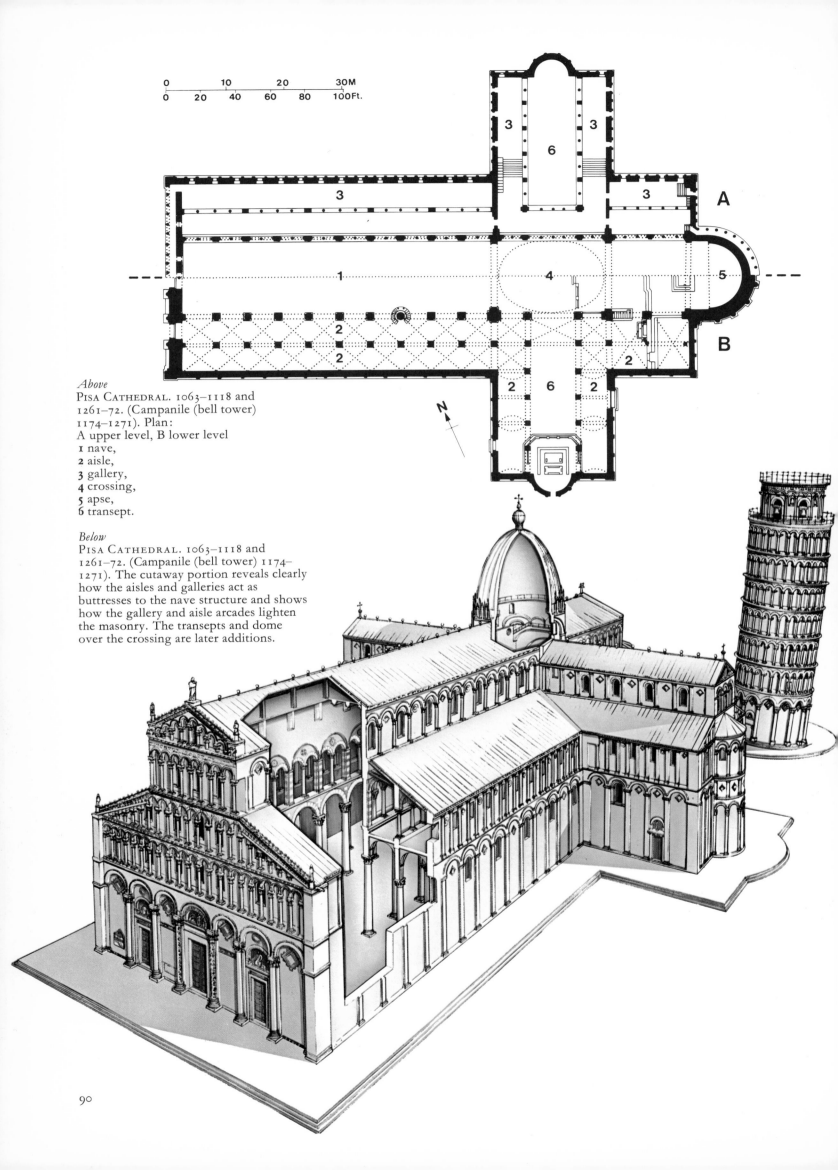

Above

PISA CATHEDRAL. 1063–1118 and
1261–72. (Campanile (bell tower)
1174–1271). Plan:
A upper level, B lower level
1 nave,
2 aisle,
3 gallery,
4 crossing,
5 apse,
6 transept.

Below

PISA CATHEDRAL. 1063–1118 and
1261–72. (Campanile (bell tower) 1174–
1271). The cutaway portion reveals clearly
how the aisles and galleries act as
buttresses to the nave structure and shows
how the gallery and aisle arcades lighten
the masonry. The transepts and dome
over the crossing are later additions.

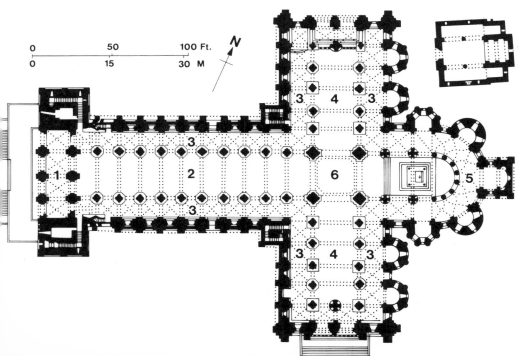

Left
SANTIAGO DE COMPOSTELA
CATHEDRAL, Spain. *c.* 1075. West front.

Above
SANTIAGO DE COMPOSTELA
CATHEDRAL, Spain. *c.* 1075.

Left
SANTIAGO DE COMPOSTELA
CATHEDRAL, Spain. *c.* 1075. Plan:
1 vestibule,
2 nave,
3 aisle with gallery overhead,
4 transept,
5 chevet (ambulatory with radiating
   chapels),
6 crossing.

tunnel vault under the wooden pitched roof. Ripoll monastery was famous for its library and school in which the monks taught many subjects including literature, music, and mathematics. Abbot Oliba who was responsible for the church was said to be a friend of Hugh, later Abbot of Cluny.

The great pilgrimage routes of this time started from Chartres and Paris in northern France, and from as far south as Arles. They stretched westwards across the Pyrenees to Ronces Valles, Burgos, and ultimately to Santiago, Galicia, northern Spain. The Cluniacs were supporters of the crusade to free Spain from the Muslims. The pilgrimages were linked with the crusade, and other orders besides the Cluniac supported them and set up hostels along the pilgrimage routes. There were other connections which favoured Cluniac influence in Spain. Queen Constance, one of the wives of King Alfonso VI of Spain, was a niece of Abbot Hugh of Cluny. King Alfonso gave considerable subsidies to Cluny as an offering of thanks, paying for much of the abbey's new church.

The great church, the old Cathedral of Santiago de Compostela, marking the end of the pilgrimage route, owed much to Cluniac tradition. Begun about 1075 and not fully completed until the end of the eighteenth century, Compostela represented Spanish Romanesque at its peak and its design influenced that of other churches. The west front, flanked by the archbishop's palace to the north and monastic buildings to the south, is deeply modelled with elaborate carvings, inset statues, and receding circular arches to the entrances, which are approached up a flight of steps because the basement contained a tomb (supposedly of St James) placed above the plaza level. Once inside the church, the full glory of the long nave comes into view, much as it must have been seen by pilgrims through nearly a thousand years. The groin vaulted aisles on either side of the nave are carried round the transepts and the ambulatory of the chevet at the east end, which has two apsidal chapels on either side of the central apsidal chapel. Four additional apsidal chapels are placed in the transepts, two on each side of the crossing. The nave is barrel vaulted in compartments, with transverse arches rising from shafts carried up on the nave piers from the floor and through the galleries which are continued round the building. The galleries are roofed with half-barrel vaults abutting the barrel vault over the nave, and

MARIA LAACH ABBEY CHURCH, Germany. c. 1093–1156. View from north west.

the nave barrel vault is continued at right angles over the transepts.

The continuous aisles, ambulatory and altars at Santiago must have been a near-perfect solution to the handling of the pilgrims and the viewing of relics, combined with the monastery's routine. The other great churches of the pilgrimage road – St Martin, Tours; St Martial, Limoges; Ste Foi, Conques; St Sernin, Toulouse – had similar plans to Santiago de Compostela.

In central Europe the Romanesque style was a mixture of earlier Carolingian church architecture and influences from Burgundy and St Michael's, Hildesheim. The great cathedrals of the period were: Mainz, dating from c. 1009, Speyer, dating from c. 1031, and Worms, from the eleventh century. The exterior was usually dominated by square or octagonal-shaped towers: a pair of tall thin towers flanking the apse roof at the east end, a shorter thicker tower over the crossing, and a similar tower between two slim towers at the west end. To throw off snow and heavy rain tower roofs were steep-pitched, meeting in a point, and usually with gable ends at the eaves, although this was not always so. The exterior of Maria Laach Abbey Church, begun c. 1093 has a particularly fine grouping of the six towers. Sometimes – a survival from Carolingian churches – the nun's choir was added. It took the form of an apse at the west end in Worms Cathedral, and a crossing at the west end in the Church of the Apostles, Cologne. The church in Cologne, begun c. 1190, has an unusual trefoil-shaped east end.

Medieval Castles

Castle remains stir the imagination. Their broken towers and windowless curtain walls dot the landscape of Europe, Britain, and the countries of the Middle East. Most were built from the eleventh to thirteenth centuries. They were added to, altered, and restored in later centuries, and bear witness to a time of rising nationhood by conquest and reconquest, and to the holy wars waged between Christian knights fighting to regain Jerusalem and the Holy Land for their faith, and the Muslims equally determined to capture and hold the same territory for Islam.

Since Mediaeval castles were built for defence purposes, their sites were chosen to command views of the surrounding country or because natural hazards like steep cliffs and sea – as at Tintagel, Cornwall – gave protection from attack.

Early defence works usually comprised a series of ramparts and ditches. Ramparts were built on stones from soil taken from the ditches. In Britain stone was used with baulks of timber as binders, even before the Roman Conquest. Important Roman defence works influenced the siting of mediaeval castles, if not their construction. Hadrian's Wall, erected as a frontier between England and the lawless lowlands of Scotland, is an example of Roman permanent fortifications. The wall stretches for more than 113 kilometres, up and down over rolling countryside, following the natural contour of the land. Usually well over 3 metres tall and 3 or more metres thick, the wall was built of stone with a concrete core, and had a walkway along the top. It was used more as a barrier than a battleground, as opposing forces armed with swords, spears, and shields usually chose open ground on which to fight. At regular intervals along the wall were watch towers, castles, and forts for housing men-at-arms.

Although Roman camps had earthen ramparts, stone was used for more permanent defences such as the castles at Pevensey in Sussex and Lympne in Kent,

in which traces of Roman work are present in the Norman remains.

The Normans built more than 1500 castles in Britain after they conquered the Saxon forces under Harold in 1066. They were built for the private use of barons or feudal lords to hold sway over the neighbouring territory. Only a proportion of them were of stone. The earliest castles were of a type known as *motte and bailey*. The *motte* was a mound and the *bailey* an area surrounding it protected by ditches and ramparts. Timber pallisades protected the motte and bailey, and sometimes there was a wooden tower on the motte. Into this system the Normans introduced the keep or *donjon*, a stone tower built on the motte in which defenders could make their last stand against a successful invasion of the bailey. The keep contained stores and there was a well for water and usually a chapel.

The Tower of London's 'White Tower' is the finest Norman stone keep in England. Roughly square with

straight walls and corner towers, it was commenced by William the Conqueror between 1076 and 1078, after the City of London became subject to him. The Caen stone used for the corners and openings (*dressings*), brought by ship from Normandy, is an indication of the Tower's importance to William, who never saw it completed as he died at Rouen in 1087. His son William Rufus finished the building some twenty years after it had been begun. The White Tower has a deep well in the crypt and a very beautiful Romanesque style chapel, the Chapel of St John the Evangelist, which extends through two of the tower's three storeys.

Castles continued to develop, and by the end of the century, timber defences round the bailey had been replaced by stone curtain walls, and the keep was retained as the citadel. Among the great castle keeps in Europe were those at Longeais, Loudun, Falaise, Caen, and along the Norman border from Domfront to Arques.

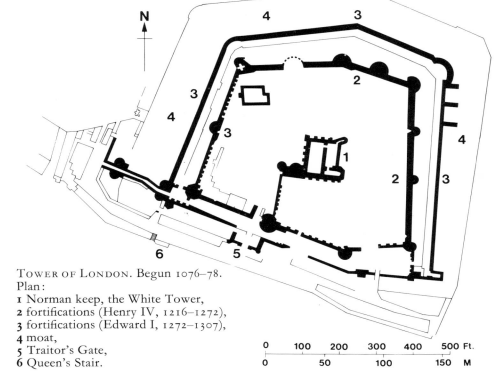

TOWER OF LONDON. Begun 1076–78.
Plan:
1 Norman keep, the White Tower,
2 fortifications (Henry IV, 1216–1272),
3 fortifications (Edward I, 1272–1307),
4 moat,
5 Traitor's Gate,
6 Queen's Stair.

WHITE TOWER, TOWER OF LONDON. Begun 1076–78. Chapel of St John. Norman style.

By the end of the twelfth century and during the thirteenth century and later, important changes were made in castle defences, some brought from the Middle East by the crusader knights. The most far-reaching was the addition of semi-circular towers standing out from the curtain wall, allowing defenders a wider field of fire than the straight wall and to infallade the vulnerable wall base. The two concentric rings of defences of the Tower of London, the inner added in the late thirteenth century, and the outer after 1300, were the result of this new idea. Windsor, begun as a motte and bailey castle, to which a polygonal keep, the Round Tower, was added, received its upper bailey stone defences by the end of the twelfth century. Both the Tower of London and Windsor Castle were added to and embellished by successive monarchs.

The result of adding concentric rings of stone fortifications and sometimes a moat to the outer defences, was to make the inner bailey the castle stronghold, and to expand the accommodation by building up against the inner bailey wall to meet ceremonial and domestic, rather than military needs.

Befitting the growing power and wealth of feudal lords, the most important of the new buildings was the great hall, the centre of social and administrative life. Kitchens and sleeping rooms were attached to it. A chapel, a guardroom, quarters for men-at-arms and retainers, stores, an area for animals, an armoury, and a water supply were included in a fairly consistent pattern, but the shape and disposition of a castle's accommodation were arranged to suit the defensive requirements of the site. Harlech Castle, Merioneth, for example, built towards the end of the thirteenth century, is sited on a hill with an outer bailey covering the difficult approaches, a middle bailey, and an inner bailey – three baileys in all. The middle and inner bailey are protected by a moat on the south and east sides. The castle is almost a square on the plan, with boldly projecting circular towers at the inner bailey corners, and a heavily fortified gatehouse in the centre of the eastern side. Opposite this entrance is the great hall and at right angles to it is the chapel, both placed against the inside of the middle bailey wall. A walkway along the curtain wall, usual in this type of castle, links the towers. The walk ends with the gatehouse tower which thus became the strong point of the castle.

Very few castles have retained their original form, and the addition of defensive devices was one of the principal reasons for making alterations.

The fortified gateway comprised a variety of defence measures. There was the drawbridge across the moat, lowered for friend and raised against foe. The rounded portals allowed a wide field of fire. Above the gateway were devices with holes, called *machiolations*, which enabled defenders to hurl stones or boiling oil down on to the heads of attackers at the foot of the wall. Machiolations were also used on curtain walls and towers, first as timber structures but later, as the idea became widespread, towers were corbelled out at the top to include the device in the masonry. The idea came to Europe from the Middle East. Parapets of towers and curtain walls were crenellated to give the defenders protection and an opening through which to fire; the opening was called a *crenel* and the upstanding stonework a *merlon*. Windsor Castle, the Tower of London, Bodiam and Hurstmoncieux Castles in Sussex all

WHITE TOWER, TOWER OF LONDON. Begun 1076–78. The drawing shows the Norman keep as it was *c.* 1610 with the changes made to the original building. The Norman-style circular-headed windows have been retained. The cutaway through the chapel of St John is taken longitudinally through the masonry barrel vault of the roof revealing the building's three floors and crypt.

95

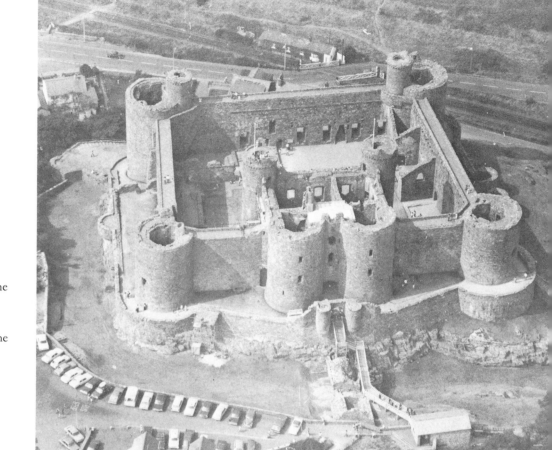

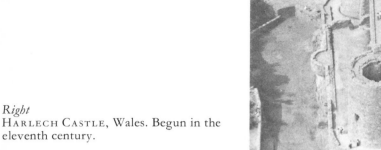

Right
HARLECH CASTLE, Wales. Begun in the eleventh century.

Below
HARLECH CASTLE, Wales. Begun in the eleventh century. Plan:
1 outer bailey,
2 middle bailey,
3 inner bailey,
4 Great Hall,
5 Chapel,
6 gatehouse,
7 tower,
8 moat.

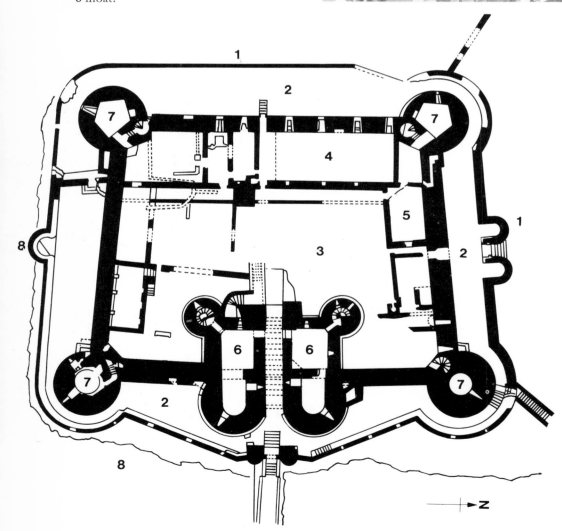

have crenellated walls, and many other examples still exist. Crenellations were also used on domestic buildings, and at one time in England a licence was required before a house could be crenellated.

The *barbican* was the defensive tower forming part of the main gateway into the castle. The circular projecting towers either side of the gateway usually contained stores and rooms for the guards. In addition to the machiolations above the gateway, there would be at least one *portcullis*. A portcullis was a heavy grating, usually made of thick oak rods tipped with metal, riding in grooves cut in the stonework, and raised or lowerd by means of chains. Where the curtain walkway met the barbican tower there would usually be a *postern*, a small door with a zigzag approach through the stonework to afford surprise. Staircases in defensive situations were usually spiral with vaulted stone steps circling upwards to the right, so that a defender's sword arm could be free. But some staircases spiralled the other way, in case a defender was forced to become an attacker! Flues for chimneys passed through castle walls at an angle, ending in a small hole, hidden from view. Latrines were also built into the thick walls with outlets passing down-

wards and outwards. Castle walls for defence were anything between 3 and 4.5 metres thick, and provided enough space for concealing such conveniences.

Another device in curtain walls and towers was the *arrowloop*, a slim opening used in Roman and Byzantine fortifications, and re-introduced into Europe by the crusaders. Arrowloops were narrow on the inside but splayed outwards to the face of the wall to give a wide field of fire in a forwards, sideways, and downwards direction. They developed decoratively from a simple slit with a circle or triangle at the base to slits in the form of a cross with one, two, or three arms, or slits opening into small circular holes at the top, middle, or bottom, a common form in the thirteenth century.

One of the great crusader castles, a model in defence works of its time, is the Krak des Chevaliers (Krak of the Knights) originally founded by the Emir of Homs in the early 1030s in Syria. The castle fell into Christian hands during the First Crusade and was captured by Tangred of Antioch in about 1109. Tangred passed it to the Counts of Tripoli who in turn ceded it to the Hospitaller Knights in about 1142. For the next hundred years or so it was reconstructed and developed as

an important citadel in the Christian campaigns. The Krak was several times unsuccessfully besieged but fell eventually to the Arabs in the last quarter of the thirteenth century. It remained a castle for hundreds of years, then fell into disuse until the French government acquired the site in the 1920s and started to restore the castle.

The site is a spur of the Husarî mountains some 610 metres high with steep slopes on all sides. The formidable citadel arises almost naturally from the surrounding terrain which it dominates with two concentric rings of defences, the inner rising high and relatively close to the outer. The outer curtain and its semicircular towers at intervals are machiolated. The south side of the inner fortress is protected by a moat, used as a reservoir, and to the east of it is the ramp by which mounted men might enter the castle. The south and east sides of the inner curtain have a remarkable batter at the base of the wall, known as a *glacis*, of quite outstanding thickness and strength. The great hall and cloisters, and the chapel rising above the inner curtain, were built in the thirteenth century. The Arabs, after defeating the Hospitallers, added three more defence towers on the south side and the great tower of Sultan Qala'un.

BODIAM CASTLE, Sussex. Begun in the eleventh century.

Above
KRAK DES CHEVALIERS, Gebel Alawi,
Syria. Begun in the 1030s. One of the
most renowned of the crusader castles.

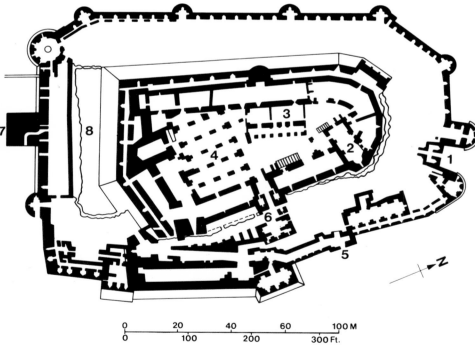

Above
KRAK DES CHEVALIERS, Gebel Alawi,
Syria. Begun in the 1030s. Plan:
1 North gate,
2 chapel,
3 Great Hall and cloister,
4 magazine,
5 lower main gate,
6 upper main gate,
7 Tower of Sultan Qala'un,
8 fosse (reservoir).

Above
KRAK DES CHEVALIERS, Gebel Alawi,
Syria. Begun in the 1030s. One of the
most renowned of the crusader castles.

Castles continued to be important as
fortifications until the fifteenth century;
then the invention of gunpowder rendered thick stone walls more vulnerable
to demolition and tactics changed. Nonetheless castles remained symbols of
power and authority in people's minds
and the term continued to be used for
important residences. Existing castles
were embellished domestically and for
pomp and ceremony, none more im-
pressively than Windsor Castle. To the
splendour of St George's Chapel, in the
perpendicular late Gothic style, begun
by Edward IV in 1475 and completed
by Henry VIII fifty years later, were
added in the nineteenth century the
magnificent royal apartments commissioned by George IV and existing then
very much as they are today. The kings
and noblemen of France, in their
châteaux near Paris and in the Loire
Valley, continued the tradition of the
castle into the Renaissance period of the
seventeenth century. In England, the
eighteenth century Castle Howard in
Yorkshire, by the celebrated architect
Sir John Vanbrugh, his first work in
the Renaissance style, is one example of
an even more domesticated kind.

Gothic Style

No architectural style was a sudden development. There was always a preparatory period when innovation was introduced into old and tried methods. This process went on until a recognizable form was apparent and received sufficient support from the architects and craftsmen of the time to give it continuity. This did not stop changes going on. Individual mannerisms occurred in buildings at all stages, and the periods themselves were often labelled with titles such as 'transitional', 'high', and 'late'. This brought a chronological sequence and an evolutionary order of recognition to the progress of development. Historians are sometimes divided on exactly when and where a style began, and different names are given to different periods. Emphasis has also been placed on the national expression – English, French, central European, Spanish, Italian, for example. But styles in Europe have been international movements as modern architecture is an international movement today. That does not mean there was no national influence. In every age there has been the national expression of a style, influenced to a stronger or lesser degree by local building traditions and materials.

Historically, the High Gothic period coincided with the increasing power of the kings of France. Philip Augustus (1180–1223) drove the English out of Normandy in 1204 during King John's reign (1199–1216), and encouraged architecture. Louis IX (1226–70) overthrew the Counts of Toulouse during the Albigenses religious wars and virtually united the country as we know France today. The power of the church was increased by the enthusiasm for the crusades which swept across Europe during the twelfth and thirteenth centuries. All those factors, with the current fervour for giving benefits to the church as a means to grace, contributed to a great period of cathedral building in France. In England, meanwhile, the French influence was strong. Henry II,

Count of Anjou, ascended to the throne in 1154, on the death of Stephen, whose disastrous reign brought misery to the English people through the unruly behaviour of his barons. Henry married Eleanor of Aquitaine, the divorced wife of Louis VII of France, and ruled over eastern France from Normandy through Aquitaine to Gascony at the foot of the Pyrenees. This made Henry more powerful than the king of France. During Henry's time and that of the later Plantagenets, the castle remained important for defence purposes but manor houses, discussed in the next chapter, began to replace them as dwellings.

Henry II's son, Richard Coeur de Lion (1189–99), spent little time in England, but the results of his preoccupation with the Third Crusade were the improvements in castle design discussed earlier. The Universities of Oxford and Cambridge were founded in the thirteenth century, not for the nobility, but mainly for the clever sons of yeomen who became clerks in holy orders. The invasion of Franciscan and Dominican friars from the continent in the thirteenth century brought more power to the church which already held much land in tithe through the parishes, in addition to its own establishments. Its power was finally crushed by Henry VIII's dissolution. Before that England had fought with France for 100 years. The Battles of Crécy, Poitiers, and Agincourt had been won by the English, who lost to Joan of Arc in her victorious campaign of 1429–31.

Gothic began with the development of the rib vault in combination with the pointed arch. The flying buttress opened up further possibilities and the development and use of stained glass in windows was important. The dates of the Gothic period are generally agreed to be about 1093 to about 1530, when innovation ceased although the style continued to be used. The first period is known as *Transitional Gothic* when Gothic charac-

teristics began to appear in Romanesque churches. *Early Gothic* (1194–1300) marked the beginning of the pure style which was called *High Gothic* in its fully developed form. The latter years of innovation were called *Late Gothic*. Within these broad classifications further terms have been used. For example in England: *Early English*, *Decorated*, and *Perpendicular*; and in France: *à lancettes*, *rayonnant* and *flamboyant*. These terms will appear as the Gothic story unfolds, but it is important to recall that there was no sudden change. High Gothic continued with Late Gothic, and Late Gothic continued when the Renaissance was dawning in Italy.

As in Romanesque, the power behind Gothic development was the Christian church. No one genius was responsible. A whole army of architects, master masons, stone carvers, painters, glass painters, and sculptors collaborated. Craftsmanship was picked up by masons as they moved between their lodges located throughout Europe. As in Romanesque times, groups of specialist workers moved from one important building to another. The building process went on a long time, anything from ten to forty years, with different teams of workers engaged. What a contrast with Coventry Cathedral, of 1962, the first to be built in England for 600 years, and to be completed in eleven years. The Gothic cathedrals are a mixture of different periods of the style, through extensions and additions, changes in patronage, and for the very significant reasons of destruction by fire or collapse. A few examples make quite astonishing reading: *burnings* – Magdeburg Cathedral and Chartres Cathedral in the twelfth century; Cologne Cathedral (Carolingian) and Amiens Cathedral in the thirteenth century; *collapses* – crossing tower, Lincoln Cathedral and Beauvais choir vault in the thirteenth century; Ely Cathedral crossing tower in the fourteenth century. Whatever the causes, English cathedrals on the whole went

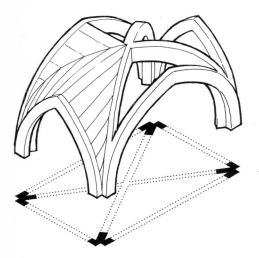

Ribbed vault.

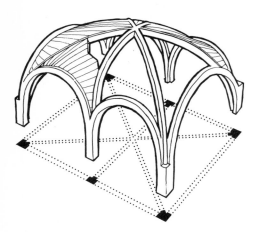

Sexpartite vault with rounded arches invented by the Romanesque masons to relate the narrow aisle bays to the wide, square, nave bays.

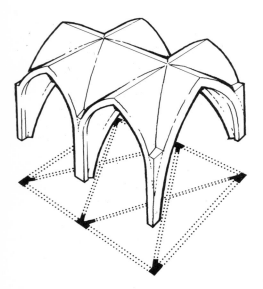

Ribbed quadripartite vault. The pointed arches enabled the Gothic masons to match aisle and nave bays of different transverse spans.

through more alteration and addition than those elsewhere in Europe.

The rib vault, which began the breakthrough from Romanesque to Gothic architecture, started in this way. Masons began to build groin vaults with a diagonal rib. This strengthened the groin and made it possible to lay the stone vault's web in sections. Ribs were taken through the vault with the web's stonework resting on rebates cut in the rib. Where the ribs met under the vault was a projection called a *boss*. The next step which gave masons the flexibility absent in Romanesque work was the use of the pointed arch in vaulting. By making the point of the arch at any height required, all the arches could be made to finish on the same level. At the same time the load became more concentrated towards the point, making the pointed arch more stable than the rounded arch. Vaults could now be constructed regardless of the plan shape below, and the effect of arches ending in a point tended to throw the eye movement upwards (instead of returning to the same level as with the rounded arch), and this brought greater unity between the lower and upper parts of a church structure.

An early addition designed to enrich the rib vault was the *ridge rib*, which became more common about the middle of the twelfth century. The rib extended along the crown of the vault between the bosses. Originally it may have been used to cover a joist. Aesthetically it helped the continuity of vaulting from bay to bay.

The pointed arch made it possible to vault any rectangular shape or square. Two common forms were the *sexpartite* vault with six compartments (*severies*) between the ribs, and the *quadripartite* vault with four *severies* to the vault. In sexpartite vaulting the extra vault ribs virtually centre on the columns below, and the vault plan is square. The quadripartite vault reached the peak of High Gothic vaulting. Its use brought symmetry to the bays and aisles. The nave bay was made a true rectangle with the span across the nave twice that of the span down the nave. One bay of the nave equalled one bay of the aisles. The sexpartite vault was originated by the Romanesque masons who used it with a rounded arch.

The flying buttress was another important Gothic innovation. It gave stability to the walls which received the thrust from pointed arches of nave and choir, and was visible as a striking external feature. Pinnacles, often elabor-

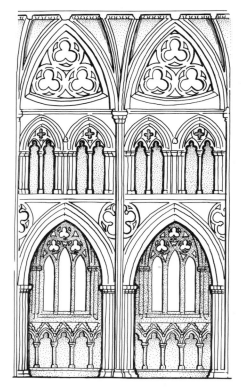

LICHFIELD CATHEDRAL. English Decorated Gothic.

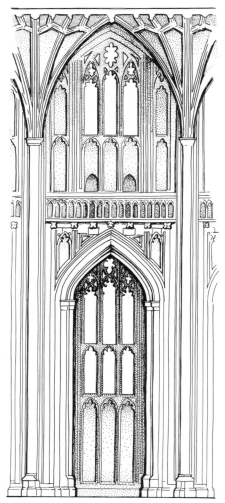

WINCHESTER CATHEDRAL. English Perpendicular Gothic.

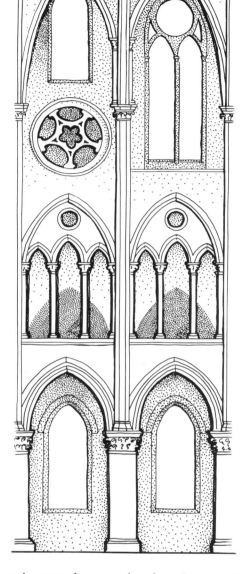

ately carved, were placed at the top of flying buttresses to add weight and increase stability.

St Denis Abbey Church, where the French kings were buried, is widely considered to be the first church to show Early Gothic work. The abbot Suger used the typical rolls and hollow of Gothic decoration, stained glass, pointed arches, and pointed vaults in the east end, in about 1135. As a young monk, Suger had been concerned with the congestion of pilgrims entering and leaving the Abbey Church on feast days – and he actually wrote about it. He planned a new porch with three doors, and above it a chamber for storing relics, flanked by two towers. Only one tower was built when the work was executed in about 1144 but the front marks the transition to Gothic, although strongly Romanesque in detail. St Denis was altered again in the thirteenth, fourteenth

and fifteenth centuries, and the west front restored about the middle of the nineteenth century.

One of the earliest Gothic cathedrals in France is Notre Dame, Paris, begun towards the end of the twelfth century, in what the French term the *primaire* or *à lancettes* period. Later additions have not obliterated the typical layout of nave, double aisles, transepts, choir, and chevet with its ambulatory and chapels. The flying buttresses of great height and ingenuity supporting the upper walls of the choir must have been a remarkable sight to mediaeval eyes, but the chapels between the buttresses, installed at the beginning of the fourteenth century, mask their full liveliness. The French Gothic cathedrals are more compact than the English, which tended to have a longer nave. Higher naves were another French characteristic. The vaulting of the nave at Notre Dame is sexpar-

Above Left
REIMS CATHEDRAL. French Early Gothic.
Centre
NOTRE DAME CATHEDRAL. French Early Gothic.
Above
AMIENS CATHEDRAL. French High Gothic.

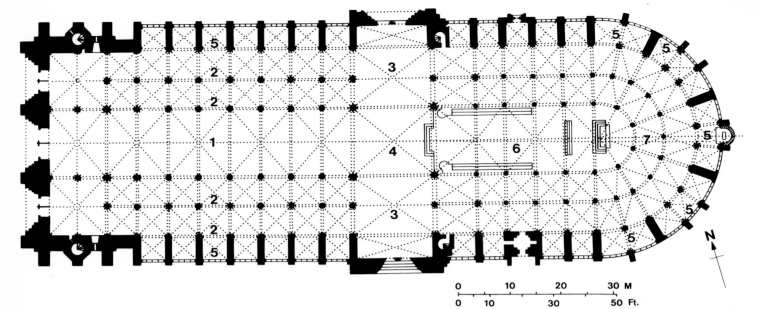

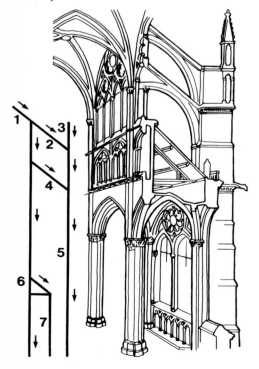

tite. The ribs of the pointed arches rise on shafts from stout rounded columns with foliage ornamented capitals. In the first half of the thirteenth century two bays were added to the nave and the west end with its towers was completed. Hundreds of tourists daily gaze at this west front from the open arena approaching it. Notre Dame is one of the most splendid of French cathedrals. The two west towers are roughly the width of the double aisles inside the church. The piers on the front mark the divisions between nave and aisles, and split the elevation into three, the centre part slightly wider than the flanks. This strong vertical emphasis is broken by the line of statues of the kings of France, above the recessed entrance ways. Above the statues is a line of windows dominated by the beautiful wheel window in the centre, and higher still an open arcade spans the whole front. Both storeys soften the vertical elements and help to bring a sense of aesthetic balance to the front which took about fifty years to build, the lowest part being completed in *c.* 1200, the window area in *c.* 1220, and the two towers in 1225–40 (south) and 1235–50 (north).

Chartres Cathedral, replanned after the fire in 1194, pointed the way to High Gothic in the treatment of the nave. Instead of galleries over the aisles abutting the nave walls, the aisle roofs were lowered, and the flying buttresses were used to support the upper part of the nave walls in place of the galleries. This exposed more nave wall to the outside and windows were made larger. There were two reasons for larger windows. They admitted much more daylight into the nave than clerestory windows, and accentuated the light-absorbing qualities of stained glass then becoming fashionable for windows. Stained glass

gave the Gothic artists the opportunity to enrich their churches with figures of saints and scenes from the Bible in a more brilliant way than the Byzantine mosaics. The problem was that large windows could not be filled with glass, as in modern architecture, without a supporting structure. Stonework tracery built up structurally was the answer to the problem. In French High Gothic the tracery usually consisted of a pair of pointed arched windows divided by a stone mullion with an *oculus* – a circular window – above the pair. These were used at Chartres and later at Rheims Cathedral (*c.* 1210–90), the coronation church of the kings of France, in which the oculi are sexfoiled. The elevation of a nave bay in the High Gothic cathedrals followed a similar pattern: clerestory windows at the top, *triforium* pierced openings corresponding with the aisle roof at mid level, and pointed arches and columns of the nave at ground level.

Amiens Cathedral, started a decade later than Rheims but completed earlier, is considered the most mature of the French High Gothic churches. There were at least three architects involved. The nave by Robert de Luzarches was begun first, followed by the choir and transepts by father and son, Thomas and Regnault de Cormont. The nave has seven bays with side aisles, the choir beyond the crossing four bays, and the chevet beyond the choir seven apses, three on either side of a central and longer apse. The transepts also have aisles. The clerestory windows of the nave, larger than those at Rheims, have an oculus above two pairs of windows, and each pair of windows also has a small oculus above. Each nave column has four protruding shafts, their small capitals carved with mouldings and leaves, and the shaft facing the nave is carried up

Above
SALISBURY CATHEDRAL. Begun *c.* 1220.

Right
SALISBURY CATHEDRAL. Begun *c.* 1220.

Below
SALISBURY CATHEDRAL. Begun *c.* 1220.
Plan:
  1 nave,
  2 aisle,
  3 cloisters,
  4 Chapter House,
  5 west transept,
  6 crossing,
  7 choir,
  8 east transept,
  9 presbytery,
 10 altar,
 11 Lady Chapel,
 12 sacristy,
 13 north porch.

to the vault ribs. The vault is 43 metres high. The diagonal view of the nave at Amiens shows how the Gothic architects mastered the art of designing 'in the round', so that from any angle the view was aesthetically complete. This was the great difference between the Gothic and Romanesque masters. In Romanesque the design was best viewed 'square on' and not at an angle.

While Amiens was being built in France, Salisbury Cathedral (begun *c.* 1220), the finest example of Early English or Lancet style, was being built in England. The plan was longer than in French cathedrals: a ten-bay nave, main transepts, a three-bay choir, east transepts, a three-bay presbytery, and a Lady Chapel. The same system of a clerestory, triforium, and arcading used throughout the church emphasizes its length. Salisbury is also distinguished by the magnificent spire over the main crossing: over 123 metres high and the tallest in England.

Early English is the name given to the High Gothic period in England,

and other examples of the style include the fine west front of Wells Cathedral, its nave, two transepts, and part of the choir. The choir and east transepts of Lincoln (*c.* 1192–1200) are believed to be the earliest examples; the main transepts, nave, and tower over the main crossing are also Early English.

Before the end of the High Gothic period in France, aisle roofs, which had been steep because of the height of French Gothic cathedrals, were made as flat as possible and the triforia became glazed windows with tracery, closely related to that of the clerestory windows above them. Architect Pierre de Montreuil is given credit for the idea first used in his alterations to St Denis Abbey Church, *c.* 1232. During the next decade his Chapel of Ste Chapelle in Paris was built, and dedicated in 1248. The chapel is beautiful and has unusual connections. It was designed as a suitable resting place for the Crown of Thorns and other relics of Christ's trial and crucifixion, brought to France from the Middle East. The sacred objects were received at the gates of Paris by Louis IX, King of France, who, barefooted, carried them back to his own chapel in the City Palace. There are two chapels at Ste Chapelle: one at first-floor level, the level of the royal apartments; the second, at ground-floor level, for the use of officials and palace staff. The main chapel, at the upper level, is remarkable for its large windows, and the cleanness of the shafts rising almost uninterrupted to the ribs of the vaults above. There are no aisles but seats for the king and his family are placed on the side walls. The relics were stored in a shrine above the altar at the end of the chapel.

As Gothic art developed and the High period merged into the Late period at the beginning of the fourteenth century, certain characteristics gradually changed. More and more wall space was devoted to tracery and stained glass. Columns and shafts were fined down and the channels cut in columns, and arches became deeper. Towards the end of the Late period, the vault was changed

Left
AMIENS CATHEDRAL. Begun 1220. Restored in later years. Nave. View to the east.

Below
AMIENS CATHEDRAL. Begun 1220. Plan:
1 nave,
2 aisle,
3 chapels (between flying buttresses added later),
4 transept,
5 choir,
6 ambulatory,
7 chapel,
8 apsidal chapel,
9 crossing.

perhaps more than any other element. The structure remained virtually the same, but ribs were added, and elaborate forms of tracery produced many beautiful forms.

In England, the Early English period of High Gothic faded into the Decorated and Perpendicular periods of Late Gothic. The more easily recognizable characteristics of Decorated work were the geometrical and curved shapes used in tracery. In the Perpendicular period these became elongated with decided emphasis on their vertical elements. Windows filled more of the wall space in Perpendicular designs than in Decorated, and shafts of columns were thin with no capitals, sometimes carried up and into the vault ribs in one uninterrupted line, as in King's College Chapel, Cambridge (1446–1515).

In Late Gothic, the rib vault changed with the addition of non-structured ribs called *liernes*, which followed the curve of the valut's web. *Tierceron*, or third rib, was a term used for another type of intermediate-structural rib. With the aid of the new ribs the pattern of English vaults became more net-like in the Decorated period, as may be seen in Gloucester Cathedral Chancel (1337–*c.* 55), or Exeter Cathedral's nave also built in the mid-fourteenth century. The next development of English Late Gothic vaulting in the Perpendicular period was the *fan vault*. The cloisters at Gloucester Cathedral dating between *c.* 1367 and 1377 are an early example. The fan vaults at King's College Chapel, Cambridge, built between 1501 and 1515 by the master mason John Wastell, are the ultimate form. Henry VII's chapel at Westminster Abbey, built between 1503 and 1519 by the brothers Robert and William Virtue has even more elaborate fan vaults with long pendants hanging from each fanning out point. The elaboration of ribs subordinates the

AMIENS CATHEDRAL. Begun 1220. The cutaway portions reveal the rib vaulting of the nave which transmits the load onto piers by means of the pointed arches. Flying buttresses brace the upper walls of the nave, the upper walls of the chancel (on the right), and the south transept. The west front is on the left.

structure, so eloquent in High Gothic, to an overall pattern of masterly decoration.

The absorption of Gothic ideas into local vernacular was the general trend in Europe outside France, and Transitional Gothic tended to persist as a style. It was not until the mid-thirteenth century, after the old Carolingian cathedral at Cologne was burnt down, that a new cathedral influenced by French High Gothic was built by the architect Gerhard. Cologne is notable for its clarity of detail and enormous size. It also has a typical feature of the central European cathedrals – the characteristic spire, of which the red sandstone minster at Freiburg im Breisgau, in its beautiful Black Forest setting, is a fine example. At Freiburg, the spire is an open structure of filigree stonework, added ten years after the square tower beneath it was completed. The spire lets in rain and snow, but a stone roof protects the tower below. It was built about the middle of the fourteenth century and became the model for the towers at Cologne. Ulm Minster's spire has similar filigree tracery to that at Freiburg, as does the spire of St Stephen's Cathedral, Vienna (fourteenth/fifteenth century).

St Stephen's Cathedral is a fine example of a hall church which became popular in central Europe in the mid-fourteenth century. Hall churches had no transepts, but sometimes chapels in their place, as at St Stephen's. The smaller churches, like the Church of the Holy Cross, Schwäbisch Gmünd, one of the earliest, were simple halls with aisles. There were no clerestory windows or triforia; the large, steeply-pitched roofs covered the building in one space. The church was usually entered through a single impressive portal in the west

Above
PRAGUE CASTLE. Fifteenth century.
Vladislav Hall. Double curved ribs.

Left
FREIBERG MINSTER, Germany,
Fourteenth century. Looking up through
the filigreed stonework of the spire.

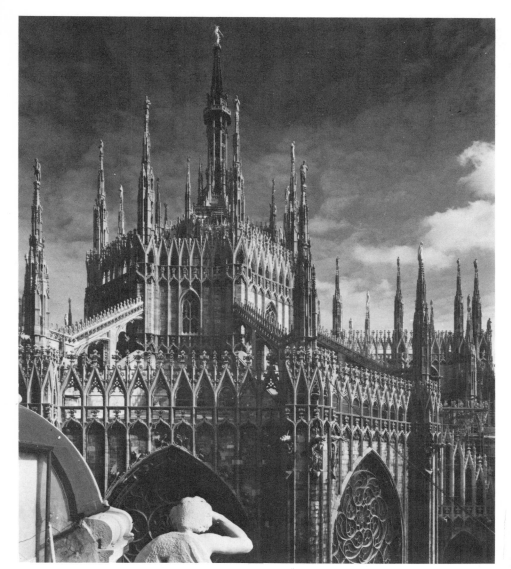

front, with a central circular window, and sometimes other windows, in the storey above. Vaulting in the hall was usually richly decorated with a network of ribs, some structural some non-structural, in the late Late Gothic style.

The final development of the rib was to use it three-dimensionally against the vault. It served no structural purpose but was effective aesthetically in a similar way to the projections on fan vaults. Examples of flying ribs are to be seen at Lincoln Cathedral, Prague Cathedral, and in the chapels of St Stephen's, Vienna. Further developments in central Europe in the fifteenth century were twisted ribs on columns (Brunswick Cathedral choir) and double-curved ribs (Vladislav Hall, Prague Palace).

In Italy the influence of northern Gothic on church architecture was less marked than in central Europe: roofs were not so steep; clerestory windows were small; flying buttresses were scarce; the west front wall was usually shaped to hide the profile of the roofs behind. In northern Italy the most important church was Milan Cathedral, begun in

about 1390 or earlier, and not completed until nearly a hundred years later. It was built as a people's church under the sponsorship of Giovanni Galeazzo Visconti. Many foreign architects took part in the work which consequently shows French and German influences. The nave, started in about 1452, has nine bays up to the crossing, and double aisles. The height to the top of the nave vault is about 45.5 metres. The aisle vaults are progressively less high under the enormous sloping roof. The nave piers, designed by a French architect, Nicholas de Bonneaventure, are octagonal with rounded corners. Above the capitals are figures carved in niches, with canopies above them from which spring the arch and vault ribs. The short transepts have aisles and end in chapels. The crossing is spanned by a domical vault with a lantern tower above. The vault's design was the result of an architectural competition won by Amadeo and Dolcebuono in 1490. The spire is a mid-eighteenth century addition. The east end has a French style ambulatory, and an apse remarkable for three very

large traceried windows filled with stained glass. The most striking features of the outside are the pinnacles and the Late Gothic detail, much of which was not completed until the nineteenth century.

In central Italy, Florence Cathedral (S. Maria del Fiore) begun *c.* 1296, almost a hundred years before Milan Cathedral, is probably less Gothic than early Renaissance. Both styles are present in the church. The first architect was Arnolfo di Cambio. He died in the first decade of the fourteenth century and the work was stopped until another architect, Giotto, took over about 1334. Two other architects, Andrea Pisano and Francesco Talenti, were appointed some twenty years later. They enlarged Arnolfo's original scheme, and further adjustments were made by a Commission of Architects a decade later. The story bears a resemblance to modern architectural schemes which have to pass through many hands before being finally approved.

The cathedral plan is roughly cruciform in shape. The crossing is an enormous octagon, 42 metres in diameter. Westwards, the unusually wide nave, with side aisles, is divided into only four very large square bays, each over 18 metres long. Beyond the octagon are three large apses forming the north–south transepts and the east end. Each apse has five chapels. The rib vaulting of the nave shows its Gothic origins, but the huge piers supporting the pointed arches are shaped with pilasters and not the rounded shafts familiar in High Gothic. The aisles are lit by a simple narrow pointed-arched window in each bay, corresponding externally with an oculus to each bay in the clerestory of the nave. The absence of larger windows make the interior rather dim, but outside this enhances the effect of the smooth marble panelling.

Florence Cathedral is renowned mainly for the huge dome, an octagonally shaped domical vault, built between 1420 and 1434. The design was the result of an architectural competition, and the famous Renaissance architect Filippo Brunelleschi was responsible for the work. The principles used in the dome's construction are Gothic. The dome has an inner and an outer shell tied together, which made it lighter than solid masonry. There are eight main ribs and sixteen intermediate ribs with the panels between built of brickwork. The bottom of the dome is strengthened by wood tie beams jointed with bands of metal to make a hoop. Stone blocks around the dome at intervals are presumed to prevent the dome exploding

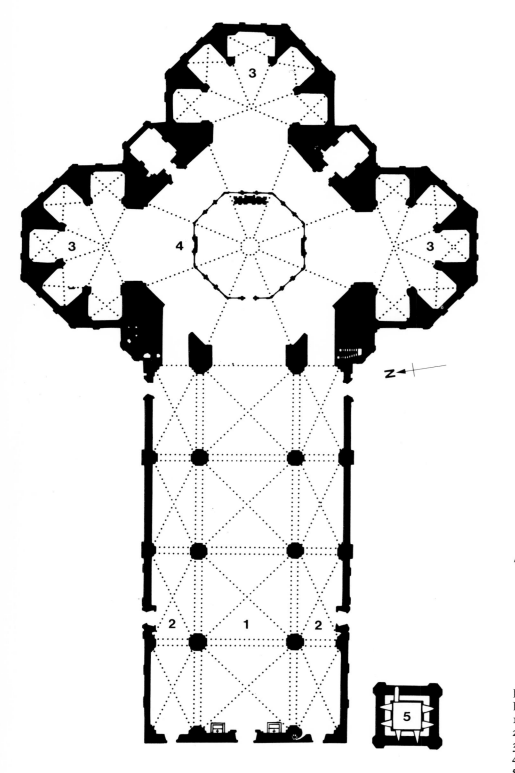

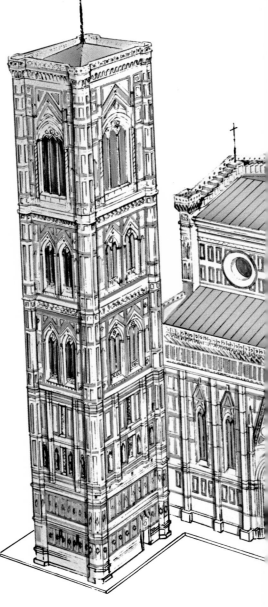

Florence Cathedral. Begun 1296.
Plan:
1 nave,
2 aisle,
3 apse with five chapels,
4 octagon (the crossing),
5 campanile (bell tower).

outwards and make it possible for the
dome to rest on the drum in a similar
manner to the Roman domes. The interior of the dome is enriched with
fresco painting by G. Vasari.

The great Gothic cathedrals of Spain
were in one respect similar to those of
England. Many of those with cloisters
had monasteries attached to them at
some time. More of the French
Cathedrals were built as metropolitan
churches, close to the townspeople.
Gothic influence in Spain came from

FLORENCE CATHEDRAL. Begun 1296.
The anatomy of the huge domical vault
designed by architect Filippo Brunelleschi
is shown clearly in the cutaway. The
domical vault was added to the cathedral
between 1420 and 1434 after a competition
won by Brunelleschi's design. The two
skins of the vault are tied together,
making a lighter structure than a solid
shell. There are eight main ribs and
sixteen intermediate ribs with panels of
brickwork in between.

Right
PALAZZO PUBBLICO, Siena, Italy. Late
thirteenth century.

Below
BURGOS CATHEDRAL, Spain. Begun 1221.
Star vaulting of the lantern over the
crossing.

France early in the thirteenth century
and was merged with Spanish tradition
and sometimes Muslim art. Detailed
work is mainly Late Gothic in expression.
The cathedrals at Burgos, Toledo, Léon,
and Barcelona were begun in the first
half of the fifteenth century, some before
and some after the establishment of the
Spanish Inquisition in 1477. Seville
Cathedral, the largest mediaeval church
in Europe, and the largest in the world
if you exclude St Peter's, Rome, was not
started until the beginning of the fourteenth century, but was completed by
the second decade of the sixteenth.

Burgos and Toledo Cathedrals both
have a French style ambulatory at the
east end. The choir is on the west side
of the crossing, the usual position in

Spanish Gothic cathedrals. Burgos has
a typical Gothic west front but with
elaborate and fine detailing. The spires
of the twin towers have filigree open-
work tracery, similar to those at Cologne
and Ulm. At the east end of Burgos is
the Capilla del Condestable, a chamber
designed by Simon of Cologne, whose
father was German and mother Spanish.
The Capilla del Condestable has a remarkable Late Gothic star vault with
star-shaped open tracery in the centre.
The west front and interior of Toledo
Cathedral is a feast of intricate and
elaborate carving and fine detailing.

In Portugal at the beginning of the
sixteenth century, King Manuel founded
the monastery of Jerónimos, Belem near
Lisbon, on the site where Vasco da

Gama landed with all his riches from a
successful voyage to India. The chapel
is an aisled hall of three bays. The
vaulting of the entire church is rich in a
texture of flamboyant ribwork.

The Gothic art was not confined to
church building although so many fine
examples came that way. Secular architecture in the Gothic period developed
its own characteristics. Towns were
growing in importance and civic authorities with more power demanded their
own kind of building. Naturally they
looked to the best buildings of the
times – the churches – for aesthetic
inspiration. The towns themselves
needed protection, and they borrowed
the idea of the mediaeval castle's curtain wall with towers and defensive

devices like machiolations (p. 95) and
portcullises at gateways. The palace
began to replace the castle as the sov-
ereign's home. Again the new building
work was Gothic in character. The
merchants and craft guilds, gaining
confidence in the expansion of trade and
their own importance in late mediaeval
life, built their own halls. The monastic
orders which had done so much for
church architecture naturally followed
the style for their own secular buildings—
hostels, tithe barns, cloisters, and so on.

Venice was one of the most important
trading centres in mediaeval Europe and
the ruler, the Doge, built his palace on
the corner of St Mark's Square. Since
the first palace was begun in the ninth
century, it has been rebuilt a number of

times. The ground and first floors on two sides have continuous arcades. The lower arcade has continuous pointed arches on rounded columns with heavily carved capitals. In the upper arcade each column is exactly above the centre of the arch or column below. The arches are termed *ogee*. Above the ogee arches is a row of oculi with *quatrefoil* (four leaf) openings, arranged so that an oculus is directly above each column. The wall above is of pink and white marble in

pieces resembling brickwork and making a pattern. The upper storey has regular and widely-spaced circular windows and is topped by an ornamental parapet. The facades were designed by Giovanni and Bartholomew Buon and date from the first decade of the fourteenth century. The part above the arcades was rebuilt in the sixteenth century after a fire.

Also in Italy are fine examples of city halls displaying great dignity, and at the same time the need for defensive meas-

ures in the form of machiolations and crenellated walls hiding steeply-pitched roofs. The Palazzo Pubblico, Siena, begun at the end of the thirteenth century, and the late fourteenth century town hall at Montepulciano in southern Italy are typical examples.

In the Netherlands, the great Cloth Hall at Ypres, destroyed in the 1914–18 War and restored since to the original design, and the Cloth Hall at Bruges with its tower more than 76 metres high,

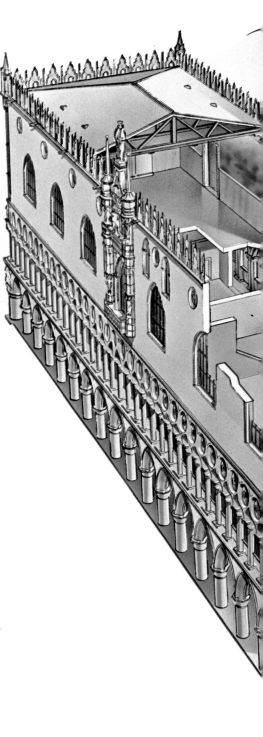

Above
HAMPTON COURT, London. Begun 1520. Entrance to the first court.

Below
CUSTOM HOUSE, Nuremburg.

both thirteenth century, show typical Gothic details, and testify to the importance of the Netherlands in the development of trade in north-east Europe.

In central Europe, the town halls usually possessed very large, steeply-pitched roofs. Dormer windows were as plentiful and as regularly spaced as those of the orderly facades. Two contrasting yet striking examples are: the Custom House at Nuremburg, built at the end of the fifteenth century, with three storeys before the roof and six storeys in the roof, the gable roof end displaying Gothic tracery work; and Markgröningen Town Hall, built between the fifteenth and seventeenth centuries and for its remarkable half-timber work, but with few dormer windows.

Early English churches and manors are discussed in the next chapter. Hampton Court Palace in England was begun about 1520 and therefore comes in at the end of the Gothic period. Historically, it has always aroused interest because of the richness of its tapestries and furniture, installed by Cardinal Wolsey, whose palace it was until he gave it to Henry VIII in 1526. The chief mason for the original building, much of which survives, was Henry Redman. Henry VIII added the Great Hall with its hammer beam roof, the chapel and wings to the west front. Christopher Wren made additions in the Renaissance style.

DOGE'S PALACE, Venice. Begun in the ninth century and rebuilt many times since. The accommodation behind the palace's well-known waterfront facade, exposed in the cutaway, is probably more extensive than might have been imagined. The facades, designed by Giovanni and Bartholomew Buon, date from the beginning of the fourteenth century, and the part above the ground and first floor arcades was rebuilt after a fire in the sixteenth century. The Cortile dei Giganti (great courtyard) by Anthony Rizzo (begun *c.* 1485) and Scala dei Giganti (staircase) (1485–89) are revealed within.

English Manor Houses and Parish Churches

When the mediaeval castles and great cathedrals were being extended, or even being built from scratch, architecture of a humbler kind but important to the anatomy of architecture made progress in England: the manor houses and parish churches that reflect the earlier history of the country.

The universal dwelling for a lord or yeoman in Saxon times was the hall – a barn-like structure, probably with rows of wooden arches rising from columns or posts, acting as struts for long purlins supporting the roof structure. The aisled hall sheltered animals as well as humans, implements, and stores. An open-hearthed fire burnt in the centre of the hall. Smoke escaped through openings at the gable points of the roof. The floor of beaten earth was covered with rushes or straw, renewed once a year. The hall was luxurious compared to the one-roomed peasant hovels, with no windows and often a sunken floor.

The importance of the hall in domestic architecture dates from classical times. Its origin seems to have been the *megaron*, the central hall of the Aegean citadel, which was adopted by the Greeks and Romans for the main apartment of their villas. With the English manorial system the hall was not only the central room of the Lord of the Manor's establishment, it was also the scene of the Manor Court where local justice was dispensed when the oak tree on the village green no longer set the scene. The tradition of the manorial system instituted by William I dies hard in England, and the local country house to this day, whatever its origins, is often called 'the hall' by villagers.

A common type of manor, popular in France and England in the eleventh century, was a hall on the first floor reached by an external staircase, possibly following the example of the stone castle keep which was usually entered at first-floor level for defence reasons. Beneath the hall was a ground floor, called an *undercroft*, which was some-times left partly open, and used for storage. Some halls had an upper floor or attic, which in later halls became the *solar*, a term for an upper room, or the withdrawing room. The manor in mediaeval times consisted of a large entrance hall for receiving visitors, with sleeping quarters at one end and service

PENSHURST PLACE, Kent. Begun 1341. Great Hall.

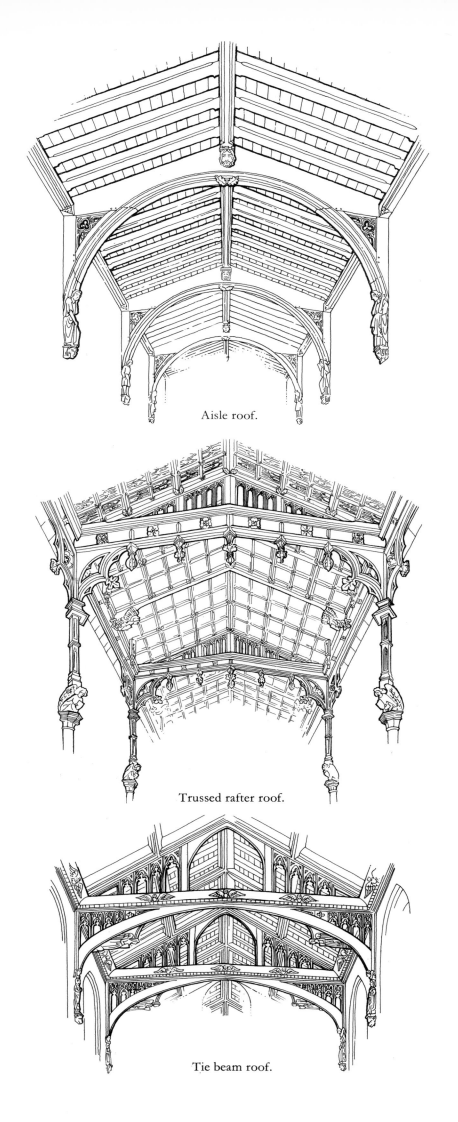

Aisle roof.

Trussed rafter roof.

Tie beam roof.

rooms at the other. The kitchen was separate. Retainers, bailiffs, or knights had hovels or small halls nearby.

Housing in general was no better than a shelter. A single room was normal in the thirteenth century, and it was not until the fourteenth and fifteenth centuries that two rooms became common for clerks in holy orders, traders, and those of similar standing.

As peace and prosperity grew in the late thirteenth and fourteenth centuries as a result of King John's humiliation and Magna Carta in 1215, the subsequent growth of trade and the work of the monasteries, the manor house also changed. The first-floor type gave way to a larger establishment with a hall on the ground floor and two-tier extensions.

One of the finest remaining halls is at Penshurst Place, Kent, built in about 1341–48 by Sir John Pulteney, a rich London merchant. The hall is about 10.5 metres wide and has a dais at one end where the family sat for meals. Retainers fed below them. Chairs would probably only be used by the Lord and his Lady. Everyone else sat on stools, the usual means of seating. Opposite the dais end three doorways lead to a passageway called a *screen*, from which the buttery and pantry were entered. A passage between buttery and pantry (terms originating from the French *bouteille*, a bottle, and *pain*, bread) led to the kitchen, now destroyed. The kitchen was kept away from the hall as a fire precaution. This was common practice, like the screen at the end of the hall. In later periods it became popular to top the screen with a minstrels' gallery. The stone walls of Penshurst Place were crenellated like the mediaeval castle. Most large manor houses adopted this practice. An example in Derbyshire – Haddon Hall – has two courtyards, a gatehouse with portcullis, and moated outer walls as additional defensive measures.

Many of the stone-built manors had private chapels adjoining the hall. The villagers had their parish church with close associations similar to those with the manor. The anatomy of both church and manor was dominated by the master carpenter's work: the open roof with its mixture of aesthetic appeal and engineering inventiveness had to cover as wide a span as possible, yet remain uncluttered. It was important that it should be uncluttered, because early roofs with rafters or *crucks* (curved baulks of timber, meeting at the top in a ridge beam) usually had their tie beams

Above
St Wendreda Church, March,
Cambridgeshire. *c.* 1500. Double hammer
beam roof over the nave.

Opposite
Church of St Mary the Virgin,
Iffley, Oxfordshire. *c.* twelfth century.
Norman. West front.

may well have been inspired by the earlier cruck roof, in which crucks became curved braces springing from the walls instead of from the floor. Variations and mixtures of these roof structures were common. The wood carving was often very fine.

The *hammer beam roof* developed in the fourteenth century was the most elaborate. The trusses were placed at regular intervals to support purlins and common rafters. The hammer beam itself was a horizontal piece of wood with a vertical member at right angles rising up to the main rafter above. A curved brace transmitted the thrust to the wall and was attached to a wall piece. The woodwork was usually carved with finials of rosettes, statuettes, and winged figures. There are many examples and variations of this type of roof. The most beautiful example in Europe is the hammer beam roof over Westminster Hall, London, by the master carpenter Hugh Herland, dating from about 1398. The fifteenth century church in Needham Market, Suffolk is another in which extra hammer beams were used to strengthen the trusses, making it a double hammer beam roof.

The parish church was well established in England before the Conquest, and the number of parishes had changed little up to the industrial revolution. But the church itself changed. There are few remains of Saxon work. We know they were simple white-walled buildings with a square east end and an entrance, usually with a porch, on the south side at the west end. Windows were narrow, set in thick stone walls of rubble faced with stone or flint. Wall openings were sometimes triangular-headed, as in the tower at Deerhurst Church, Gloucestershire, or round-headed with lintels cut from a single stone. Towers were added, usually over the porch on the south side.

After the Conquest the Normans rebuilt many of the Saxon churches on a grander scale and made additions to others. They introduced aisles with rounded arched arcades to suit changes in ritual. A few Norman parish churches had cruciform plans. The tower was usually placed centrally, and the main entrance became a south door, at the west end of the nave. Like the hall, the church floor was covered with dried rushes. There was no heating and no place to sit down. People stood and the weakest literally went to the wall (hence the expression) where a ledge gave some support. But the church had an enormous following. The power of the monasteries

placed on the ground. The next step was to raise them up to the top of the wall (or columns, in an aisled hall) to produce the trussed roof. The ties prevented the ends of rafters from spreading outwards.

A common form found in some Norfolk churches was the *trussed rafter roof*. In this roof, rafters were prevented from spreading outwards by means of collars and diagonal ties or braces placed high up in the fork. The system was useful for high roofs with steep pitches and for gaining headroom. The nave roof of Ely Cathedral and Needham Church, Norfolk (9.5 metres) are wide-spanned examples. The *tie beam roof* was frequently used in the Late Gothic English Perpendicular period for low-pitched roofs. They were often beautifully adorned with figures of angels at the base of the vertical wall pieces to which curved braces were attached. The braces gave support to the tie beam which sometimes sloped upwards from sides to middle. The *collar braced roof*

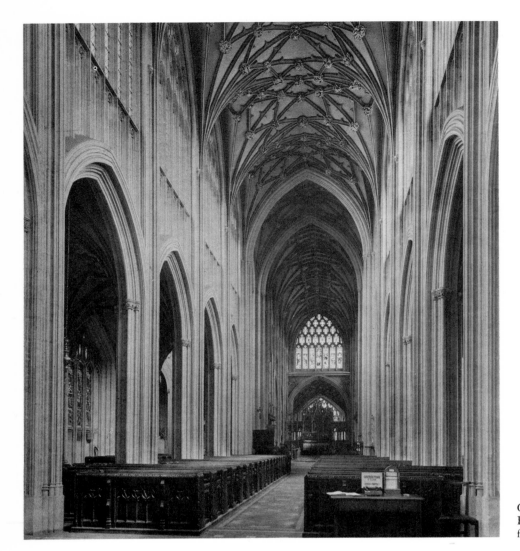

CHURCH OF ST MARY THE VIRGIN, Redcliffe, Bristol. Fourteenth and fifteenth centuries.

had grown, and by the middle of the twelfth century their number was approaching 500. They received most of the tithes of the parish churches under their control, and rules had to be introduced at the beginning of the thirteenth century to check the monasteries' control of parishes, and to give the parish priest a stipend. Understandably, perhaps, the monarchy either feared or became anxious of the monastic wealth, culminating in their suppression by Henry VIII in 1536.

The gradual change from Romanesque to Gothic architecture with the Transitional period (p. 99) gradually affected the parish church. Examples of Gothic alterations and additions to Norman churches are evident by the juxtaposition of pointed and rounded arches, and the rolls and hollows of Gothic decoration next to the chevrons and birdbeak carvings of Norman work. As architecture moved into the High Gothic then later Gothic periods the parish church continued to reflect the changes seldom complete in any one style because, like the cathedrals, changes were made at different times. Local builders and masons were responsible

for the work. They copied the craftsmanship of the local cathedral, adding ideas and sometimes idiosyncrasies of their own. St Mary Redcliffe, Bristol is one of the few great parish churches which faithfully reproduces Gothic in the Late period.

In the fourteenth/fifteenth centuries, in the period between the Black Death (1349) and the Reformation (1536), one of the influences in the plan of the parish church came from the addition of the chantry chapel. Chantries were small colleges, usually consisting of up to six priests, attached to a parish church by a benefactor, sometimes no doubt with an eye to a means of salvation. Rich merchant guilds also endowed chantries and had their own guild chapel in the local church. Chantry priests said mass every day. They took part in parish duties when the priest was non-resident or had several parishes to look after. The chantry chapel was not confined to any particular part of the church plan. Well-known examples may be seen at Long Melford, Suffolk, and at Berkeley in Gloucestershire, but many exist in other churches.

Renaissance Architecture

The Renaissance in Europe was not just the rediscovery of the classical art and architecture of Ancient Greece and Rome, it was a period of great expansion in philosophy, science, and literature and the opening up of the New World, in preparation for the modern world we know today. In architecture it all began in Florence, Italy about the second decade of the fifteenth century and went on until the Baroque forms of Late Renaissance changed back into the classical forms and revivals, beginning between 1760, when George III ascended the throne of England, and the end of the eighteenth century. The Renaissance period was a time of political and religious upheaval. In England, the period included the reigns of Henry VIII, Elizabeth I, James I, Charles I, the English Republic, Charles II, James II, William and Mary, Anne, George I and George II. On the continent of Europe, great monarchs of France and Spain vied with each other to become the greatest in Europe. There were constant wars over successions, and between Protestant and Catholic factions during the dreadful 'Thirty Years War'. There were other events of equal importance, and as each country's architecture is discussed, the extent of their influence will be apparent.

In 1420 the principal powers of Italy were the three republican states of Venice, Florence, and Rome, corresponding roughly to the northern half of Italy as we know the peninsular today. Florence was a centrally-placed city state. Venice was prosperous and well established through her international trade, and controlled the country to the north-east almost as far as Milan, and also the south-west parts of Istoria and Dalmatia. Rome was dominated by the papal state, extending northwards to link up with Venice, and Florence which also had an outlet to the sea through Pisa.

Florence, the chief state, was ruled by the Medici family in 1420. Four gener-

ations of them were heads of state in succession. Their principal business was banking and trading, besides politics. Like other wealthy Florentines, the Medici were great patrons of the arts and sciences. Scholars, painters, sculptors, astronomers, and mathematicians were among their friends. It was an age in which men excelled in many things and tried to develop all the talents with which they were born. The Florentine way of life at the beginning of the fifteenth century was greatly influenced by the rediscovery of the classical arts of Greece and Rome. Sculptors and painters had already begun again to include the naked human form in their art, but in a more enlightened way than the Greeks and the Romans. When writings on architecture by Vitruvius, a Roman military engineer of the first century B.C., were re-read, their content was eagerly absorbed. Vitruvius based his architectural theories on the human figure, the circle, and the sphere. More simply, proportion was the hallmark of beauty in any form, a theory which persisted in the minds of the Florentines leading them on towards a new style of architecture.

FOUNDLING HOSPITAL, Florence. Begun c. 1421. Architect: Brunelleschi.

One of the founders of the Renaissance was Filippo Brunelleschi, who had already designed the dome for the Cathedral of Florence (1420). Born in 1377, Brunelleschi was trained as a goldsmith, became a sculptor, invented machinery especially for the construction of Florence Cathedral's dome, and visited the ancient works in Rome before his successful career as an architect in Florence. Between 1419 and 1426, he designed the Foundling Hospital. The famous loggia with its delicate Corinthian capitals, generous circular arches, and medallions ornamented with swathed figures of children over the columns, is a breathtaking piece of sensitive design after the flamboyance of the Gothic. Brunelleschi, who through his dome and hospital became one of the foremost architects in Florence, designed work for the Medici (Sacristy of S. Lorenzo) and the Pazzi family.

Brunelleschi's design for S. Spirito (c. 1436), generally considered to be an improvement on his earlier S. Lorenzo, is a Latin cross shaped plan with identical transepts and east end, and a slightly longer nave. The proportions of the church were based on the square bay of the aisles which was half the width of the nave; the height of the nave is double its width. Roman influence is strong in the Corinthian-style capitals with portions of entablature above them. The ceiling is flat and there is a dome over the crossing. The ordered regularity of the church is helped by the single windows in each bay of the aisles, corresponding to similar windows in the clerestory of the nave, and by the proportion of solid wall to window opening. There is order too in the regular arrangement of niches against the walls around the church. The church, like other work by Brunelleschi, was completed after his lifetime. He died in 1446.

Other products of the new style were the magnificent palaces built for the great families of Florence: the Palazzo Pitti, begun in 1458; the Palazzo Strozzi, begun in 1489; and the palace designed for the Medici in 1444 and sold to the Riccardi family in 1659. All these palaces were largely similar, with household rooms arranged around an inner court. The fronts were finished with ashlar masonry, heavily rusticated at ground floor level, that is finished with a rough surface and recessed joints to give it a coarse appearance. The rounded headed windows were regularly spaced with well-defined arches, and there was usually a cornice or balustrade at the top. The designer of the Medici palace was

Michelozzi, a friend of Cosimo de Medici, who was Florence's head of state from 1434–64. His son, Piero de Medici, and grandson, Lorenzo de Medici, used the palace for their splendid courts, particularly those of Lorenzo the Magnificent, who succeeded his father and grandfather as head of state.

In 1472, the year he died, Leon Battista Alberti's Church of S. Andreas Mantua was begun. Although its shape is that of a Latin cross, S. Andrea is unlike S. Spirito. The west facade is remarkable for the massive pilasters flanking three levels of windows and the 'triumphal arch' appearance of the entrance way, typical of Roman architecture. Great pilasters against the piers, entablatures and rounded arches with all surfaces richly ornamented are evident in the interior. Chapels on either side of the nave, identical to those in the transepts, are used instead of the aisles at S. Spirito. The crossing is domed. An apsidal east end was added in the late sixteenth and early seventeenth centuries. Alberti was one of the first Renaissance architects to re-introduce pilasters to the front of a building, a style which became widely used in the Baroque period of Late Renaissance.

Early Renaissance is the term usually used for the first part of this period. Leon Battista Alberti was one of its great exponents. He was born in 1404, the son of a banker. Like Leonardo da Vinci, he was illegitimate, scarcely a stigma in Florentine society in which

many of the great princes rose from such beginnings. Weak as a child, Alberti nonetheless excelled at jousting and horseriding as a young man, and was proud of his physical prowess. He could speak Greek and Latin, took a degree in law, wrote ballads to his ladies, and a book on horsebreeding. There was perhaps none other quite like him.

Political trouble started for Florence when Charles VIII, King of France, occupied the city in 1494 in an effort to sustain his claim to the Kingdom of Naples. The Medici were overthrown because of Piero de Medici's unsatisfactory handling of the French affair. Savanarola came to power and was overthrown by the Spanish emperor Charles V, who captured Florence and restored the Medici. Meanwhile the power of the Popes was gaining in strength. Architecturally, Rome was influenced by Florence. Alberti had been a secretary to the papal chancery in Rome, and had been made architectural adviser to Nicholas V, when he became Pope in 1447. Other architects of the Renaissance were employed in the papal service, and Rome carried on the developments started in Florence. The great High Renaissance period followed. Donato Bramante (1444–1514), one of its greatest architects in Rome, was born near Urbino, Italy, and settled as a young man in Lombardy. He was a painter before becoming an architect. He studied the work of Brunelleschi and, when the French invaded Milan in 1499, moved to Rome, entering the service of Pope Julius II.

The old basilican church of St Peter had been pulled down, and Julius II, a great pope and patriot, wanted a new church to be a tomb for himself. An architectural competition was held. Bramante's design won, and the foundation stone was laid in 1506. It took 120 years, from 1506 to 1626, to complete the great church which marked the peak of High Renaissance in Italy. Pope Julius II died in 1513, and new architects, Giuliana da Sangallo, Francesca Giocondo, and Raphael were appointed in Bramante's place. All three were dead

Left
S. Spirito Church, Florence. Begun 1436. Plan:
1 nave,
2 transept,
3 crossing,
4 choir,
5 aisles,
6 cloisters.

Opposite
S. Spirito Church, Florence. Begun 1436. Architect: Brunelleschi. Nave.

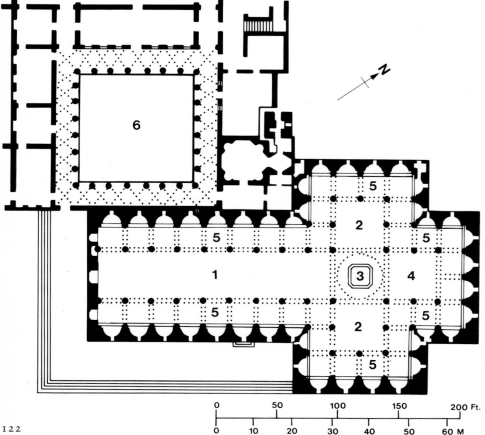

by 1520. Baldassare Peruzzi and after him Antonio da Sangallo the Younger were appointed, but they had both died by 1546. All these architects made changes to the original design, which was again changed by Michelangelo who was finally appointed at the age of seventy-two. Much of the completed church is his work.

Bramante's original plan for St Peter's, a classic example of proportion and rhythm, was a completely symmetrical inscribed Greek cross with apses at the ends of the arms. Much of the original Bramante design was retained in the final plan of the cathedral as built. Michelangelo reduced the number of bays and made the ambulatories around his huge central dome into more of a square. Another architect, Carlo Maderna, extended the nave in a westerly direction to form a Latin cross shaped plan, and added the huge entrance portico and imposing west facade.

Between 1655 and 1667, the famous piazza in front of St Peter's with colonnades of Tuscan order columns was finally added by the Baroque architect, Gian Lorenzo Bernini, who was a sculptor, painter, and stage designer, as well as an architect. His most famous work for St Peter's is the great Baroque gilt-bronze *baldacchino* (canopy) over the

high altar: the tomb of St Peter is alleged to be in the crypt below. The baldacchino's twisted columns, highly decorative carving, including heraldic devices and the papal tiara, blend into an outstandingly free and lively composition, rising at least 30.5 metres high. The baldacchino and high altar stand at the crossing where they are dwarfed by the great dome above, its interior richly decorated with frescoes and mosaics.

The dome is Michelangelo's masterpiece. The distance from floor level to the base of the dome is about 76 metres. Sixteen equally spaced stone ribs support the huge lantern on top of the dome, and the web between the ribs is of brickwork, commencing 2.74 metres thick and parting into two skins of brickwork as it ascends. Iron chains have been inserted in the base of the dome from time to time to prevent its spreading. The weight of the dome is transmitted through pendentives and arches on to four gigantic piers below. The piers are faced with Corinthian order pilasters. The exterior of the church is finished in Travertine stone. There is Baroque influence in the tall Corinthian order pilasters and entablature which adorn all sides of the building, with smaller pilasters and balustrading above.

Antonio da Sangallo the Younger,

who worked for Bramante, and followed him in the work on St Peter's, designed the finest High Renaissance palace in Rome, the Palazzo Farnese (*c.* 1530). It is monumental in scale, arranged symmetrically, with a vast colonnaded central courtyard entered through a long vaulted passage from the front, which faces a piazza. The building is in three storeys, stucco-faced with stone dressing at the corners. The rows of windows, each flanked by orders with pediments: triangular on the top floor, alternately triangular and segmented on the second floor, and straight on the ground floor, are the striking feature of the front facade. The heavy cornice and the top floor were added later.

Towards the end of the High Renaissance period in Italy, from somewhat before the mid-sixteenth century until the beginning of the seventeenth, architects either adhered too closely to the classical origins of the Early Renaissance or used it in a self-conscious way, which historians have termed *Mannerism*. Baroque in a sense was the reverse: the harmonious use of curved surfaces or plan forms, great orders with small orders, balustrades, all used freely and boldly to produce a unified design.

In northern Italy, Andrea Palladio became one of the most important architects, particularly through the individual style of his villas, which have been copied in other countries in a manner known as *Palladian*. Born in 1508, Palladio as a boy trained with a sculptor, became a mason and worked on the Villa Trissino. He visited Rome, measured old Roman buildings, studied the works of High Renaissance architects: Bramante, Raphael, Peruzzi, and Michelangelo, and returned to Vicenza, where his first major public work was the local town hall. His villa Chiericati, Vicenza, illustrates his individuality. He retained the High Renaissance Roman orders, Tuscan on the ground floor and Ionic on the first floor, but the open colonnades on either side of a solid-fronted centre on the first floor are his own invention. His most famous villa, certainly the most copied, was the Villa Capra, or La Rotonda, near Vicenza (1550–51). The villa, sited on a hill, has a symmetrical plan. Ionic-columned porticoes with flights of steps are centred on each of the four sides. The central hall of the villa is circular, reached through passageways from the porticoes, and there are rooms to the sides to make up the square plan. A shallow dome over the central hall first appears above the tiled roof covering the remainder

of the building. In 1570 Palladio published his literary work *I Quattro libri dell'architettura* summarizing his studies and the principles of Roman architecture. There were four books and some of the illustrations were of Palladio's own designs.

Gian Lorenzo Bernini (1598–1680) and Francesco Borromini (1599–1667) were great architects of the Late Renaissance, Baroque period, in Rome. In his youth, Borromini worked as a stonemason in the Rome office of his relative, Carlo Maderna, who died in 1629. Borromini also worked with Bernini on the baldacchino of St Peter's. Bernini's much admired church, typical of Italian Baroque, is S. Andrea del Quirinale in Rome. The plan is an oval, measuring over 24 metres across on the long axis facing the entrance. Eight chapels, four ovoid and four rounded, radiate from the central space. Curved walls form a

concave enclosure to the entrance facade, contrasting with the semicircular canopy over the porch, and its semicircular steps. Great Corinthian ordered pilasters, architrave, and pediment dominate the front. The smaller circular arch above the porch canopy, and the smaller columns and pilasters of the porch bring the scale down to the entrance door with a still smaller triangular pediment above it. The orderly way in which the elements are reduced in size, and the exuberant use of curves make this small church a masterpiece of the period.

One of Palladio's disciples was England's Inigo Jones, born three years after the publication of Palladio's four books on architecture. Jones visited Italy in his early life, became proficient as a painter and designer, and returned there in about 1613–14, with the Earl of Arundel, to study Roman remains and

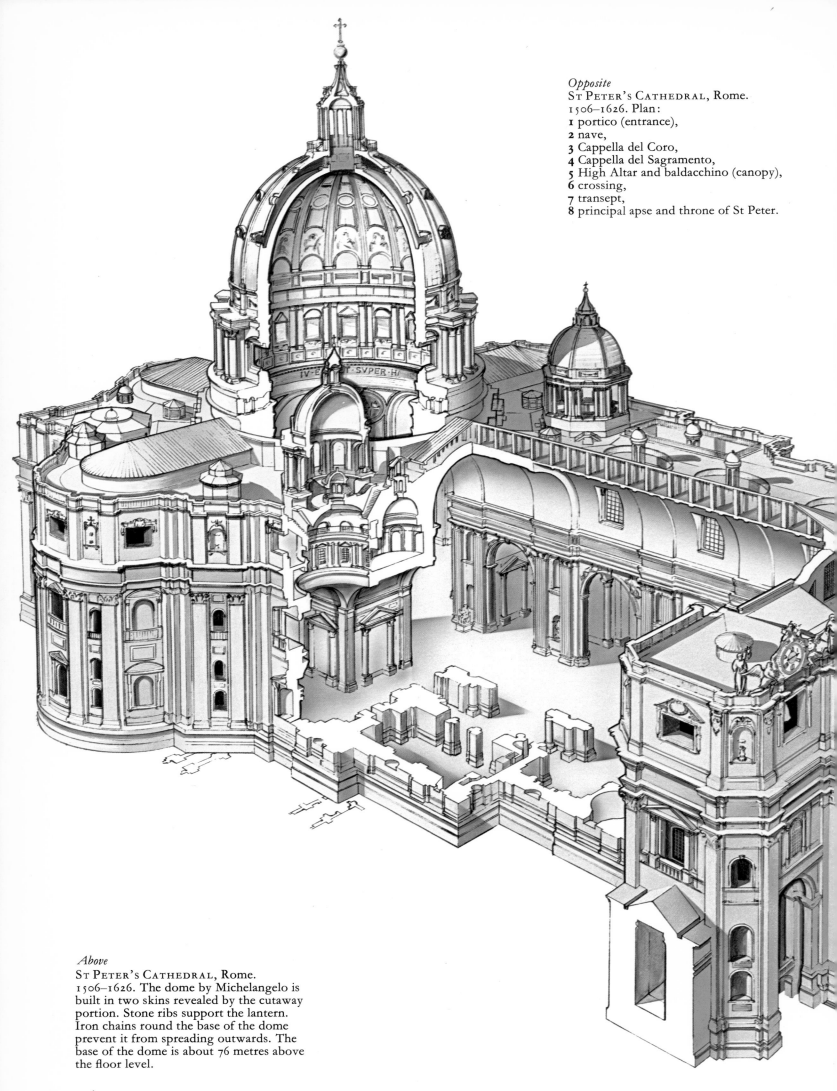

Opposite
ST PETER'S CATHEDRAL, Rome.
1506–1626. Plan:
1 portico (entrance),
2 nave,
3 Cappella del Coro,
4 Cappella del Sagramento,
5 High Altar and baldacchino (canopy),
6 crossing,
7 transept,
8 principal apse and throne of St Peter.

Above
ST PETER'S CATHEDRAL, Rome.
1506–1626. The dome by Michelangelo is
built in two skins revealed by the cutaway
portion. Stone ribs support the lantern.
Iron chains round the base of the dome
prevent it from spreading outwards. The
base of the dome is about 76 metres above
the floor level.

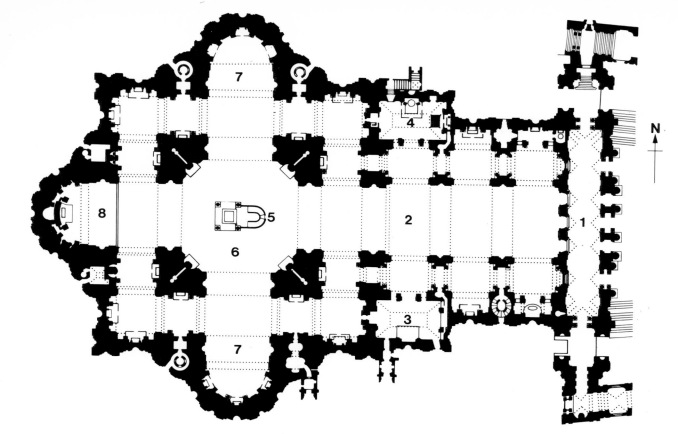

the work of the great masters of the Renaissance. On his return to England, Jones was appointed surveyor to James I, a post he continued to hold under Charles I, James's son. Jones's first great work as Surveyor of the King's Works was the Queen's House, Greenwich (1616–1635), now the National Maritime Museum. The similarity to Palladio's Palazzo Chiericati is immediately evident, apart from the colonnade in the centre of the first floor flanked by solid walls at the sides.

Inigo Jones's equally well-known work was the Banqueting House, Whitehall, London (1619–22) – a classically elegant building with carefully ordered superimposed columns and pilasters flanking the evenly arranged windows in two tiers. The alternate triangular and segmented pediments to the first tier of windows and straight pediments to the second tier are reminders of the Palazzo Farnese, Rome. Inside, these two tiers of windows illuminate one grand floor. The Banqueting House was incorporated later on in a plan for a vast royal palace by John Webb, a pupil of Inigo Jones. The palace, if it had been built, would have extended to the River Thames to the south-east and St James's Park on the other side, absorbing today's Whitehall and neighbouring streets. Inigo Jones worked on a new St Paul's Cathedral from 1634 to 1642, when he lost his job because of the Civil War against Charles I. He was captured and disgraced, which meant losing his estates, then pardoned by Parliament. His patron Charles I was executed in 1649, and the great portico to St Paul's west

front disappeared in the rebuilding by Christopher Wren after the Great Fire of London of 1666.

Sir Christopher Wren (1632–1723) came in contact with the court early in life as his father was Dean of Windsor to Charles I until the Civil War. He was first and foremost a geometrician and astronomer before becoming an architect. Indeed, he was Professor of Astronomy at Oxford when he worked on the Sheldonian Theatre there, and, through his contact with Bishop Sheldon, was working on St Paul's before the Great Fire occurred which gave him his chance. Wren had already gained experience of the great Renaissance works during a visit to Paris in 1665 which had afforded him contacts with the court of Louis XIV, the work going on at the Louvre, and at the Palace of Versailles.

After the Great Fire which destroyed the greater part of the City of London, including more than eighty churches, there were great difficulties in rebuilding because of the question of compensation, laying down new roads, and the vexed problems of ownership and property improvement. A number of persons produced plans for the rebuilding of St Paul's, Wren amongst them, but little progress was made. Charles II had been restored to the throne six years before the Great Fire, and his surveyor died in 1669. Here fate played a part. Wren, who had already demonstrated organizing ability in the debates going on after the Great Fire, was appointed the King's Surveyor in 1673. This accounted for the fact that Wren played

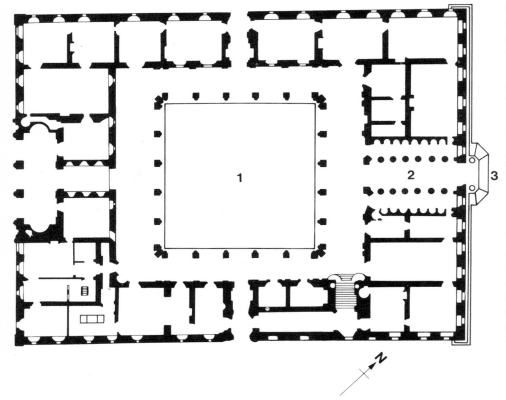

such a large part in the 150 or more new churches which were built in London after the Great Fire, but his most famous work was St Paul's which he used to watch being built from a little house across the River Thames in Southwark, which still exists today.

The construction of the cathedral is a story in itself, full of controversy, cunning, and criticism of the architect. It took thirty-five years to build and, unlike St Peter's, Rome, there was only one architect. After a number of early designs, the 'Grand Model' was produced, preserved in the cathedral today. This was of a centrally planned church of splendid size in the shape of a Greek cross. Over the central area was a huge dome ringed by eight smaller domes over the aisles surrounding the central area. A large domed vestibule was entered from a broad portico on the west front. The clergy who wanted a traditional form of church with a nave, side aisles, transepts, and a choir, more suited to their liturgy, objected to the Grand Model. A new plan known as the 'Warrant Design' was drawn up and approved by the King and construction went forward. The outward appearance showed little resemblance to the Gothic form of the plan. It seemed a compromise.

Top
PALAZZO FARNESE, Rome. Begun *c.* 1530. Architects: Antonio da Sangallo the Younger. Michelangelo completed the top floor and added the cornice *c.* 1546.

Above
PALAZZO FARNESE, Rome. *c.* 1530. Plan:
1 courtyard,
2 vestibule,
3 entrance from piazza.

QUEEN'S HOUSE, Greenwich. 1616–35.
Architect: Inigo Jones.

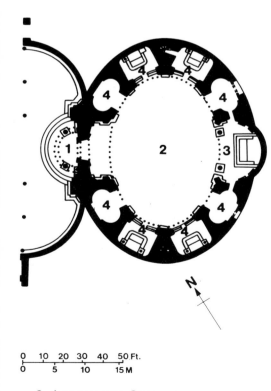

0 10 20 30 40 50 Ft.
0   5   10   15 M

S. ANDREA DEL QUIRINALE
CATHEDRAL, Rome. 1658–70. Plan:
1 entrance porch,
2 central oval,
3 High Altar,
4 chapel.

The essential Gothic structure is hidden behind the Baroque exterior. The central dome is full of ingenuity. A high colonnaded drum supports the three structures: a shallow inner dome of brick with an eye at the apex; a cone-shaped dome of brick reinforced with iron chains that support the enormous lantern weighing more than 812 tonnes; and an outer dome of framed timber, covered in lead, that rests on the cone-shaped dome. The weight of this great structure descends through pendentives and circular arches on to the piers below. The interior of the church is over 122 metres long by over 30.5 metres wide, including the aisles which are only half the height of the nave. From outside they appear higher because the exterior wall is disguised by a screen hiding short flying buttresses which stay the outward thrust of the nave's walls. Although hidden, the structural system is nonetheless Gothic. Beneath the church the great crypt contains the tombs of many famous English heroes including those of Lord Nelson and the Duke of Wellington. A modern addition in the crypt is a chapel designed by Lord Mottistone, Surveyor of the Fabric of St Paul's (1957–63) for the Order of the British Empire, instituted by King George V in 1917.

Unevenness in architectural development in Europe was as true for the Renaissance as it was true for other architectural styles. A few years after Palladio's Palazzo Chiericati and Villa Capra in Italy, half a century of great mansion building began in England. The evident prosperity of Elizabeth I's reign (1558–1603) had prompted nobles and rich merchants to establish themselves in this way. One of the earliest, Longleat House, Wiltshire, begun in 1547 but burnt down, and rebuilt between 1567 and 1580, is rectilinear and symmetrical, with main rooms facing outwards placed around a central court. The stone-mullioned plain windows, regularly spaced, are typical of the Elizabethan manor house which is mainly Gothic in appearance with some Renaissance detail, such as the balustrading to the roof parapet. Other country houses followed, for example, Wollaton Hall (1580–88), Hardwick Hall, Derbyshire (1590–97), and the present Hatfield House, Hertfordshire (1607–12), an English Jacobean mansion. During both the Elizabethan and Jacobean periods of architecture many colleges were founded at the Universities of Oxford and Cambridge.

In France, the great period of châteaux building in the Île de France, the region

Right
PALAZZO CHIERICATI, Vicenza. 1550–80.
Architect: Andrea Palladio.

Below
VILLA CAPRA OR LA ROTONDA,
Vicenza. Begun *c.* 1550. Architect: Andrea
Palladio. The design has been much
copied and gave rise to the so-called
Palladian style. The structure is
extremely logical. The tile-covered roof
helps to brace the walls supporting the
dome. The porticoes help to buttress the
outside walls of the villa.

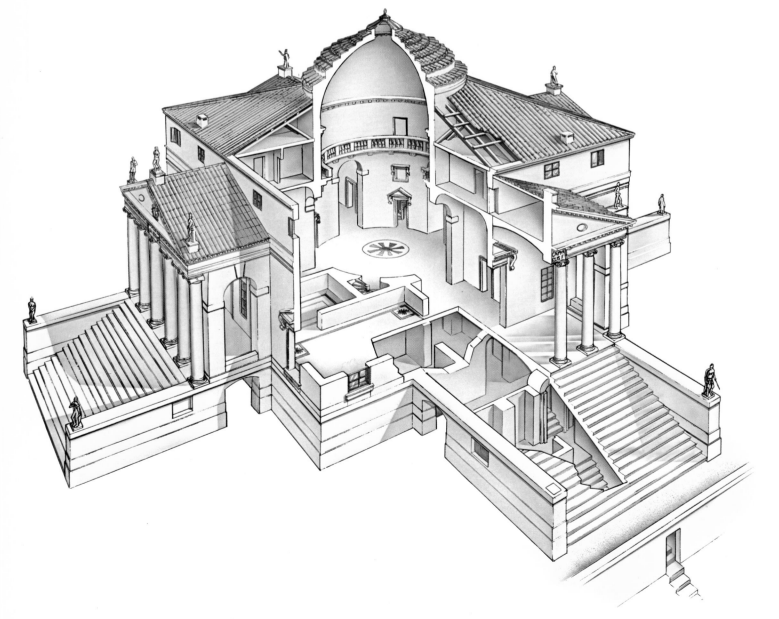

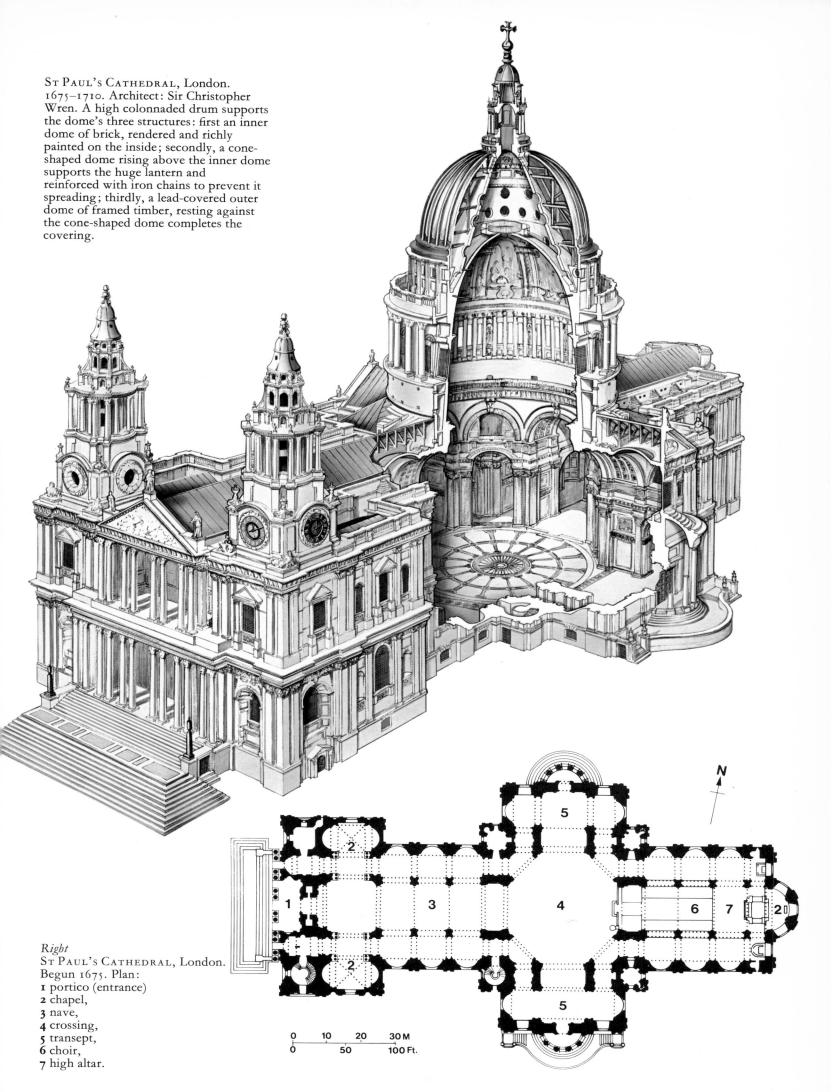

St Paul's Cathedral, London.
1675–1710. Architect: Sir Christopher
Wren. A high colonnaded drum supports
the dome's three structures: first an inner
dome of brick, rendered and richly
painted on the inside; secondly, a cone-
shaped dome rising above the inner dome
supports the huge lantern and
reinforced with iron chains to prevent it
spreading; thirdly, a lead-covered outer
dome of framed timber, resting against
the cone-shaped dome completes the
covering.

Right
St Paul's Cathedral, London.
Begun 1675. Plan:
1 portico (entrance)
2 chapel,
3 nave,
4 crossing,
5 transept,
6 choir,
7 high altar.

131

Below
CHATEAU DE CHAMBORD, Loire Valley.
1519–47. Architect: Domenica da
Cortona. Plan:
1 inner donjon (similar to mediaeval
  castle keep),
2 double staircase,
3 moat,
4 disused moat,
5 outer accommodation in the mediaeval
  manner.

Bottom
CHATEAU DE CHAMBORD, Loire Valley.
1519–47. Architect: Domenica da Cortona.

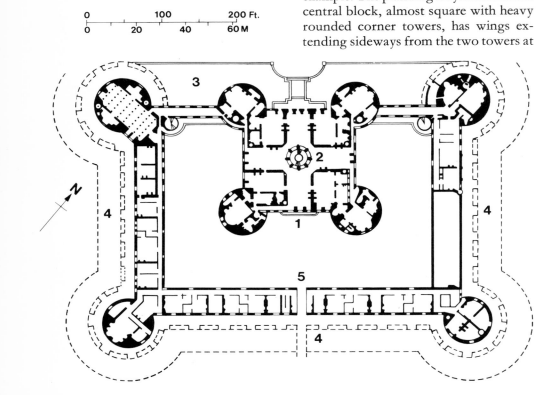

centred on Paris, and in the Loire Valley lasted until the end of Louis XIII's reign, about half way through the classical period of the Renaissance in that country. As already discussed, France came into contact with the Renaissance at the time of Charles VIII's dealing with Florence over his claim to Naples, but it was some years before its influence had much effect. Up to the reign of Louis XIV, when the King centred his administration and court at Versailles and expected those in favour to attend there, the great nobles had lived mainly on their estates outside Paris and on the Loire.

Chambord (1519–47) is one of the best-known châteaux of the Loire Valley. The layout is not dissimilar to that of a Mediaeval castle, Harlech for example. The planning is symmetrical. A central block, almost square with heavy rounded corner towers, has wings extending sideways from the two towers at the rear. In front is a vast courtyard enclosed on three sides by low buildings; the entrance to the courtyard is in the centre of the far side facing the main inner block or *donjon*. The donjon is divided into four vaulted halls with a curious double spiral staircase in the centre, which different people can ascend or descend at the same time without seeing one another. The style is mainly Gothic, particularly the corner towers with conical roofs and stone-mullioned windows, and the high-pitched ornamental roofs. Other well-known examples in the Loire Valley are the Château de Bury (c. 1520). the Château de Chenonceaux (1515–23) and the Château d'Azay le Redeau. All these were built forty to fifty years before the spate of mansion building in England previously described. France has the greatest number of châteaux of any country. Over 1400 are believed to be occupied today by private owners and many more are abandoned ruins.

Louis XIV was so jealous of his minister Fouquet's splendid mansion at Vaux-le-Vicomte, designed by the architect Louis Le Vau, that he commissioned Le Vau to reconstruct the château at Versailles as an enormous and splendid palace. Le Vau's work began in 1661 around Louis XIII's old hunting château (1624–26) designed by the architect de Brosse, but another architect, Jules Hardouin Mansart, extended the palace from 1678 to 1710. While building was going on, the grounds were laid out with fabulous landscaping including canals, lakes, formal gardens, statues, and fountains. The fountains were so numerous that there was insufficient water to have them all on at once – something of a problem requiring skilful management when the Sun King (Louis XIV) and his Court walked around the grounds. The famous garden front of the palace has rusticated stonework to the ground floor, orders flanking the tall windows on the first floor, and attic windows only a little higher than they are wide. The roof parapet has a balustrade.

The garden front at Versailles has been compared with Late Renaissance work in England, particularly Queen's Square, Bath (1728) by John Wood the Elder, and the Royal Crescent, Bath (c. 1770) by John Wood the Younger. But the greatest influence, from Late Renaissance through the Revivalist period of the nineteenth century, came from Palladio's work. The classic Palladian examples were Chiswick House, Middlesex, a villa begun c. 1721–

22 by Lord Burlington, and incidentally extremely well restored by the old Ministry of Public Buildings and Works in the 1950s, and Holkham Hall, Norfolk (c. 1734) by William Kent.

Twenty years earlier than Chiswick House, Castle Howard, Yorkshire (1699–1712) had been started by Sir John Vanbrugh, who was a soldier and playwright before becoming an architect. The symmetrical plan was fairly typical of the larger mansions of the Late Renaissance period, known in England as Georgian houses. The main central block had principal rooms facing out over the garden. On the other side of the main block was the entrance court facing a terraced entrance with the kitchen wing to the left and the stable wing to the right. The accommodation in each wing was arranged around a central court. Both wings were set back from the main block on the garden side.

Blenheim Palace, Oxfordshire (1704–20), by the same architect, a grateful nation's gift to John Churchill, first Duke of Marlborough, after his victory over the French at Blenheim, was similar in layout, but not in detail. The characteristics of the style are present in both mansions: rusticated stonework to the ground floor, ordered pilasters flanking tall windows, and balustrading to the parapet. The side wings were dispensed with in smaller Georgian-style mansions, the principal rooms being contained in a single block, usually with a carefully ordered arrangement of windows, and the central entrance em-

phasized with classical ornamentation. Later Georgian details were available in pattern books of the period.

Chatsworth House, Derbyshire (1681–96), designed for the Duke of Devonshire by William Talman, is a typical single block mansion. The symmetrical garden front has a grand external staircase leading to the first floor, the *piano nobile* of Italian origin. The great hall still existed in the mansions of the day, usually ascending through the ground and first floor. It became more and more associated with the entrance and grand staircase, and other rooms took over the functions of reception areas and private

living quarters.

A particularly English feature of great houses, dating from the early seventeenth century, was the long gallery. A grand example with windows along one side exists in Hatfield House, built at the beginning of James I's reign. Blenheim Palace has one on the west side of the main block, overlooking the Italian garden.

The development of Renaissance architecture outside Italy, France, and England was influenced by the politics of the time and the effect it had on the movement of people and the flow of ideas. Maximilian I (1493–1519), Em-

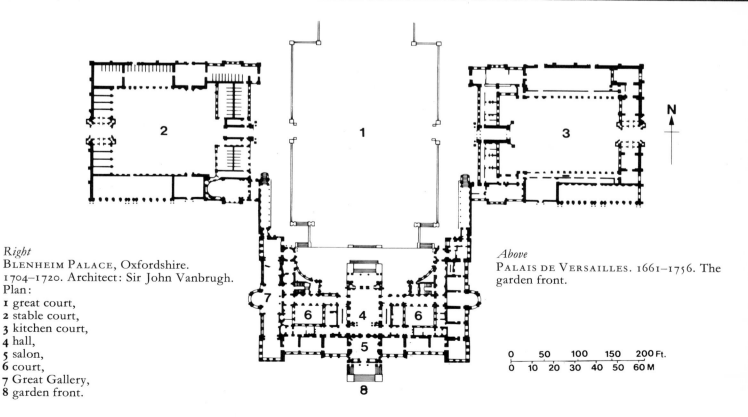

Right
BLENHEIM PALACE, Oxfordshire.
1704–1720. Architect: Sir John Vanbrugh.
Plan:
1 great court,
2 stable court,
3 kitchen court,
4 hall,
5 salon,
6 court,
7 Great Gallery,
8 garden front.

Above
PALAIS DE VERSAILLES. 1661–1756. The garden front.

0   50   100   150   200 Ft.
0   10 20 30 40 50 60 M

peror of what remained of the Holy Roman Empire, had enlarged the territory of his dynasty (the Habsburg family) by hereditary marriages linking Spain, the Netherlands, and Austria, forming the basis of the empire of Charles V (1519–55). Spain had grown wealthy from the successful voyage of Vasco da Gama to India (he returned to Madrid in 1499), and from the gold from Mexico and Peru following their conquest by Hernán Cortés in the early part of the sixteenth century, shortly after Christopher Columbus's discovery of America in 1492. Charles V spent most of his life trying to keep his huge empire together. He failed, and in despair abdicated the Spanish throne to his son Philip II in 1555, and gave up the remainder of the Holy Roman Empire to Ferdinand I in 1556. Charles V died in 1558 in Spain. Thus, the Habsburg line was split in two: one relative living in Spain, another in Central Europe

controlling Germany, Austria, Bohemia, and Hungary. The introduction of the Inquisition into the Netherlands by Charles V had already caused outbreaks of discontent, which, in Philip II's reign, brought open revolt under William the Silent, Prince of Orange from 1533. In the bitter struggle that followed, the northern provinces under William gained independence and became the Dutch Republic, Spain retaining what now roughly corresponds to Belgium. The Prince of Orange was murdered, after many attempts on his life, in 1584.

The palace of Charles V, Granada (1527–68), never in fact completed, was designed by the architect Pedro Machuca. His son, Luis, continued the work after Pedro Machuca's death in 1550. The great central court is High Renaissance in style and possesses a fine classical feeling, very different from the great palace-monastery built for Philip II – the Escorial (1559–84), out-

ESCORIAL PALACE, near Madrid. 1559–84. The great palace-monastery, originally built for Phillip II as a monument to the power of sixteenth century Spain, has an austere dignity. The great entrance block can be seen in the centre of the facade on the left. immediately inside the palace is the Patio of the Kings. Beyond the Patio are two square towers flanking the vestibule of the Basilica of San Lorenzo el Real. The dome of the Basilica dominates the huge palace.

side Madrid. The Escorial's first architect was Juan Bautista de Toledo, who died in 1567 when the work was given to Juan de Herrera. The whole complex, erected as a monument to the sixteenth century power of Spain, has an austere dignity, befitting the character of Philip II. The layout is symmetrical with the tall buildings arranged around courts of different sizes, the majority of them square. The grand entrance block has eight superimposed giant Doric order columns and an entablature across the front, with windows on three levels between the columns. The central part of the entrance block rises still higher, with four superimposed Ionic order columns, with an entablature and a pediment. Immediately inside the entrance, the Patio of the Kings, leads to the vestibule of the Basilica of San Lorenzo el Real, flanked by square towers. The church plan is an inscribed Greek cross with a central dome supported by four piers and pendentives. South of the church is the large Court of Evangelists surrounded by cloisters, and to its north is the Royal Palace. Extending outside the rectangular complex and immediately east of the church are the apartments of Philip II, around a small central court. The college and monastery buildings are each set around four square courts to north and south of the Patio of the Kings. The disciplined order of the window openings and consistency of detail, helped by the yellowish-grey granite of which the Escorial is built, gives the enormous palace a unique quality.

In the Netherlands, towards the middle of the sixteenth century, the Renaissance movement became better established through the publication of books of engravings. The Town Hall, Antwerp, by Cornelius Floris is typical of Early Renaissance style in that country. Much later, the Mauritshuis at

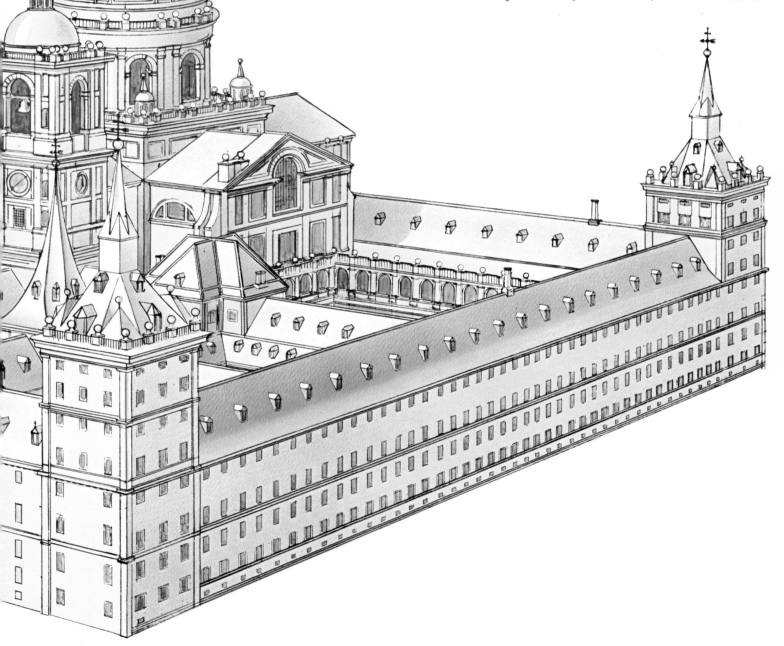

VIERZEHNHEILIGEN CHURCH,
Franconia. 1744–72. Architect:
Balthasar Neumann. The nave illustrates
his fine Rococo interior.

the Hague (1633–35), by Jacob van Campen illustrates a restrained form of Baroque with none of the exuberance shown in central Europe. The Maurit-shuis has tall pilasters through two storeys and a classical pediment.

Central Europe in the seventeenth century was a conglomerate of small states and imperial cities. The preachings of Martin Luther (1483–1546) had fanned the flames of religious rivalry between Roman Catholics and Protestants, at a time when each believed the other's doctrine to be heresy, punishable by death or expulsion. Torture of all kinds was acceptable to bring about conversion. The powerful kings had their vested interests: the Habsburgs and the Roman Catholic church in Spain; expansionist policies in France. The Hanseatic League of trading towns had declined as the power of the princes grew. These growing pressures culminated in the Thirty Years War, which ended in the Peace of Westphalia in 1648. Much rebuilding of damaged property took place after the war, and this coincided with the acceptance of the Late Renaissance Baroque style from Italy. In north Germany, this was to develop into the highly decorative form known as *Rococo*, a visual style little related to structure. Italian archi-

tects were employed first. One of the earliest examples was the front of the Czernin Palace, Prague, begun *c.* 1667 by Francesco Caratti. Passau Cathedral interior by another Italian, Carlo Lurago, was begun about the same time. But the greatest Renaissance works of Germany and Austria were by German architects who had trained in Italy or had connections there. Johann Bernhard Fischer von Erlach (1656–1723) was a sculptor and mason who had worked under Carlo Fontana in Rome. Johann Lukas von Hildebrandt (1668–1745) was born in Genoa of an Italian mother, studied in Italy, and worked as an engineer there. The most brilliant was probably Balthasar Neumann (1687–1753).

An example of von Erlach's work is Holy Trinity Church, Salzburg (1694–1702). The elegant and restrained Baroque facade is curved, with towers flanking the entrance. The interior shape is oval, with a commanding dome over the centre. Von Erlach's most famous work is the Karlskirche, Vienna (1716–37), completed after his death. The front facade shows a remarkable assortment of influences, with a classical portico in the centre; columns like Trajan's Column, Rome, on either side, built with a balcony each at the top, similar to Islamic minarets; a typical dome and

Left
ABBEY CHURCH, Zwiefaltern, Germany.
Begun 1738. Nave. Architect: Johann
Michael Fischer.

Below
TOLEDO CATHEDRAL. Completed 1732.
Transparente by Narciso Tomé. Section.

drum of the period; and side towers
topped by curved roofs showing eastern
influence. The total effect is a splendid
essay in exuberant Baroque architecture.

Exuberance of a different kind is
illustrated in Balthasar Neumann's pilgrimage church, Vierzehnheiligen, in
Franconia (1744–72) which has one of
the finest Rococo interiors. The elaborate decoration, principally white and
gold, impresses by its sheer vivacious-
ness and the constant movement of its
curved forms. The late Baroque in Spain
climbed to a similar pitch of enthusiasm
as Neumann's church, in the famous
Transparente in Toledo Cathedral by
Narciso Tomé, completed in 1732. The
Transparente was a glass-covered recep-
tacle above the high altar in which the
sacrament was kept. Between ornamental columns on either side and above
is a whole galaxy of carved figures and
curving classical forms, illuminated from
a small window formed high up in part
of the vault opposite the high altar, but
disguised from below by more figures
and other elaborate carvings.

The effect of the Renaissance was felt
beyond Europe to America and the
colonies of the British Empire, as discussed in a later chapter. To the north
and north-east of Europe there are
examples from the mid-seventeenth to

the early eighteenth centuries. The Riddarhus (House of Lords) Stockholm (*c.* 1653), is a typical Palladian-style building with tall pilasters flanking the windows along the front. The roof is notable for the 'break' about two-thirds of the way up – a *säteri* or manor house roof, typical of country houses in Sweden at this time. The Riddahus was begun by Joost Vingboons, a Dutch architect, and completed by Jean de la Vallée whose father, Simon de la Vallée, a French engineer, had been appointed royal architect, and designed the Oxenstierna Palace, Stockholm (*c.* 1650).

In Russia, St Petersburg (Leningrad) was founded by Peter the Great in 1703. At the time there was no shortage of European-trained architects. Peter the Great's architect was Domenico Tressini of Swiss-Italian origin, who favoured Baroque in the Dutch style. But he chose a French engineer, Alexandre le Blond, to begin his great palace, Peterhof (now Petrodvorets) (1747–57), on the coast, which was extended by an Italian architect, Bartolome Rastrelli. The palace has some of the features of Versailles which Peter the Great wished to emulate. The most memorable *tour de force* is the terraces cascading down in descending tiers of golden statues and fountains to the canal leading to the sea. The surrounding park is laid out with follies and splendid areas of semi-wild planting. Rastrelli also designed the Winter Palace, Leningrad (1754–62), one of the most important buildings in the city. It now houses the State Hermitage Museum, which has one of the finest collections of French Impressionist paintings to be seen. Like Petrodvorets, it was among a great many buildings damaged in the vast destruction of Leningrad in World War II. The truly remarkable restoration work carried out since is one of the great rebuilding feats of the twentieth century.

Nineteenth Century Revivals and Innovations

The exact course of the move to the classical forms of Greece and Rome in the latter half of the seventeenth century is less important perhaps than the fact that further development of Late Renaissance was not possible. It may therefore have seemed logical to return to the classical source. The new movement tended to use the classical forms in an unadulterated way in what was called *Neoclassical* or *Classical Revival* or *Romantic Classicism*. The Neoclassical movement was almost universal across Europe at about the same time. It spread to America, Australia and New Zealand, and India, indeed, wherever there were strong ties with Europe or Europeans. Neoclassicism was not the only revival in the nineteenth century. A revival in Gothic architecture, if it had ever actively ceased, became strong in the last half of the nineteenth century and continued well into the twentieth century. Other forms – Byzantine, Chinese, Egyptian, Etruscan – were used, and, at the end of the century, *Art Nouveau* flourished for a short period, in the search for a new kind of architecture. Another important movement in the

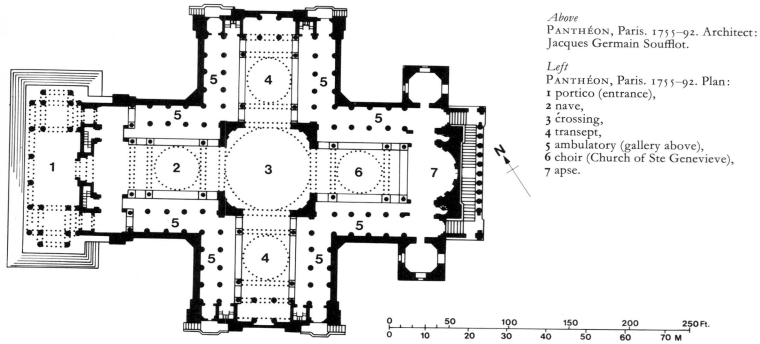

Above
PANTHÉON, Paris. 1755–92. Architect: Jacques Germain Soufflot.

Left
PANTHÉON, Paris. 1755–92. Plan:
1 portico (entrance),
2 nave,
3 crossing,
4 transept,
5 ambulatory (gallery above),
6 choir (Church of Ste Genevieve),
7 apse.

nineteenth century, discussed in the next chapter, was *Functionalism*, brought into prominence by the needs of the industrial revolution and the development of the use of iron. The growth of towns brought about the need for greater care in the planning of towns and cities, and it gave birth to town planning as an art.

One of the great neoclassical buildings in Paris is the Panthéon (1755–92) by Jacques Germain Soufflot (1713–80), one of the most notable architects of his time. He visited Rome to study classical architecture in 1754, or thereabouts, and, on his return, commenced work on the Panthéon which at that time was called the Church of Ste Geneviève, only later becoming the mausoleum of France's heroes. The plan of the church is shaped like a Greek cross; in fact there are two crosses: a thin lower cross sunk inside another, with broad steps leading up from the lower cross on all sides to a columned ambulatory with a gallery above it. Each arm of the plan has a small circular dome over its centre. The great dome over the crossing is based on that of St Paul's, except there is a tall colonnaded drum with tall windows carried round it. These give good light and expose the dignity of the interior, achieved by the skilful placing of decoration and sculpture by well-known French artists. The exterior brickwork is remarkably plain. Apart from an entablature and festoons it is unrelieved. This helps to concentrate the eye on the great dome from a dis-

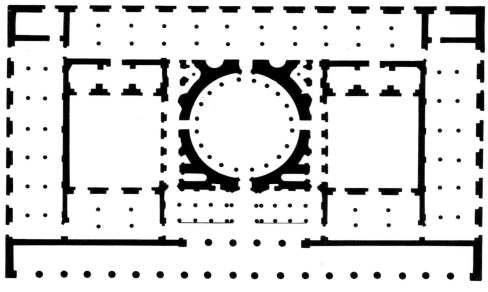

tance, and, nearer to, on the huge Corinthian-columned portico across the front, in which the columns are unusually arranged.

It was after the French Revolution in 1789 that the Church of Ste Geneviève was given its new name, the Panthéon. France's political changes shook the other establishments in Europe, and the rise of Napoleon Bonaparte, in succession to the revolutionary power, the Directorate, led to conflict enflamed by Napoleon's personal territorial ambitions. By 1793 England was at war with France, and not very successfully, until Napoleon's ambitions in Egypt and the Far East were thwarted by the battle of the Nile (1798). The end of the war came with Nelson's sea Victory

Top
ALTES MUSEUM, Berlin. 1824–28.
Architect: R. F. von Schinkel.

Above
ALTES MUSEUM, Berlin. 1824–28. Ground floor plan.

141

at Trafalgar (1805), and Wellington's victory over Napoleon's armies at Waterloo (1815). Nearly twenty-three years of war did not much affect building in France and England, but left its mark in the commemorative architecture. In Paris, the Arc de Triomphe, by V. E. T. Chalgrin, built between 1806 and 1808, and today the meeting place of the Champs Elysées and the avenue de la Grande-Armée, is a splendid monument to the credit of Neoclassicism. There were open fields beyond the Champs Elysées when it was built, untrue of Nelson's Column and Trafalgar Square, London, by Walter and Pickon (1852).

Neoclassicism or Romantic Classicism found favour in Germany at the turn of the century. Such well-known landmarks as the Schauspielhaus, Berlin (1819–21), by Karl Friederich von Schinkel (1781–1841), and the Altes Museum, Berlin (1824–28), by the same architect, are dignified and use classic elements with great skill. The Altes

Museum is one of the most impressive buildings of the style. The long front has a colonnade of Greek Ionic order columns with its entablature carried round the building. The colonnade is closed at the ends. Inside, a central circular hall the full height of the building has a coffered dome with a large eye (opening at the top of the dome). The circular hall is inscribed between four long two-storeyed galleries, connected at first-floor level by an ambulatory around the hall. The Greek revival was also evident in Scandinavia during the first half of the nineteenth century, for example, the Palace of Justice (1805–15), and Bindesboll's Thorwaldsen Museum (1839–48), both in Copenhagen, Denmark. A museum building also illustrates the best of Greek revival in London: Sir Robert Smirke's British Museum, begun in 1823, a year before the Altes Museum in Berlin, and not completed until 1847. Smirke was a pupil of Sir John Soane (1753–1837),

Below
CUMBERLAND TERRACE, Regent's Park, London. *c.* 1820–30. Architect: John Nash.

Opposite
ROYAL PAVILION, Brighton, Sussex. 1815–21. Architect: John Nash.

142

the designer of the Chelsea Hospital, London, and one of the greatest architects of the period, with a style of his own.

It was another John, John Nash (1752–1835), who left the greatest mark on London. Nash was the son of a millwright and became the protégé of the Prince Regent (later George IV). This gave him confidence and he drew up his bold plan for London embracing Regents Park, Portland Place, and Regent Street down to Carlton House Terrace. Nash's neoclassical palatial compositions, embracing individual

houses with porticoes and terraced houses with columned entrance porches, are among the most significant buildings overlooking Regent's Park (c. 1820–30). Behind the facades restored in the last two decades there is now modern accommodation. Nash introduced the painted stucco fronts in imitation of stone. They became fashionable immediately and were widely used during the next fifty years.

In the surge of building which took place in the peace following the war with France, the Royal Pavilion, Brighton, Sussex (1815–21), was rebuilt by John

Nash for the Prince Regent. The rambling plan with interior columns of cast iron, a development discussed in the next chapter, is surmounted by a forest of domes and minarets in a mixture of Indian and Islamic forms. The well-restored interior is a bizarre mixture rich in the Chinese-style decoration (*Chinoiserie*) of the period. What a contrast the Royal Pavilion is with the Nash terraces of Regent's Park, or Nash's rustic thatched cottages in Blaise Hamlet, Gloucestershire (1811).

George III had come to the throne at the end of the Renaissance period in

1760, and before his death in 1820 a new phase had developed in architecture, helped by the Prince Regent's interest in building which continued during his reign as George IV. George IV adopted Buckingham Palace as his home in London after extensive alterations to what had previously been Buckingham House, and entirely remodelled the royal apartments at Windsor Castle, which are largely the same today. After William IV (1830–37), Queen Victoria acceded to the throne of England to reign until the beginning of the next century (1901).

The mood in architecture had already begun to change again. The old Palace of Westminster had been burnt down in 1834 and an architectural competition had been held to replace the old palace with new buildings for the English Houses of Parliament, the style of which had to be either Gothic or Tudor. Sir John Barry's design won and the resulting building (1836–68) was the first important Gothic Revival building in London. The difference from the true Gothic is clear. Authentic Gothic detail has been retained, but the facades are regularized and flattened. The skyline and irregular grouping of towers and spires in a picturesque way is typical of the romantic attitudes of the time. This attitude was reflected in the follies and eccentric buildings erected during the period. Barry obtained the help of A. W. N. Pugin, an expert in Tudor detailing, for the Palace of Westminster. Barry was more of a classical-revivalist and one of his best works is the neo High Renaissance facade of the

Traveller's Club (1829–31), in Pall Mall, London.

It would be a mistake to think there was any sequence in the revivalist styles. They appeared, disappeared, and reappeared throughout the nineteenth century and in the early part of the twentieth century. But there were major influences which converted both architect and laymen to their way of thinking. Pugin, a zealous Catholic, published three books extolling the virtues of Gothic architecture and proclaiming it the only style for Christians. The ten volumes of the *Dictionnaire raisonné de l'architecture française du XIe au XVIe siècles* (1854–68), by the French architect Viollet-le-Duc (1814–79), may have had more influence. It must also be remembered that the nineteenth century saw the beginning of relatively new building types for which there was no precedent.

The needs and improving education of a much larger population than before made individual buildings necessary for: libraries, museums, railway stations, offices, colleges, and so on. Railways and steamships had arrived making travel relatively easy compared to the past. Between 1830 and 1890 more Europeans moved to other countries than in any previous generation. Better conditions for child birth and improved medical knowledge had reduced early deaths, and there were enormous increases in world population. In Britain, France, and Germany these increases in population were accompanied by industrial development which brought people off the land into cities and towns. The cities and towns therefore needed

rapid expansion. At the same time more land was brought under the plough. This unprecedented expansion in many directions brought an undercurrent of restlessness in architecture. Most men in such circumstances were unable to come up with fresh ideas for the occasion, and were persuaded to look for inspiration in the familiar styles of the past, in which they believed.

After Napoleon Bonaparte's exile to Elba in 1814, the French monarchy was restored for a time under Louis XVIII (1815–24), Charles X (1824–30), and Louis Philippe (1830–48). A second revolution in 1848 produced the Second Republic, and a nephew of Napoleon Bonaparte, Louis Napoleon Bonaparte, was elected President and took the title of Napoleon III. Napoleon III's disastrous policy in Mexico was followed in 1870 by an even more disastrous war declared against Prussia. The French were promptly defeated. By the Treaty of Frankfurt the French lost the provinces of Alsace and Lorraine, had to suffer an army of occupation, and pay heavy reparations to Germany. The elated German princes elected William I Emperor of Germany, thus fulfilling William's Chancellor, Prince Otto von Bismarck's dream of uniting the southern states of Germany: Bavaria, Württemberg, and Baden, with the North. Thus, Germany became the strongest military power on the continent of Europe.

After the defeat of France, a vow was taken to erect a church in Paris as a votive offering, in the belief that the situation would improve. The site chosen was the hill of Montmartre (Mons Martyrum), which was closely associated with the heroes of the past – Louis XIV and Joan of Arc had worshipped there. St Dionysius, the first apostle of the capital, was supposed to have spent a night with his disciples in the gypsum caves of the hill. Funds were raised from the people, rich and poor alike. An architectural competition was won by Paul Abadie with a design in Byzantine style which he had already used in restoring St Front at Périgueux. The building of the church, the Basilique du Sacré-Coeur, began in 1875, but it was found that the ground was unstable and foundation piles had to be driven 30 metres down, which used up the money collected. There was delay while more money was subscribed. Then World War I (1914–18) delayed matters again, and the church was not consecrated until 1919. The plan is typically Byzantine with the nave shaped like a Greek cross and the dome over the crossing

carried by piers and four pendentives. The exterior is of white fine-grained stone. The church, at the top of the great flight of white steps, overlooks Paris and is one of the city's great landmarks, its most outstanding feature being the elongated cupolas. The architect made the cupolas longer than the usual Byzantine rounded dome, so that they would not look too flat from the bottom of the hill.

London as well as Paris possesses a revivalist building in the Byzantine style: Westminster Cathedral (1895–1903), by J. F. Bentley. The cathedral is conspicuous on the outside for its

Opposite
HOUSES OF PARLIAMENT, London. 1836–68. Architect: Sir John Barry.

Left
SACRE-COEUR BASILICA, Paris. Begun 1875. Architect: Paul Abadie.

Below
SAGRADA FAMILIA CHURCH. Plan:
1 Portal of the Glory,
2 nave with double aisles,
3 transept,
4 altar,
5 apse with ambulatory and seven chapels.
6 Chapel of the Resurrection,
7 sacristy,
8 cloister,
9 Portal of the Nativity,
10 Portal of the Passion,
11 baptistry.

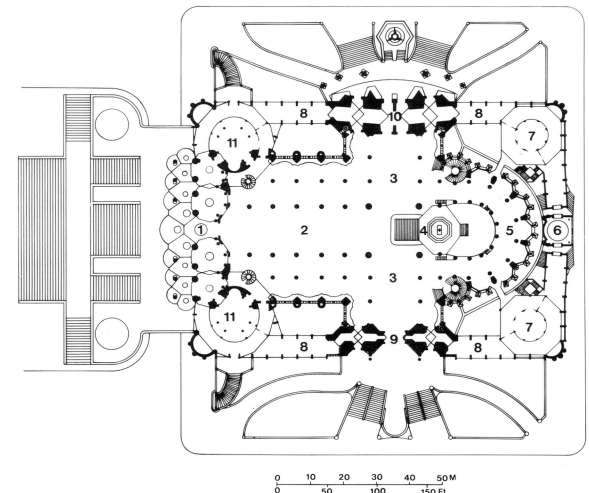

| 0 | 10 | 20 | 30 | 40 | 50M |
| 0 | | 50 | | 100 | 150 Ft. |

Left
SAGRADA FAMILIA CHURCH, Barcelona.
Begun 1882. Architect: Antonio Gaudi.

Opposite
PARC GÜELL, Barcelona. 1900–14. Part
of a garden suburb laid out by Gaudi.

horizontal bands of stone and brick alternately. The cathedral's campanile, St Edward's tower, is a well-known landmark and the view most usually associated with the building until recently. With the rebuilding of the south side of Victoria Street (1975), a small piazza was created exposing the entrance front.

One of the most original architects of the nineteenth century, whose pioneering spirit has helped the development of the *Modern* movement in the twentieth century, was Antonio Gaudi (1852–1926). Gaudi was born in Catalonia, Spain, and lived most of his life there. He attended the School of Architecture, Barcelona, and designed buildings to help fund his studies. It was eight years before he qualified as an architect. Gaudi laid emphasis on the sculptural quality of buildings, and on the logical develop-

ment of structure; but he was concerned also with the romantic and picturesque and many of his patterns and detail, original though they are, stem from natural forms. Gaudi died in 1926, in the Hospital of Santa Cruz. Tragically, he was knocked over by a trolley bus on his way from his unfinished Church of the Sagrada Familia, Barcelona, or Expiatory Church of the Holy Family (begun 1882), where he is buried in the crypt. The Sagrada Familia is remarkable for its plastic Gothic form. Gaudi disbelieved in the flying buttress, and in the last change of many he made to the church's design, he concentrated all the loads on to the supporting parts of the building. He also made them of different materials to suit the load they had to carry. The curiously shaped towers which mark the exterior (the original design had fourteen) are pierced with

openings with horizontal stone louvres to throw off rain water. The work is still unfinished. Domenec Sugranes continued with Gaudi's design until 1935. Gaudi's style, which is illustrated also in the Casa Batlló (1905–07), and the Casa Milà (1905–10), both in Barcelona, has often been criticized, or considered of no consequence, but he was a great thinker and builder and his work is probably more of an inspiration to architects today than in his own time.

Besides Gaudi, there were other well-known innovators towards the end of the nineteenth century, Charles Rennie Mackintosh (1868–1928) from Scotland, and Charles Voysey (1857–1941) from England, for example. Mackintosh's Glasgow School of Art, and Voysey's carefully designed houses were both admired in Europe, where Art Nouveau was the new mode.

Nineteenth Century Iron and Glass

Below
CLIFTON SUSPENSION BRIDGE, Bristol.
1830–64. Designer/Engineer: Isambard
Kingdom Brunel.

Opposite Top
PADDINGTON STATION. 1852–54. Railway
sheds. Engineer: Isambard Kingdom
Brunel.

Opposite Bottom
GALLERIA VITTORIO EMANUELE, Milan.
1865–77. Architect: Giuseppe Mengoni.

The two major happenings of the nineteenth century, which were to show the way towards an entirely different kind of architecture in the twentieth century, were the technical changes in building materials and the industrial revolution. The second event was principally responsible for a change in attitude towards the function of a building in the process of its design and planning, to what has been called *Functionalism*. Functionalism had always been present in architecture, for example, in the buildings of the ancient world, or in mediaeval churches, the practical needs of which had always been taken into account, but the emphasis had been placed on pomp, ceremony, or adornment. Defence fortifications and the mediaeval castle were the nearest to purely functional buildings, in which the fundamentals of the design were based on their relevance to defence.

Architects of the nineteenth century generally believed in the romantic and pictorial qualities of their work above all else, as discussed in the last chapter; but the Industrial Revolution brought a new kind of client, a proprietor who needed a building to serve the functional purposes of his new industrial processes, and little else. Matters of heat, light, unobstructed space for machinery, and so on became all-important. At this point the paths of Functionalism and of newly invented materials fortunately coincided, with fashion as always playing a part in the appearance of the new kinds of buildings. The philosophy of Functionalism was necessary to the development of new building types. By the twentieth century, if not before, the first task of the architect was to analyse very carefully the purposes which his building was required to serve.

The technical changes which were to revolutionize design and building methods began in this period with the use of cast iron, followed by wrought iron, and then steel. The development of other building materials was not standing still, particularly improvements in the production of glass. The first iron beams were used in the latter part of the seventeenth century. One of the earliest examples was the Late Renaissance style Marble Palace, St Petersburg (1768–72), by the Italian architect Antonio Rinaldi, who built a number of palaces after going to Russia in 1755. Before the end of the century iron was being used in a number of other ways. In Paris, iron framing with hollow tiles was used for floors in an effort to reduce the risk of fire. Sir John Soane designed a lantern of iron and glass (1794) to

cover the top of one of the vaults in his Bank of England building, London. By the beginning of the nineteenth century in England, mill owners were adopting fire-proof floors of brick or tile arches between cast-iron girders, supported by cast-iron stanchions.

The same engineers who installed the steam machinery were at work on the new structural systems. The Industrial Revolution was more than a revolution of industry, with its effects on the movement of people and the growth of towns. New canals, new roads, the building of the railways, brought new forms of construction, many of them in iron. Although strictly speaking not architecture, some of the new bridges were beautiful examples of the use of iron. One of the great bridge builders was Thomas Telford (1757–1834), the son of a shepherd, and a mason by trade. Two of his more famous bridges were the Craigellachie Bridge (1815) across the River Spey in which he used latticed iron in one span, and his suspension bridge across the Menai Strait (1819–26), in which he used masonry towers tapered like Egyptian pylons. Telford was the first president of the Institution of Civil Engineers, London. He was elected a fellow of the Royal Society in 1827.

Another great engineer, Isambard Brunel (1806–59) was appointed to the newly formed Great Western Railway in England in 1833. His design for the famous Clifton Suspension Bridge near Bristol, built between 1830 and 1864, was the winning entry in a competition. The Clifton Bridge was completed by W. H. Barlow who was also the engineer for the great St Pancras train sheds. These have a single span of over 73 metres, rising about 30 metres and are over 213 metres long (1863–67). Brunel was also responsible for the train sheds at Paddington railway station, London, in which historic decorative work by the architect M. D. Wyatt was incorporated in the structural ironwork.

The use of cast iron in architecture reached a high point in the London Coal Exchange (1846–49), a circular hall covered by an iron and glass cage, by J. B. Bruning, elegantly detailed and now demolished. Sydney Smirke, brother of Sir Robert Smirke, the architect for the British Museum, designed a wrought-iron dome over the Reading Room (1852–57) of the museum. The catalogue of cast-iron and wrought-iron constructions could be extended. What had become established before the middle of the nineteenth century was

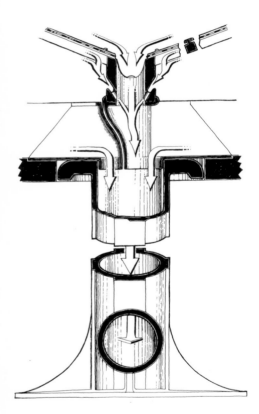

the use of cast iron and glass, not only for transport buildings, but for commercial purposes throughout Europe. A classic example of commercial use is the Galleria Vittorio Emanuele (1865–77) by Giuseppe Mengoni, the shopping centre close to the Cathedral Square, Milan, covered with a barrel vault of cast iron and glass.

The Great Exhibition of 1851 in England provided the opportunity for the finest example of an iron and glass structure in that country. An archi-

tectural competition had been held for the design of the exhibition building. The exhibition's Building Committee had rejected all the designs, and had produced one of their own, about which controversy raged, when a last-minute entry was allowed from Joseph Paxton (1803–65). Paxton had been head gardener to the Duke of Devonshire, had been promoted to become the duke's general overseer, and was also a director of the Midland Railway Company, when he produced his unique design. It was

based on principles he had already used for the Great Conservatory at Chatsworth (1836–40), the Duke of Devonshire's country house, and more especially on those used for a smaller greenhouse (1849) to house the duke's rare lily, *Victoria Regia*. The design was accepted, but was not without its severe critics who thought it was either unsafe or unbuildable. The weekly humourist paper *Punch* called the design 'The Crystal Palace', a name used ever since.

The Crystal Palace (1850–51) covered 7.7 hectares under glass. It measured 563.3 metres long by 124.4 wide and 19.2 high. There was an extension on the north side, 285.3 metres long by 14.6 wide. The huge structure, three times the length of St Paul's Cathedral, consisted of a central house, side aisles with galleries over them, and transepts, carried to a height of 32.9 metres to include elm trees growing on the site in Hyde Park, London. Other growing trees were left inside the building. Columns were regularly spaced and girder lengths coordinated, so that off-site mass production of building components was possible, an idea well understood and exploited more in the twentieth century than at the end of the nineteenth century. The glazing of the roof over the house and aisles was the ridge and furrow principle Paxton had used for the Chatsworth conservatory. A specially designed covered trolly with its wheels running in the roof gulleys enabled the glaziers to carry on putting glass over the roof regardless of the weather.

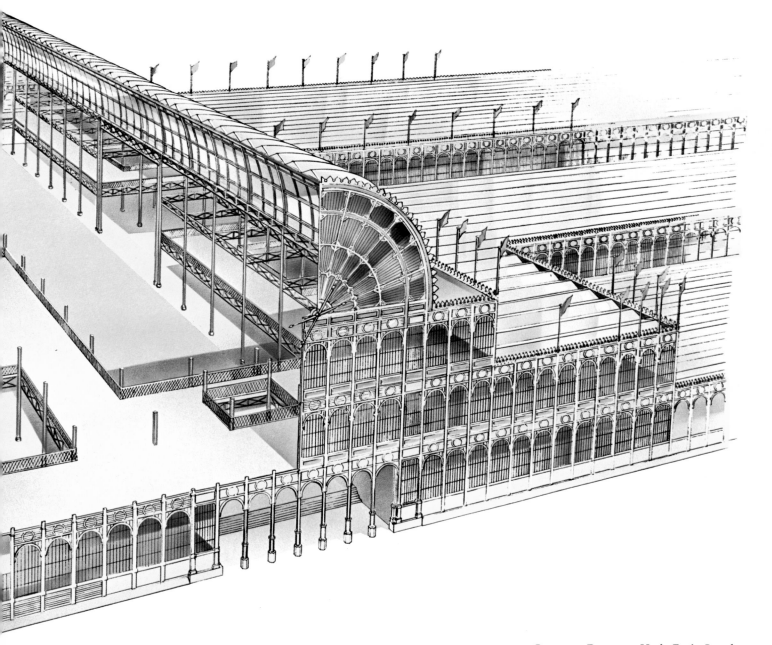

CRYSTAL PALACE, Hyde Park, London. 1850–51. Engineer: Sir Joseph Paxton. The drawing shows the transepts and part of the nave as it was built for the Great Exhibition of 1851. Paxton's 'ridge and furrow' roof glazing is clearly identifiable. The regular spacing of columns and girders made it possible to mass-produce the different elements. The Crystal Palace, so named first by the humorist weekly, *Punch*, took only nine months to build.

Paxton's guttering was very carefully thought out. A single component possessed a main channel outside to catch rainwater, and either side of it *under* the glass a smaller channel caught condensation running down the glass inside. All the water ran from the gutters down inside the iron columns. In the great work, built in the remarkably short time of nine months, Paxton was helped by the engineers, Fox and Henderson. Both Paxton and Fox were knighted in 1851. After the exhibition, the Crystal Palace was dismantled and re-erected in Sydenham (1852–54). Changes were made to the plan, and the nave was roofed with an iron and glass barrel. The building was destroyed by fire in 1936.

In the second half of the nineteenth century the rise of cast iron and glass became widespread. Examples in

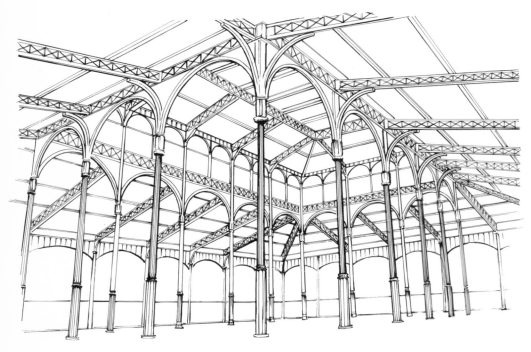

England have already been mentioned. In Paris, the Reading Room of the Bibliothèque Nationale (1862–68) by Henri Labrouste is an example of cast-iron and glass architecture at its best. The roof is a series of domes with delicately designed lattice iron arches descending on to very slender iron columns. Each dome has a central eye and concentric rings of metal work supporting the terracotta web. The contrasting planes of the various curves give vitality to the composition.

The earlier Les Halles (1853–59), the famous central market of Paris, by Victor Baltard, was demolished in 1971 to make way for redevelopment. None of the twelve pavilions, two of which were added in the 1930s, was rescued from the demolition. Les Halles was a typical market of stalls with pedestrian ways between, intersecting at right angles. The area was entirely covered over with a structure of iron and glass. The pitched roof over the circulation routes was higher than the roofs over the stalls, and windows were placed in the clerestory between.

In the 1850s a cheap and fast method of producing steel was discovered by Henry Bessemer (1813–98), the son of a Frenchman who had settled in England. The process was used for ships in the 1860s, and spread to France, Germany, Belgium, and Austria, becoming widely used in building to replace iron from the 1880s onwards.

In the last decade of the nineteenth century, perhaps in a final effort to initiate a new style, a movement started known as *Art Nouveau*, which continued throughout the first decade of the twentieth century. It gained impetus from Eiffel's Tower, and later from his structures at the Paris Exhibition of 1900. The movement was far from being purely structural; it influenced decoration, and not least the graphic arts. It was international in scope, and its zenith is associated with the work of Victor Horta (1861–1947) in Brussels, Belgium, and later with Louis Sullivan's work in America, discussed in the next chapter.

One of Victor Horta's celebrated works is the Tassel House (1892–93), in which structural iron is freely displayed and the decorative forms illustrate mature Art Nouveau. Horta's Maison du Peuple (1896–99), in which the iron beams supporting the roof are visible from inside, is now demolished, and his Innovation Department Store (1901), with its mainly glass and metal facade, was destroyed by fire in 1967.

Colonial and Nineteenth Century American Achievements

From the latter part of the eighteenth century and during the first half of the nineteenth century, architecture in North America, Canada, Australia, and elsewhere among the colonies followed closely the traditions in Europe. This was not in the least bit surprising since the men who were bringing development to these countries were either Europeans or were led by Europeans, and, with few exceptions, there was little indigenous architecture to draw on as a source of inspiration. Bengal in India had fallen to Lord Clive in the reign of George III of England (1760–1820), but not until 1858 did the British gain full powers of sovereignty over all India.

The reign of George III had also seen the loss to Great Britain of her thirteen American Colonies. Infuriated by the heavy taxes and, to them, the unfair trading arrangements of the mother country, the Colonists aligned and declared their independence, leading to war with the British in 1776. When peace came in 1783, Britain recognized the independence of all thirteen Colonies. Four years later the liberated Colonies formed a federation, drew up a constitution, valid to this day, and elected George Washington, the successful general of the war, to be the first president of the United States of America. Only three years after India was united under British rule, the northern and southern states of America were at war with one another, ending in 1865 with the unification of all the American states. Progress was rapid after that, and the country moved forward towards its

Opposite
LONGFELLOW HOUSE, Cambridge, Massachusetts. *c.* 1759.

Below
WHITE HOUSE, Washington, D.C. 1792–1829. Garden front. Architect: James Hoban.

destiny as a great industrial power.

Since 1791, Canada had consisted of two independent states, Upper and Lower Canada, the latter a former French settlement conquered by the British. The two Canadas became a single country – United Canada – in 1840, and were joined by the independent states of Novia Scotia and New Brunswick in 1867 to form the Dominion of Canada.

In Mexico, Spanish rule had been overthrown in 1821 after a decade or more of fighting. Revolt had been stirred up, first by the American War of Independence, and then by the French Revolution of 1789. Trouble in Mexico led the Mexican leader, Benito Juarez (1806–72), to break faith with France, Britain, and Spain over money, and the three powers moved in with military forces. Spain and Britain withdrew when it was discovered that Napoleon III wished to set up a monarchy in Mexico, as a hedge against American expansion there, and Archduke Maximilian of Habsburg was offered the crown. He took over in 1864 supported by French troops, and arrived in Mexico with his wife Charlotte Amélie (Carlota). When

the American Civil War ended in 1865, the United States demanded the withdrawal of French troops. Napoleon III agreed as he needed his troops for the Russian front, and warned Maximilian to leave the country. Maximilian stayed in Mexico, as he believed the Mexicans wanted him there, while Carlota rushed to the Vatican for help. The story ended in tragedy. Napoleon's troops withdrew. Juarez took Mexico City (1867). Maximilian was captured, tried, and shot. Carlota, who was inclined to insanity, failed to get help from the Pope and went completely mad while still in the Vatican. She is believed to have been the only woman to have slept a night there. Maximilian's Castle of Chapultepec, and his Palace on the Cerro de las Companas, are memorials of the French Empire style of the period with Italian and Spanish influences.

Outside the Americas, the rest of the world was feeling the influence of European commercial progress and exploration. China virtually closed her doors to Europe, until after the Opium War with Britain (1839–42), when China ceded the Port of Hong Kong to Britain,

and the Manchu empire was opened to European influences. Japan was also opened up to Russian and American influences in the second half of the nineteenth century. Africa, north of the Sahara, was already influenced by France and Britain; the Suez Canal was opened in 1869. South of the Sahara, exploration of the continent begun in the eighteenth century by Mungo Park, continued with David Livingstone's remarkable series of explorations in the 1840s, culminating in his disappearance in the 1860s and his memorable meeting with Henry Stanley. West Africa began to be colonized by the French and British, followed by the Belgians in the Congo. In South Africa, the Dutch Cape Colony established in the seventeenth century was annexed by the British in 1814, and the abolition of slavery throughout British colonies in 1834 resulted in the Great Trek of Boers from the Colony between 1835 and 1837. The British were the first to begin the colonization of Australia, where a penal settlement was established in 1788, following the loss of the American Colonies. By 1840 there were more free immigrants in Australia than convicts. Local government for the different colonies, set up on the British system of two chambers, was established by 1850. New Zealand adopted the same line in 1852.

The central point of this review of colonial expansions is the relatively short period of history in which it all began to happen. The importance for architecture was that it marked the beginning of the social, economic, and political launch pad from which the international style rocketed in the twentieth century. The influence of nineteenth century European architectural ideas in other parts of the world was obviously uneven; in Canada it continued to come from both France and Britain; in Australia, the influence was from British architects; up to the end of George III's reign in 1820, American architecture was a mixture of Georgian and Classical Revival, with more influ-

Below
UNITED STATES CAPITOL, Washington D.C. 1793–1867.

Opposite
AUSTRALIAN HISTORICAL SOCIETY, Sydney. Built 1853.

ence from France than Britain. As in Europe, Greek and Gothic Revival continued well in to the second half of the nineteenth century. In the last decade of the century, the work of American architects, such as Louis Sullivan, established their position in the international field of architecture.

Early architecture in America in this period is to be seen in the stucco-fronted White House, Washington (1792–1829), the residence of the President of the

United States of America. A neo-High Renaissance feeling is unmistakable in the tall Doric order pilasters of the front, flanking the centrally placed curved portico with dual staircases, and also in the eaves balustrading. James Hoban, an Irishman, was the architect. Another architect, Benjamin Henry Latrobe, designed the porticoes in 1807 or 1808. The earlier American Georgian style is present in Westover (c. 1730–34) by Richard Taliaferro, and in the Governor's House in Williamsburg, the capital of Virginia, rebuilt in the 1930s. Both houses have typically symmetrical facades, dormer windows set against high-pitched roofs, and regularly spaced windows. Thomas Jefferson (1743–1826), Secretary of State to George Washington, a legislator, then later U.S. President, and also an architect, favoured Classical Revival and this helped to increase the style's popularity between 1820 and 1860. Jefferson was architect for the state capitol build, Richmond, Virginia (1789–98), which he based on the Roman temple, Maison Carrée, Nîmes. The United States Capitol, Washington (1793–1867) was originally designed by William Thornton, as the result of a competition. Successive architects worked on the building, including a French architect, E.S. Hallett (1755–1825), Benjamin Latrobe, and Thomas

Ustick Walter (1804–88). Walter added the great dome over the central rotunda, which was part of Thornton's original design. The grand central area of Washington was planned by a Frenchman, Major Pierre L'Enfant, who of course was familiar with the Palace of Versailles. L'Enfant was also the architect for the rebuilding of New York City Hall as a federal hall.

The first architect of importance in Australia was Francis Greenway (1777–1837), who was deported to Australia as a convict in 1813. His Georgian work survives, much restored, in St James's Church, Sydney (c. 1824). Examples of Gothic Revival are to be seen in St Mary's Cathedral, Sydney, by William Wardell, the foundation stone of which was laid in 1868 by Bishop Polding; also in Government House, Sydney, occupied about 1845, and generally supposed to have been designed by Edward Blore in England. Much more representative of Australian architecture perhaps than the revivals imported from England or Europe, are the colonial style houses. A typical example, showing fine proportions and detailing, is the Sydney headquarters of the Australian Historical Society, originally a doctor's house in 1815. Another fine example is the house for J. W. Marshall (1877) at Parawai, New Zealand, similar in the careful metalwork details of the verandah and balcony, and excellent proportions. In India, where, unlike Australia and New Zealand, there was already a long tradition of architecture, the Classical Revival period was tempered with local traditions. St James's Church, Delhi (c. 1830), believed to have been designed by Colonel James Skinner of Skinner's Horse, combined a mixture of Neo-classic and Renaissance elements applied in that environment.

At the end of the century in America, the work of Louis Sullivan showed the way buildings were going in the future. Sullivan, the son of an Irish dancing master, was born in Boston in 1856. He joined Dankmar Adler and the Adler & Sullivan partnership was formed in 1881. Adler's chief draughtsman between 1887 and 1893 was Frank Lloyd Wright. Sullivan's first skyscraper was the

Above
HUNTERS' HILL, Sydney.

Opposite Top
GUARANTY BUILDING, Buffalo. 1894–95. Architect: Louis Sullivan.

Opposite Bottom
CARSON PIRIE SCOTT & CO. STORE, Chicago, Illinois. 1894–1904. Entrance Pavilion. Architect: Louis Sullivan.

Wainright Building, St Louis (1890–91), but his best skyscraper was the thirteen storey Guaranty Building, Buffalo (1894–95). The upper part of the Buffalo building rises from a ground floor and mezzanine of columns and piers. The interval between columns and piers is halved in the upper part, therefore only every other pier contains steelwork. The piers meet in rounded arches at the top of the building with an eye over every arch and a projecting cornice running along the top. Surfaces are covered with decorated red and green terracotta sheathing. The design is symmetrical with doorways placed in the centre of the ground floor facades. The Reliance Building, Chicago (1890–94) by Burnham and Root, originally four storeys and then increased to sixteen, is also metal-framed faced with terracotta, but the horizontal bands at floor levels are given emphasis and break the upward vertical sweep so characteristic of Sullivan's skyscrapers. The Reliance Building, although earlier, is perhaps more closely linked with the twentieth century than the Buffalo skyscraper. Sullivan's entrance pavilion to the Carson Pirie Scott department store, Chicago (1899–1904), illustrates his decorative approach, in this case apparently related to European Art Nouveau.

Twentieth Century
Early Modern Movements

At the start of the twentieth century, no great political or economic landmark indicated the revolution in architecture which was to take place in the next fifty to sixty years. The period of industrial expansion in the latter part of the nineteenth century had given western nations enormous potential. With railways and steamships communications were made possible as never before, and the travels of nineteenth-century explorers had opened up the world for unprecedented expansion in trade.

The rising powers of European nations led to jealousies and disputes between them over territory. Worst of all were the excessive ambitions of Kaiser William II, emperor of Germany, who was bitter and resentful towards Britain, even though he was Queen Victoria's grandson, and was cold towards Britain's approach for an alliance with Germany. Edward VII, who acceded to the throne of Britain in 1901, when Queen Victoria died, made friends with France. The 'Entente Cordiale' (1904), as it was called, led to an understanding, which amounted to a defensive alliance between the two countries to counterbalance the growing might of Germany's military position. Later, Russia joined the alliance. Meanwhile, Bulgaria had gained her independence from Turkey whose power was weakening. Greece, Serbia, Montenegro, and Bulgaria formed the Balkan League in 1912, and local wars in the Balkans between 1912 and 1913 ended with Serbia in a strong position and Austria suspicious of her intentions. The murder of Archduke Ferdinand, heir to the Austrian throne, in Sarajevo, Serbia, in June 1914 produced a series of unfulfilled demands, followed by mobilizations and ultimatums among the aligned powers. Austria declared war on Serbia; Germany declared war on Russia, then on France; the Germans invaded Belgium in flagrant abuse of her neutrality; and Britain declared war on Germany. Sarajevo was the spark

that set off the worst war ever in cost of human lives. The suffering in four years was 40,000,000 killed and wounded in a relatively limited field of operations.

The damage to property and architecture was complete in the theatre of war, but relatively little elsewhere. Famous buildings like the Gothic Cathedral of Amiens became a blackened ruin from shell fire. The social and economic changes resulting from the devastation altered the conditions under which architecture was produced. It did not suddenly bring to an end in Europe the revivalist styles or speed up the change to modern forms. They continued to evolve and were interrupted, rather than hastened or changed, by the carnage and severity of World War I; nor were they affected to any marked degree by the new national boundaries laid down by the Treaty of Versailles in 1919.

But the political and economic climates in Europe were not healthy. In Germany, Kaiser William II's policy of war had failed. The Germans had revolted, the Kaiser was thrown out and lived the rest of his life an exile in Doorn, Holland. There was nearly a revolution in Germany, like that in France in 1789. But the parties compromised, and a coalition government was formed known as the Weimar Republic, after the German town where the Republic's National Assembly met. The situation in Germany continued to deteriorate. The French had occupied the Ruhr, the centre of German industry. Under the Treaty of Versailles, there was a huge reparations debt to be paid off, and the communists were causing the government trouble. Strikes followed, and the worst inflation ever known hit Germany. By 1929 the whole world was plunged into a slump. Germany had over six million unemployed; Britain at least three million.

In this atmosphere the National Socialist party, the Nazi party, founded in 1921 with Adolf Hitler as its president,

started to gain power. Hitler had been a corporal in World War I and a sign writer in Vienna before that. By devious means he became Chancellor of Germany in 1933, and in 1934 was Head of State and Commander of the Armed Forces. Hitler next repudiated the Treaty of Versailles, reoccupied the Ruhr and rearmed Germany. Like the Kaiser before him, his territorial ambitions led to the occupation of Austria, followed by Czechoslovakia, then Poland. These acts violated the conditions of the League of Nations, set up after the Treaty of Versailles to preserve peace among the nations. The League had already failed to stop the ambitions of Mussolini, dictator of Italy, who had invaded Abyssinia in 1935, nor had it intervened in the Spanish Civil War (1936–39) in which General Franco was successful with help from Germany and Italy. The invasion of Poland ended uncertainty. In 1939, Britain and France went to war with Germany, and in 1940, with Italy. This was the atmosphere in which, surprisingly perhaps, the new style of architecture developed.

The technical basis of the Early Modern movement was reinforced concrete. A mixture of rubble and mortar reinforced with metal had been used in the Panthéon, Paris, by Rondelet, the architect Soufflot's associate, in the eighteenth century. Later, in 1849, a French gardener, Joseph Monnier, used metal rods to reinforce concrete flower pots. Thanks to the systems developed by François Coignet (1814–88), and François Hennibique (1842–1921), reinforced concrete was fully developed by the end of the nineteenth century. In English it was called *ferro-concrete*, in French *béton armé*. in German *Eisenbeton*, and in Italian *cimente armato*.

One of the first architects to exploit the new material was a Frenchman, Auguste Perret (1874–1954). He never completed his architectural course at the École des Beaux Arts in Paris, but left early to enter his father's building firm.

In Perret's early flats (1902–03) in the rue Franklin, Paris, the reinforced-concrete frame clad in glazed tiles was exposed on the facade. This was a new idea. But the exposure of the structure was part of the philosophy of Functionalism. After it had come into fashion at the beginning of the twentieth century, it remained a consistent feature of much twentieth century modern architecture. Perret's early flats were transitional between the classical and modern approach. In his later work he produced his own finish to reinforced concrete and left it unclad. Sometimes he used coloured aggregate in the concrete to achieve the finish he desired.

Perret and his contemporaries, Peter Behrens (1868–1940) and Otto Wagner (1841–1918) in Germany, Adolf Loos (1870–1933) in Austria, and Frank Lloyd Wright (1867–1959) in America represent what historians like to call the first generation of modern architects. They threw off any tendency to continue Art Nouveau, which after about 1905 began to wain in popularity as quickly as it had arrived. There was a complete absence of ornament in their buildings. They relied for their aesthetic appeal on a building's function, and an honest external expression of the structure, interpreted in a lively manner. Early Modern buildings were few and far between. The great majority of architecture was either still revivalistic, or Georgian, or what has been called 'traditional'. Indeed, up until the end of the second decade of the twentieth century, the majority of architects did not follow the Modern movement. Many thought it was merely a passing phase.

The Steiner House, Vienna (1910), by Adolf Loos was Early Modern – flat-roofed, symmetrically designed, with starkly unadorned, carefully shaped windows. Peter Behrens, Schröder House (1908–09) at Eppenhausen, new Hagen, has the same 'block' image, but the window arrangement is more interesting. The roof is pitched, the lower walls, masonry and the upper walls white rough-cast cement rendering. After Behrens was appointed architect to the German Electric Company (AEG), he designed a number of industrial buildings. The first and best known of these for AEG, and one which had an immense influence on the work of later architects, was the Turbine Factory, Berlin (1909). For so early a factory it proclaimed what strides had been made in the design of a purely functional building type. Large areas of window are set between regularly spaced steel

FAGUS FACTORY, Alfeld-Anderline, Germany. 1911–14. Architect: Walter Gropius and Adolf Meyer.

uprights which taper towards the base. The uprights are tied to the roof structure at eaves level. Solid walls on the front facade are of concrete with horizontal incisions at regular intervals. The response of the architects of the day to the need for abundant natural light for factory processes, shows their single-mindedness over Functionalism.

Another pre-World War I building with an astonishing structure for its time was Max Berg's Centennial Hall, Breslau (1912–13) in Germany. The hall was covered over with a vast reinforced concrete skeleton-like dome, consisting of a series of radial ring beams, reducing in size and supported by curved spokes radiating from a compression ring at the top of the dome. Above each ring beam was a row of continuous windows, giving the dome a stepped appearance from the outside.

It would be wrong to give the impression that in these early days more traditionally-minded architects were not making progress. Eliel Saarinen (1873–1950), for example, designed the Finnish pavilion of the Paris Exhibition of 1900, and won the Helsinki railway station competition with Lindgren and Gesellius in 1904. Saarinen changed the design before it was built (1906–1914). It is functional in style, but ornamented, and the enormous circular arched entrance

is flanked by two huge figures. Saarinen was the leading architect in Finland until he left for America in 1922. His son Eero Saarinen became one of the best-known mid-twentieth-century architects in that country. In America, Eliel Saarinen was as well-known as Frank Lloyd Wright.

Although Wright is counted amongst the first generation of modern architects, his long life and inspired output gave him a period of activity spanning from the Sullivan era of the nineteenth century, referred to in the last chapter, until well into the fifties, and the international movements discussed in the next chapter. Wright was born in 1867 and belonged to the nineteenth century. He loved the natural landscape of America. In much of his work he was inspired by Japanese and Pre-Columbian American architecture, especially Mayan. After 1938, until he died in 1959, Wright spent most of his time at Taliesen West, his home and studio near Phoenix, Arizona, on the edge of the desert. The characteristics of Wright's early 'prairie houses', dating from the first decade of the twentieth century, were rambling asymmetrical plans, with floors interwoven at different levels, and roofs, verandahs and balconies extended to provide an essentially horizontal feeling. The general massing of the buildings was fitted carefully into the landscape. The Kaufman House called 'Falling Water' (1936–37) is best known. It was constructed with cantilevered floors and balconies of reinforced concrete over a stream by the name of Bear Run, in Connesville, Pennsylvania. Heavy vertical walls in rough stone, in contrast with the smooth finish of the concrete, counterbalance the cantilevered horizontal elements. Windows are arranged in continuous areas of glass. The interplay of different horizontal and vertical planes set against the natural landscape gives the building astonishing life.

Wright was sixty-nine when he started to build 'Falling Water'. New directions in architecture had already been taken by a second generation of modern architects in Europe more than twenty years earlier. The architects were Walter Gropius (1883–1953), Erich Mendelsohn (1887–1953). J. J. P. Oud (1890–1963) and Ludwig Mies van der Rohe 1886–1963), and the Swiss-born architect, Charles Edouard Jeanneret, known as Le Corbusier (1887–1965), Gropius and Mies van der Rohe were Germans

and both had worked as assistants to Peter Behrens, establishing the link with the first group of modern architects.

J. J. P. Oud was a Dutchman who had worked in association with William Marinus Dudok (b. 1884). Dudok was outstanding in the 1920s when he was city architect for Hilversum, Holland. His work was outside the mainstream of modern architecture. His buildings were usually of brick, with clean lines, no decoration, and windows with a horizontal emphasis. His compositions were always sharp and clear, like his Dr H. Bavinck School (1921). Dudok belonged to the influential Dutch group of abstract artists of the period, known as *de Stijl*, founded by Theo van Doesburg. Piet Mondriaan, George Vantongerloo, a sculptor, and J. J. P. Oud were also members of the group, which believed in designing with geometric abstract forms in asymmetrical arrangements. It influenced the work of painters, sculptors, and furniture designers, as well as architects. Oud developed the idea of de Stijl. Workers' houses in the Hook of Holland illustrate his classic style with long balconies projecting as a canopy to the ground-floor shops below. Also in Holland, the housing estates in Amsterdam by Piet

Kramer built in 1918–23, and those of Michel de Klerk (1884–1923) of 1917, follow the characteristics of the Amsterdam school of that time, with clean brickwork, flat roofs, and the right-angle corner junctions of flats enlivened with bulbous or concave brickwork. The De Dageraad Housing Estate by Piet Kramer is an example of this corner treatment.

Walter Gropius had achieved distinction before the First World War. He left Behrens' office in 1910 and, in partnership with Adolf Meyer, was architect for the Fagus Factory, Alfeld (1911–14). The factory was a brick building but unmistakably modern. Gropius used continuous windows, projecting slightly between slim piers. The windows met at the corners, a feature which heralded the continuous curtain walls of glass in later modern architecture. After the First World War, Gropius had no practice. He succeeded van der Velde as Director of Applied Art at Weimar. Here he founded his famous Bauhaus, in which a unique form of training, half craftsmanship and half academic, took from the best of both spheres. The principles expounded at the Bauhaus did more to spread the philosophies of the Modern movement

Opposite
EINSTEIN TOWER, Potsdam (near Berlin).
1920–21. Architect: Erich Mendelsohn.

Above
SCHRÖDER HOUSE, Utrecht, Holland.
1924–25. Architect: Gerrit Rietveld. This
is an outstanding example of the Dutch
de stijl concepts applied to architecture.

than the comparatively few examples executed. Gropius left Germany in 1934 after the Nazis came to power. He worked in Britain for three years, then settled in America on his appointment as Professor of Architecture at Harvard University.

Erich Mendelsohn left Germany for the same reason as Gropius and eventually followed him to America. In Germany, Erich Mendelsohn's notable work was the Einstein Tower, Potsdam, near Berlin (1920–21), an observatory and laboratory with rounded forms appropriate to the use of optical instruments. It was not in the mainstream of modern architecture, but Mendelsohn followed that in his later work. The Einstein Tower, designed for reinforced concrete, was built in brickwork and cement rendered, because of a cement shortage in Germany after the war. The design followed Mendelsohn's original pencil sketch faithfully. In the trenches during the war, Mendelsohn made sketches of his ideas for modern buildings, but nobody then believed they could be built. Mendelsohn's work was

always intuitive. He worked from his sketches, and referred drawings back to them, although he considered the primary objective was the functional requirement. Mendelsohn liked to work to music and preferred Bach's compositions to those of others. Once he was asked to design a building to Brahms. This of course was not the purpose of the music, which was there to create the right atmosphere for his imagination to be fully released. After leaving Germany in 1933, Mendelsohn teamed up with Serge Chermayeff to win the competition for the De La Warr Pavilion, Bexhill in Sussex, England. It helped to advance modern architecture in that country. The pavilion (1934–35), a very straightforward building, was notable for its wide terraces facing the sea and semicircular staircase tower. Mendelsohn left England for a period in Palestine and reached America in 1941.

Auguste Perret's most notable building in this post World War I period was the Church of Notre Dame, le Raincy (1922–23), a remarkable structure in

reinforced concrete, with the concrete left in an unfinished state, as it came from the formwork. The building is a vast hall with slender square-shaped columns rising to support shallow rounded vaults over the nave and aisles. The walls between structural supports are filled with a network of reinforced concrete and glass. The plain concrete surfaces devoid of applied decoration are typical of the Modern movement, but the feeling of the church is transitional, as can be seen by comparing it with designs of reinforced concrete churches in central Europe of the fifties and sixties.

The traditional work in Scandinavia during the second and third decades of the twentieth century is represented in Sweden by the works of Ragnar Östberg (1886–1945), architect for Stockholm's Town Hall (1911–23), a brick-built, carefully detailed building with elegant turrets and finials. The Grundtvig Church, Copenhagen, Denmark (1913–

late 1920s) is closer to the country's revivalist traditions than to modern architecture. Modern architecture did not make much impact in Scandinavia until the 1930s, when Alvar Aalto (1898–1976) began his tuberculosis sanatorium at Paimio, Finland, after a competition in 1928. The reinforced-concrete structure and wholeheartedly functional form places the building with those of the second generation of modern architects. The planning of the sanatorium is arranged so that the rows of patients' bedrooms in the long multi-storey wing catch the early morning sunshine. After the Second World War, Aalto, who had designed the Finnish Pavilions at the Paris Exposition of 1937 and the New York World's Fair of 1939, developed his own particular form of modern architecture, moving away from the white reinforced-concrete International style, to the use of brick-work, more suited to Finland's shortage of steel reinforcement in that period.

In England, the chief traditionalists of the 1920s and 30s included Sir Edwin Lutyens (1869–1944), renowned for his country houses using Renaissance-style features, and the planning of New Delhi, India. Lutyens was the last of three architects who, in their own way, produced very English-style houses, usually with spreading gabled roofs, large chimneys and mullioned windows, at the end of the nineteenth century and early part of the twentieth century. The other two were Norman Shaw (1831–1912) and Charles Voysey (1857–1941).

We must turn to the Americas to complete this chapter which finishes with the end of World War II. 'Falling Water' was nearly completed. Frank Lloyd Wright was commissioned to design the administration building for the Johnson Wax Co., Racine, Wisconsin, (1936–39). His interest in the circular form, which found its ultimate expression in the Guggenheim Museum's spiral, (p. 175), is certainly

apparent in the horizontally based building for Johnson's. The clean lines of the enclosing red-brick walls have no sharp edges, but rounded corners. The central portion rises in a series of circular masses. Some of the wall surfaces have thin bands of Pyrex glass tubes arranged at regular intervals. The interior of the main hall is filled with reinforced-concrete columns like some ancient temple. The columns taper towards the base where they are fitted with metal shoes. Huge circular mushroom heads at the top of the columns form the roof structure, and almost touch. The spaces between the mushroom heads are filled with Pyrex glass tubes, similar to those used on the outside of the building. The glass tubes allow light into the hall.

We have seen the use of reinforced concrete for churches in Perret's Church of Notre Dame le Raincy. He used precast as well as site-formed (*in situ*) concrete work. A more fluid form of reinforced-concrete work than Perret's

rectilinear design began to be used, particularly in South America. Oscar Niemeyer's little Church of St Francis of Assisi, Pampulha, Brazil (1942) is a classic example. Niemeyer used a complicated form of reinforced-concrete vaulting, known as *parabolic* vaulting, in which the stresses are distributed evenly throughout the thin shell. In Niemeyer's church the roof and walls are a single flowing structure using the parabolic vault. Over the nave is a shape rather like a section of a cone. At right angles to the nave is a large parabolic vault over the altar, and there are three smaller vaults, two to south and one to north, making a single rolling structure. The four vault ends on the east side are filled with a solid wall faced with *azulejos*, glazed tiles, depicting a continuous mural. The single vault end on the west side of the church is filled by the entrance way with glass above it. Vertical louvres in the upper portion of the vault end control the light filtering

Below
JOHNSON WAX CO., Racine, Wisconsin, U.S.A. Administration building. 1936–39. Architect: Frank Lloyd Wright. The cutaway shows the reinforced-concrete columns of the main administration area, with their huge mushroom heads and stems tapering towards the base. The spaces between the mushrooms heads are filled with Pyrex glass tubes which let light into the hall.

Opposite
GRUNDTVIG CHURCH, Copenhagen. Begun 1913. Architect: P. V. Jensen Klint.

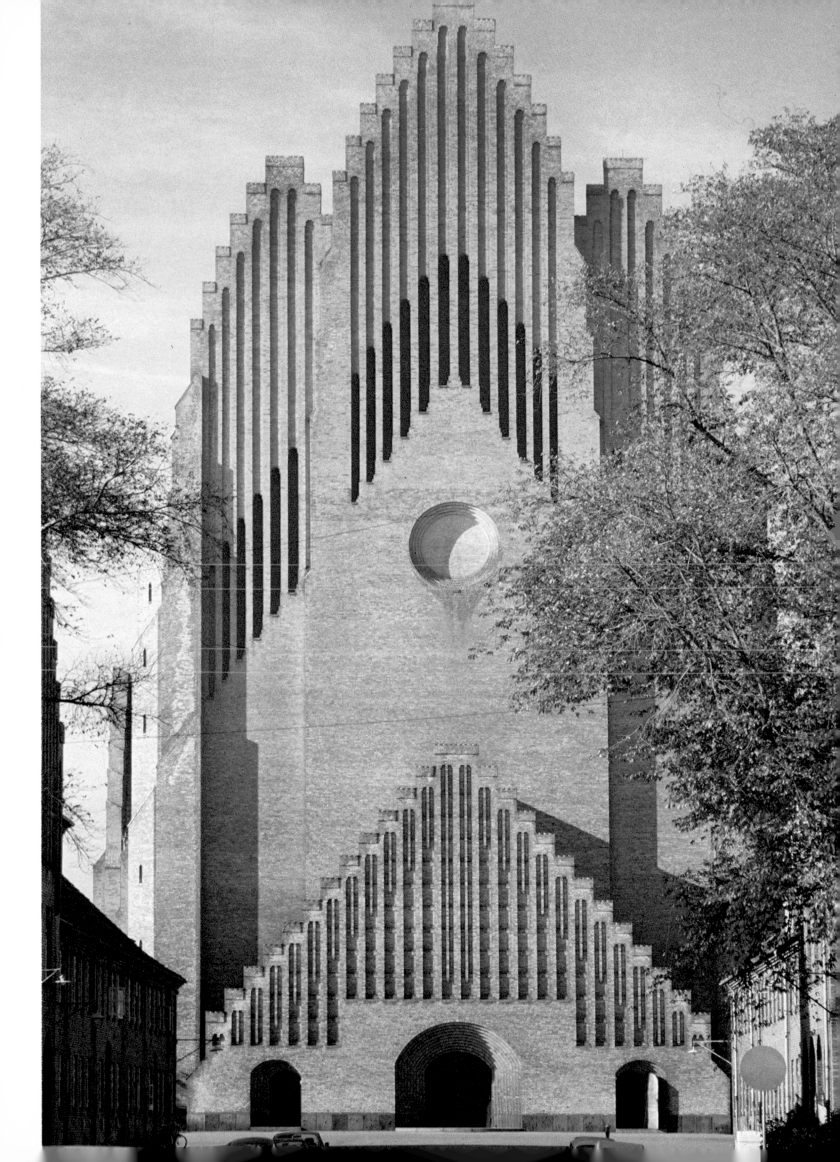

into the nave. To the south of the entrance is a free-standing, inverted, wedge-shaped bell tower, linked to the entrance by a slightly slanting reinforced-concrete canopy. The composition is wonderfully unified by the different white shapes of the structure enclosing apparently darker areas.

Niemeyer is among the early twentieth century generation of modern architects. Born in 1907 in Rio de Janeiro, he was still a student when he joined Lucio Costa's office. He has worked on his own since starting an office in 1939, except for a short period (1957–60) when he was chief architect for Nova-cap, the building authority of Brasilia, discussed in the next chapter. His output of projects and executed works has been prolific.

The Church of St Francis was part of a larger scheme around the curved artificial lake at Pampulha, created as a recreational centre for a new suburb of Belo Horizonte. President Kubitschek of Brazil was at that time Mayor of the city, the capital of the state of Minas Gerais. In addition to the church, the scheme included a casino, a restaurant, and a yacht club. All these buildings were constructed in white reinforced concrete in rectilinear or flowing forms, with windows forming glass walls, characteristic of Niemeyer's style at this period. The casino complex includes a main hall with a gaming room and an oval-shaped restaurant on the next level. Open and enclosed areas flow into one another in an extremely logical and clean-cut design. The separate restaurant at Pampulha was less rigid in design than the casino. The dining area is circular,

enclosed by windows, except where it is joined to a semicircular service space. A covered way with a reinforced-concrete canopy on pillars follows a path along the shores of the lake to another section of the restaurant area. The yacht club at Pampulha is a long two-storey building with a flat roof of two unequal inverted slopes. The upper-floor lounge and restaurant have an open terrace facing the lake. There is a boathouse, with locker rooms and storage space on the floor below.

The Pampulha buildings were designed for pleasure, and they must be among the earlier moder reinforced-concrete buildings to be so created. They underline the fact that the International style, the name given to the established Modern movement, had become universal for all building types.

Twentieth Century International Movements

NOTRE DAME DU HAUT CHAPEL, Ronchamp, France. 1950–55. Architect: Le Corbusier.

The war in Europe changed dramatically in 1941. Hitler's forces attacked Russia. In the Far East, the Japanese attack on the American fleet at Pearl Harbour brought America with its great resources wholly into the war on the side of Britain and her allies. Britain was drawn fully into the Far East struggle. In 1945 the war ended in Europe with the destruction of Nazi Germany and the death of Hitler. It was also all over in the Far East after atom bombs had been dropped on Hiroshima, killing 78,000 people, and on Nagasaki. Politically, the war in Europe and the Far East had changed the world: Germany was split into two; there were now two world powers – Russia and America; Russia possessed a ring of satellite communist states around her western frontier: East Germany, Poland, Czechoslovakia, Hungary, Rumania, and Bulgaria; in the Far East, India and Pakistan became separate dominions in 1947; the communists took over China in 1949; the British withdrew from Malaya which formed a federation in 1957; in the Third World, politically independent African states followed swiftly: between 1951 and 1964, for example, Libya, Algeria, Nigeria, Kenya, and Tanzania. All these changes heightened the expec-

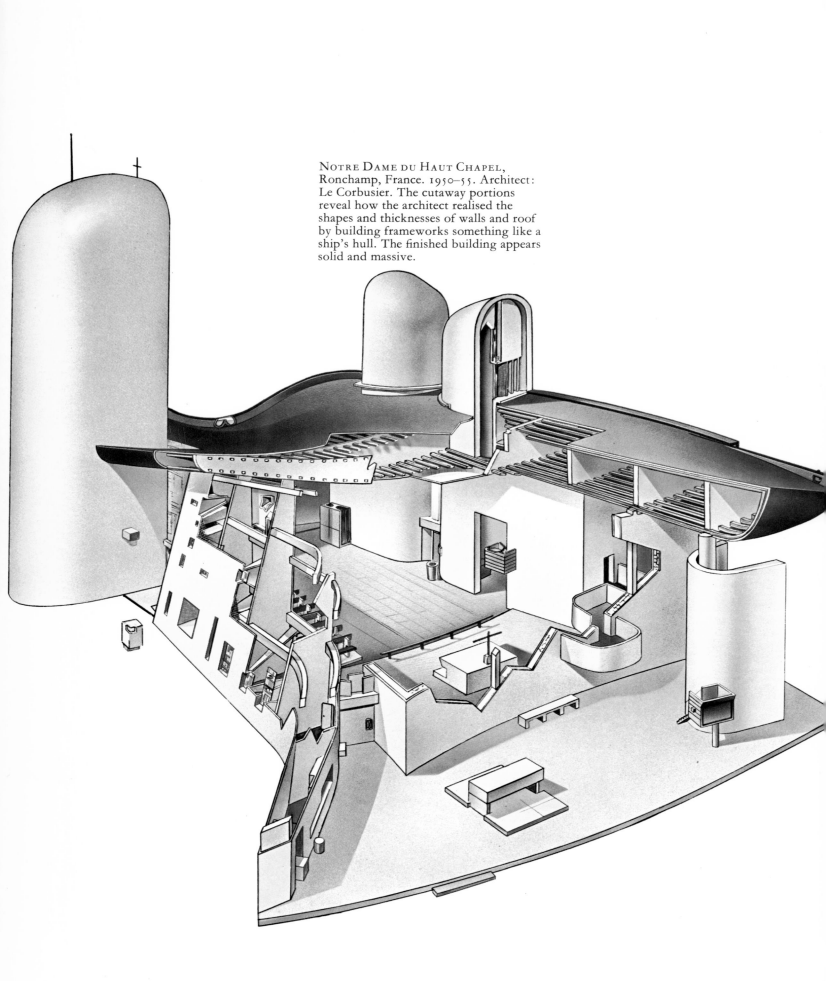

NOTRE DAME DU HAUT CHAPEL,
Ronchamp, France. 1950–55. Architect:
Le Corbusier. The cutaway portions
reveal how the architect realised the
shapes and thicknesses of walls and roof
by building frameworks something like a
ship's hull. The finished building appears
solid and massive.

tations of new indigenous forms of architecture based on the modern International style.

The destruction of property in Russia, Germany, France, England, Italy, Japan, and elsewhere during the six years of war was on a scale never experienced before. Whole cities needed restoration or rebuilding, not only as a result of destruction by bombs, but because of the decay which set in during the years of neglect afterwards. The ravages of 'blitz and blight' were the first to be made good when peace came. The priority was housing the homeless, a task undertaken in Europe with great shortages of building materials. The worst shortages had to be met by lowering standards or finding substitutes. In Britain, the quantity of timber used per house was rationed. Amidst the gloom of devastation there was hope for a better architecture – new towns, new city centres, better working conditions and better housing for the people. The problems were immense, and, in the case of housing, the task is still incomplete in areas where populations started to increase unexpectedly.

The situation helped the progress of modern architecture in two ways. A great deal of construction needed to be done. New techniques had been developed to help modern building. Also the Modern movement was generally accepted. Traditional architecture had become stripped of decoration in the post-war need for economy. The technique of reinforcing concrete had improved

NOTRE DAME DU HAUT CHAPEL, Ronchamp, France. 1950–55. Architect: Le Corbusier.

enormously, both in the material for aggregates and in the mixing. A new form of reinforcement, using wires as thin as piano wires, could now be tensioned to take the required loads. Prestressed concrete, as the improved material was called, meant that individual concrete units could be finer and less bulky, designed for a more precise performance. Techniques for producing reinforced concrete and prestressed concrete units in off-site factories were also developed. In the sixties this led to the widespread use of prefabricated units for whole walls including windows and doors, and for whole roof units.

An early form of prefabrication had already been developed in 1947 in Hertfordshire, England, by the county council's architect, C. H. Aslin and his deputy Stirrat Johnson Marshall, to meet the programme of school building under a new education act, at a time when bricks were in short supply or unavailable. The Hertfordshire schools became world famous. The later forms of prefabrication were essential for rehousing in the devastated areas of eastern Europe. The mass production of units could not be expected to produce architecture in the accepted meaning of that word, but the prefabrication of specially designed elements is quite a different operation, and played an important part in post-war design. The manufacture of improved steel for construction, the development of aluminium as a building material, and the use of plastics were among the new techniques employed in the post-war range. As the architecture of the fifties and sixties developed, it became increasingly difficult to identify building types. The traditional merged

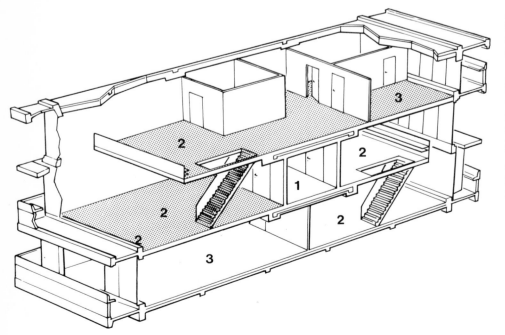

Above
SEAGRAM BUILDING, New York. 1956–58. Architects: Mies van der Rohe and Philip Johnson.

Left
UNITÉ D'HABITATION, Marseilles. 1946–52. Architect: Le Corbusier. Plan:
1 internal street,
2 two-level living space,
3 children's rooms.
Two overlapping family apartments occupy three floors. The darker floor indicates an 'upper' apartment entered from the 'street' at the lower level.

with the modern, and only a few buildings could claim to be worthy successors to those of the early masters.

Le Corbusier, one of the second generation of modern architects, was one of the influential leaders from the beginning. As a boy, Le Corbusier was apprenticed as an engraver and in 1908 he joined Auguste Perret's studio. Later, he spent time in Peter Behren's office and thus became closely acquainted with the work of the first generation of the Modern movement. In 1920 he founded an avant garde architectural magazine and before World War II wrote books on his ideas. One of these ideas was the concept of the vertical city. After the war, Le Corbusier was commissioned by the French Government to build a huge block at Marseilles, the Unité d'Habitation (1946–52). The immense building, 137 metres long, 24 metres wide, and 55 metres high, was built in reinforced concrete. It contains 337 apartments broken down into over twenty different types. The logic of Le Corbusier's planning is illustrated in the ingenious arrangement of the typical family apartment, which occupies all the space from front to rear of the block on one floor, plus not quite half the space on the second floor. By arranging the apartments in pairs, interlocking, the two short floors leave a space in the middle for a corridor or street. The living rooms are 5 metres high through two floors, making it possible to have entrances from streets arranged on alternate floors, and to enter either at the upper level of the sitting room or at the lower level. A family aprtment of this kind contains a living room, a parents' room with bathroom, two long children's rooms with a balcony and built-in furniture. The living room also has a balcony with some sun protection. The apartments generally fit into the structural frame like drawers in a wardrobe, and are carefully insulated from the structure to reduce noise. The whole building rests on giant *pilotis*, leaving the ground floor open. At mid level the building contains two service floors with shops and stores. The roof is used for recreational and entertainment purposes: there are gymnasia, a kindergarten, an open air theatre, and a small race track. The Marseilles block demonstrates a logical approach to housing where there is a land shortage or prices for land are exorbitant. The experiment seemed worthwhile at the time.

Le Corbusier's Chapel of Notre Dame du Haut, Ronchamp, France (1950–55), shows another side of the architect's

character. The requirements were for a shrine which would be suitable for a solitary pilgrim or for large groups. The irregularly shaped plan will seat about two hundred people in the nave and from ten to about thirty people in side chapels. An outside pulpit is provided for preaching to a multitude. The chapel has the qualities of a painting or sculpture. It is a small jewel of a building, whether viewed from a distance, peeping through the trees at the top of the hill, or at close quarters. The huge dark roof sweeps outwards and upwards at the eaves forming a canopy on two sides, but presses down inside. The massive south wall bends inwards and is punctuated with scattered windows of different sizes and fitted with coloured glass.

Le Corbusier went to immense trouble in the preparatory stages of his work.

LA TOURETTE MONASTERY, France. 1956–60. Architect: Le Corbusier.

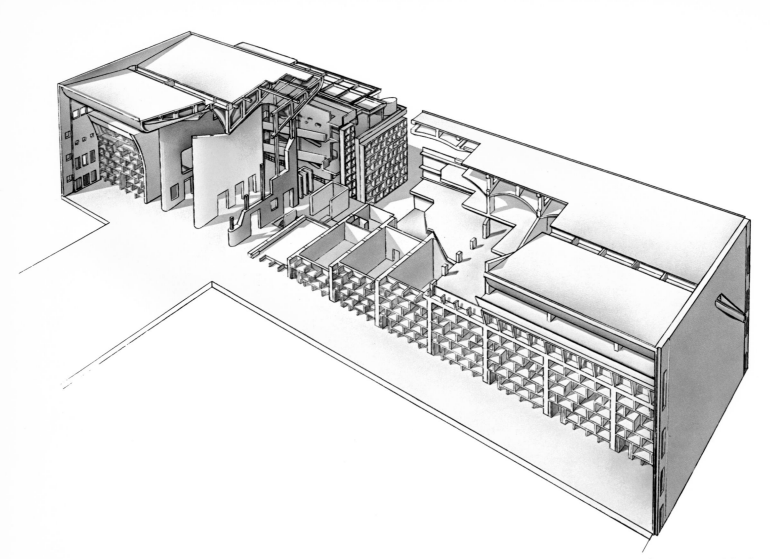

For the Monastery of La Tourette (1956–60) which he designed for the Dominicans, he studied the ancient Abbey of Le Thoronet. He also studied the rules of the Dominican order, and the problems of a building in which silence, meditation, and devotion were the rules of the day. The constitution of the Dominicans laid down rules for the building of their monasteries, as was done in earlier times, and is still done in some other denominations and religions, but the shape and arrangement of the required spaces and the design of the structure was left in the architect's hands. The site for the new monastery is steeply sloping. The monastic accommodation was arranged on three sides of a central court. The monastery church occupied the fourth side. The structure is of reinforced concrete, left unfinished straight from the formwork, with no decoration except for the use of exposed aggregate round the projecting window of the monks' cells on the two upper floors of the monastery accommodation. The forms and massing, an arrangement of void to solid, and the use of pilotis to overcome the slope of the ground, make their own statement. The church and monks' cells apart, the other principal accommodation includes refectory and kitchens, libraries, common rooms, an oratory, and cloisters. In spite of the generous enclosure of space, La Tourette needed to be built economically. The Dominicans are a mendicant order and money was not plentiful. There is very little paintwork and all the service pipes, electric cables, and plumbing are left exposed.

Le Corbusier's final work, still incomplete when he died in 1965, was the city of Chandigarh, the new capital of the Punjab. Maxwell Fry, who designed a school in England with Gropius, and Jane Drew from Britain joined him. The High Court building (1952–56), the Secretariat, and the Assembly buildings were completed and show the full flowering of Le Corbusier's ideas after Marseilles, Ronchamp, and La Tourette. The High Court building illustrates once again the flexibility of the architect's design in reinforced concrete: the smaller pattern of *brise-soleil* (sunbreaks) on the front, the gigantic vertical elements flanking the entrance, and the wide spreading canopy. The concrete is left unfinished as it came from the shutters.

Le Corbusier, Frank Lloyd Wright, and Mies van der Rohe were probably the three architects to make the most impression and gain the greatest number of followers of their work. All three were leaders of modern architecture in their own ways, both before and after World War II. Wright had completed his administration building for Johnson Wax just before World War II. In 1946 he added a tower of laboratories, completed in 1950. This building was constructed on what Wright called the 'tap root' principle: the central core of the reinforced concrete structure contained the lifts and services and the floor structure was cantilevered from it, like horizontal branches from a tree trunk. The central core was taken down as a foundation, so that the building 'floated' like a ship, the subsoil reacting to its compression from the weight of the building with an equal and balancing set of forces. The cantilevered floors permitted a free choice of materials for cladding the outside of the building. For this Wright used alternate bands of brickwork and glass with the four corners of the tower rounded. The projecting top of the central core is circular. The general treatment of the tower matched the earlier administration building.

Wright's interest in the circular form continued. In the Guggenheim Museum (1946–59), Fifth Avenue, New York, he introduced the spiral. Inside the building a great void is enclosed by ramps spiralling upwards through seven floors. Outside, the building billows outwards like some monstrous shell creature. Over the top of the void inside is a circular glass dome. The art exhibits are viewed while descending the ramp, having reached the top floor by lift. The material used for the structure is reinforced concrete. In no way does the building pretend to relate to its prosaic neighbours on either side.

Mies van der Rohe (1886–1969) followed Walter Gropius and Le Corbusier to the office of Peter Behrens in 1908. His father was a stonemason and, as a young man, Mies (his mother's surname was van der Rohe) worked in his father's business and designed stucco ornament for local architects, until he moved to Berlin to the office of Bruno Paul, an interior designer and furniture maker, where he learnt to work in wood and to design furniture. He came to the notice of the world in 1929 when his Germany pavilion for the International Exposition, Barcelona was acclaimed. The pavilion was destroyed when the exhibition closed, but he used the same principles for his Tugendhat House in Brno, Czechoslovakia (1930), again unfortunately now destroyed. Already Mies's approach to architecture, expressed by himself as 'less is more', was clearly evident in its planning and detailing. The site was a superb one – a slope overlooking the town. Mies planned the accommodation in a wonderfully open way on two levels, in a manner which would have been modern thirty years later. The entrance was at first-floor level, where the spacious bedrooms with furniture designed by Mies were fairly conventional and faced out on to generous terraces. A wide staircase enclosed within an opaque glass screen lead downstairs. The lower level was entirely free, the floor structure above being carried on slender chrome-plated columns. Mies used free-standing partitions to mark off the various living areas: eating, resting, entertaining, and so on. A wall faced with onyx appearing as a single sheet marked off the sitting area, a semicircle of ebony the dining space. Door handles and curtain tracks, as well as the furniture, were designed by the architect, and composed as part of the architecture.

Mies continued to design houses, expanding his architectural philosophy, until he left his post as head of the Bauhaus which had moved from Weimar to Dessau, and from Germany itself in 1937 because of the Nazis. He settled in America and became Director of Architecture at what is now the Illinois Institute of Technology, at that time the Amour Institute. It was good fortune for Mies, and indeed for America, that the development of steel construction was pre-eminent there. Mies was able to refine his ideas on steel structure to

Opposite
HIGH COURT BUILDING, Chandigarh, India. 1952–56. Architect: Le Corbusier. The built-up roof structure with its enormous front canopy is similar in concept to the Ronchamp roof. The towering portals contrast with the square pattern of the *brise-soleil*.

Below
GUGGENHEIM MUSEUM, New York. 1946–59. Architect: Frank Lloyd Wright. The cutaway portion reveals the spiralling ramp and galleries, and a circular glass dome above the void.

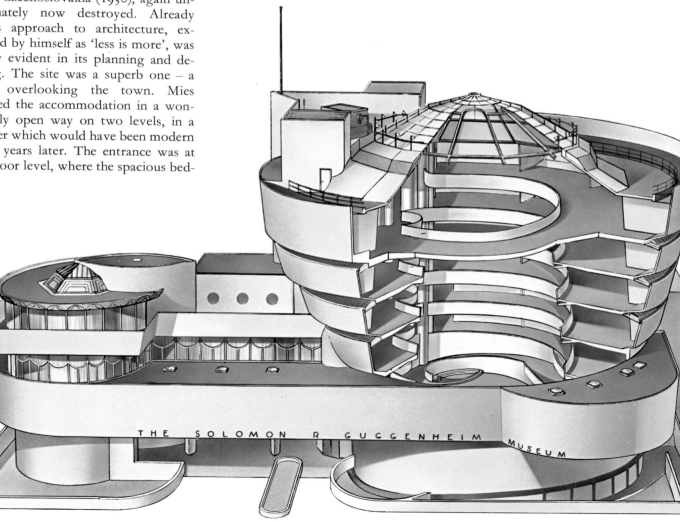

THE SOLOMON R GUGGENHEIM MUSEUM

such an extent that they have been copied since in most countries of the world where steel of the right kind is available. The 'Miesien' style, as it has been called, rationalizes the skeleton steel structure and its curtain-wall glass cladding to the simplest vocabulary. The first examples created a major stir when they appeared. They were the twin rectangular glass-clad twenty-six storey blocks of apartments on Lake Shore Drive, Chicago (1949–51). Raised on steel pilotis, the towers seem to dance together when seen from different points by a moving person. They are completely glazed on all four sides. The core of lifts and services rises in the centre. The Seagram building, New York, (1956–58), by Mies van der Rohe and Philip Johnson (b. 1906) is a block with thirty-seven floors of offices in a similar style to the Lake Shore Drive apartments, but clad in glass and bronze-coloured steel. The ground-floor piazza treatment with careful land-scaping and detailing under the giant pilotis is one of the outstanding features of the scheme.

Architecture in the form of buildings for practical purposes such as hangars, exhibition halls, and stadia, perhaps the logical successor to the functional iron structures of the nineteenth century in type, but not in construction, is to be found in Europe in the work of the Italian engineer Pier Luigi Nervi during this period. Nervi's structures often look complicated but they are in fact ex-

tremely logical. He is the follower, in reinforced-concrete terms, of what Paxton, Telford, and Brunel did a century earlier. Nervi was born in 1891, graduated from the Civil Engineering School of Bologna in 1913, and then worked for two years for the Società per Costruzioni Cementizie, Bologna. He was an officer in the Italian Engineering Corps in World War I, and in 1920 formed his own firm, Nervi e Nebbiosi, in Rome, which changed to Nervi e Bartoli twelve years later. In 1932 he completed the Florence Municipal Stadium begun in 1929, winning a competition with his design. The great grandstand was protected by a shell concrete canopy supported on curved, cantilevered, reinforced-concrete beams, integrated with the raking structural supports of the tiered seating. Nervi used precast-concrete lattice girders for the huge spans of his Italian Air Force hangars (1937–43). For the Turin Exhibition Hall (1948–49), he used his own brand of reinforced concrete – *ferro cimento* – which consisted of layers of fine steel mesh sprayed with a thin coating of cement mortar. For greater loads, he placed reinforcing rods between the layers of mesh and mortar, resulting in a very tough, flexible material of light section and great strength. It made the precasting of units much more precise. Nervi improved precasting too by making moulds of plaster instead of a more rigid, conven-

Opposite
COVENTRY CATHEDRAL, England. 1951–62. Architect: Sir Basil Spence. Nave.

Below
COVENTRY CATHEDRAL. Plan:
  1 old cathedral ruin,
  2 porch,
  3 great glass screen with doors,
  4 Chapel of Unity,
  5 baptistry,
  6 nave,
  7 chancel,
  8 Lady Chapel,
  9 Chapel of Christ in Gethsemane,
 10 Chapel of Christ the Servant,
 11 refectory.

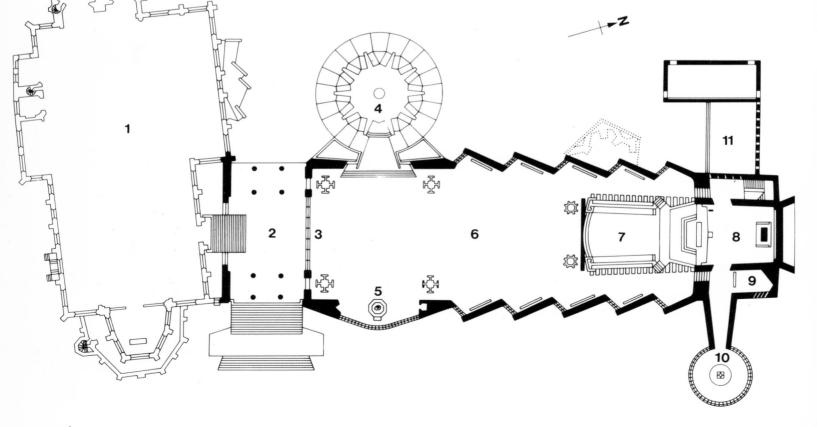

tional material like wood. In this way, he was able to prefabricate and cast his special shapes and the curves he used in his designs. Nervi, 87, died in 1979.

Because of its pleasing appearance and structural simplicity, the Palazzetto dello Sport, Rome, designed with the architect Annibale Vitellozzi, has been much admired. The Palazzetto is one of three buildings designed for the 1960 Olympic Games. In the other two, the larger Palazzo dello Sport, and the Stadio Flaminio, Nervi worked respectively with the architect Marcello Piacentini and his son Antonio. The palazzetto's dome is a graceful network of diamond-shaped ribs and straight ribs in reinforced concrete, rising to meet a compression ring, surmounted by a roof light. The edges of the flat dome are triangulated before the outward thrust is received by Y shaped struts set at an angle and carried round the entire circular building. Vertical walls of glass ring the building below the overhanging edges of the dome. Inside, tiers of seats for 5000 surround the central arena. The elegance of the Palazzetto dello Sport is reminiscent of the elegant bridges by the Swiss engineer, Robert Maillart (1872–1940), thirty years earlier, for example the Salginatobel Bridge, Switzerland

(1929–30) or the work in Mexico of Nervi's younger contemporary, the Spanish-born Felix Candela (b. 1910). Nervi tended to work intuitively, using a basic approach to structure and not relying on structural calculations for the design work. He used these later to check stability and to decide thicknesses of structural members and so on.

An American architect, Buckminster Fuller, born in 1895, developed a method of covering large areas of space without supports. His work was quite different from Nervi's. Fuller developed his Geodesic principles for domes, using three-dimensional, triangular-shaped units which he built up piece by piece to form an enclosing ball-shaped structure. A Fuller dome was used as the U.S.A. Pavilion at Expo '67 in Montreal, Canada, and a remarkable dome using Fuller principles was created as a Concert Hall for 1800 people in Hawaii (1957). The skeleton and covering skin were put together in panels of aluminium with cross-bracing struts. It was erected in twenty hours by its designers, the Kaiser Aluminium and Chemical Corp.

Parallel with the work of the second generation of modern architects, were many buildings of merit by their contemporaries, whose work in the fifties

and sixties was traditional rather than modern, or was modern without being conspicuously so. The Cathedral of St Michael, Coventry (1951–62) by Sir Basil Spence makes no pretence of following the concepts of the Modern movement in reinforced concrete. It has something of a mediaeval character. Spence worked in Sir Edwin Lutyens' office, and like Lutyens was an individualist. Spence's cathedral has unusual features and a romantic history, both worth the telling.

In 1940, Coventry's old Gothic cathedral was bombed with incendiaries by the German Air Force and burnt to the ground. An international competition was held and Spence won it. He preserved the whole of the old cathedral ruins by turning it into a garden of remembrance, placing his new cathedral at right angles to it. Thus, the altar of the new church faces north instead of the usual east. The exterior of the cathedral is unadorned Hollington stone, a pinkish-grey colour, similar to the stone of the old cathedral. Between the entrance to the new cathedral and the ruins is a right of way down one long side of the ruins, leading to the city centre. Passers-by can see the vast screen between vestibule and nave, if not the

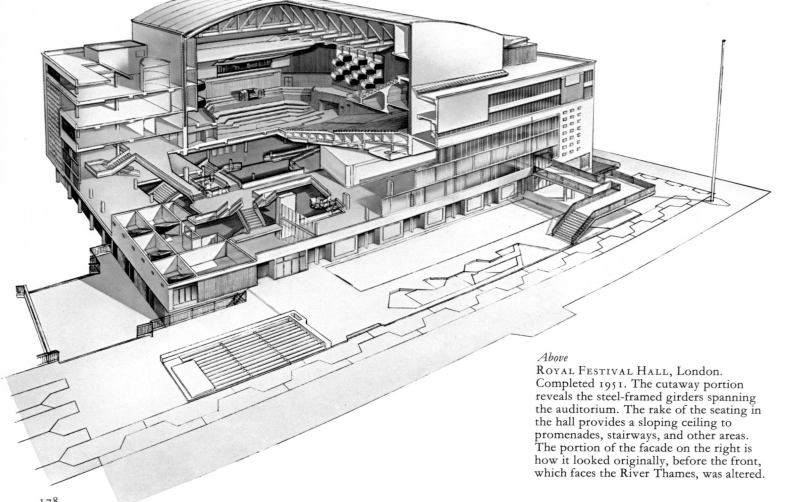

Above
ROYAL FESTIVAL HALL, London. Completed 1951. The cutaway portion reveals the steel-framed girders spanning the auditorium. The rake of the seating in the hall provides a sloping ceiling to promenades, stairways, and other areas. The portion of the facade on the right is how it looked originally, before the front, which faces the River Thames, was altered.

high altar backed by the huge tapestry showing a figure of Christ the King, seated in glory, by the English artist Graham Sutherland.

The adornment of the cathedral is remarkable for the numbers of the eminent English artists whom the architect chose to help with the work. The great glass screen, 21 metres high, with figures of saints and angels in rows, was engraved by John Hutton. The great tapestry was executed in Bayeux, France, to Sutherland's design. Stained glass for the great baptistry window was designed by John Piper and executed by Patrick Reyntiens, and Sir Jacob Epstein sculpted the figures of St Michael and the Devil near the entrance to the cathedral on the east

Below
METROPOLITAN CATHEDRAL OF CHRIST THE KING, Liverpool. 1960–67. Architect: Sir Frederick Gibberd. The cathedral has a circular plan with the high altar in the centre. Above the altar rises the huge reinforced-concrete ribbed lantern. Round the base of the lantern is a reinforced-concrete compression ring. From the ring, huge reinforced-concrete struts descend to the ground in support of the lantern and tent-shaped roof.

side. As the high altar is approached, five sets of nave-high windows, arranged in echelon so that their light shines towards the altar, reveal themselves in pairs. By night, when the tapestry is floodlit it is visible to passers-by along the right of way as they cross the entrance of the cathedral's vestibule.

Beyond the tapestry is the Lady Chapel, and there are two smaller, independent chapels. The Chapel of Christ the Servant for the use of local industries follows the tradition of the earlier Guild Chapels. It projects in an easterly direction from the Lady Chapel, is circular in plan, with walls of stained glass between green slate fins extending from floor to ceiling. The outside appearance is like a huge cylindrical cog-

Below
PALAZZETTO DELLO SPORT, Rome. 1956–57. Architect: Pier Luigi Nervi. The Palazzetto was the smaller hall for the 1960 Olympic Games in Rome. The cutaway portion reveals the inside seating and arena, also the precast elements of the dome relaying their thrust down to the Y-shaped supports carried round the circular building. The construction is in reinforced-concrete.

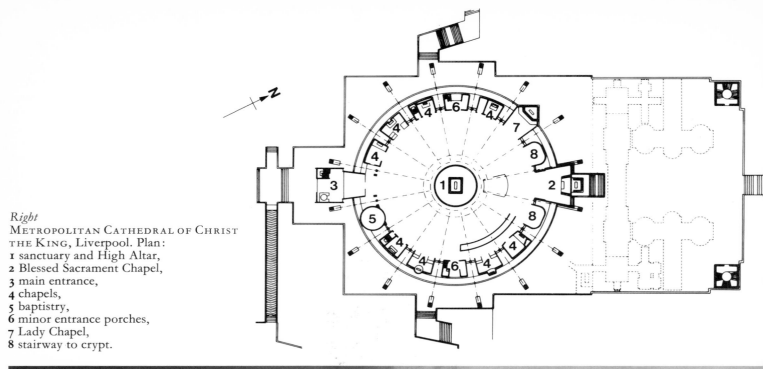

Right
METROPOLITAN CATHEDRAL OF CHRIST
THE KING, Liverpool. Plan:
1 sanctuary and High Altar,
2 Blessed Sacrament Chapel,
3 main entrance,
4 chapels,
5 baptistry,
6 minor entrance porches,
7 Lady Chapel,
8 stairway to crypt.

wheel placed on end. The Chapel of Unity projects westwards opposite the great glass screen and may be used by any denomination or by any religion – Hindu, Muslim and so on – a remarkable, if not unique, act of faith. It is circular and larger than the Chapel of Christ the Servant, built in reinforced concrete and faced in green slate.

In the year Coventry Cathedral was begun, the Festival of Britain exhibition opened on London's South Bank to mark the centenary of the Great Exhibition of 1851. The coordinating architect was Hugh Casson, knighted after the event. The pavilions and other structures showed the extent modern architecture had progressed in Britain. One of the permanent buildings completed for the occasion was the Royal Festival Hall, the great post-war concert hall by architects of the Greater London Council, at that time Robert Matthew, Leslie Martin (both knighted later), Edwin Williams and Peter Moro. In the original conception, the auditorium seating 3000 people was to be slung in a glass box, so that its oval shape might be apparent from outside the building. In execution, the box needed more solid areas for efficient sound absorption, as the railway passed nearby. Nonetheless, by suspending the auditorium in its structural frame, splendid vistas through several levels were obtained, particularly under the rake of the auditorium's floor, and from the stairways and promenades. In contrast with the transparent lightness and flowing space surrounding it, the auditorium is enclosed, rich in walnut, teak and leather, in red and black colours. White boxes thrust their way outwards towards the stage in striking fashion. The design started a new chapter in theatre decor at the time. The structural supports are reinforced concrete pillars, faced with white stucco marble arranged in a grid pattern at each floor level.

Since the Royal Festival Hall was completed, other buildings have been added to the complex. The Queen Elizabeth Hall and Purcell Rooms were completed in 1967, the arts centre, the Hayward Gallery, in 1968. The new buildings have mainly windowless walls finished in shutter-marked concrete, very different from the smooth stone and glass elegance of the Festival Hall to which they are connected by stairways, terraces, and walkways. The system of pedestrian ways is continued under Waterloo Bridge, downstream to Sir Denys Lasdun's National Theatre opened in 1976, a resolutely modern

reinforced-concrete building with strong vertical and horizontal elements.

In most countries, the fifties and sixties produced widespread variations in the International style, sometimes influenced by local traditions in architecture or adapted to suit what building materials were available. In Paris, the UNESCO Headquarters (1958) by Pier Luigi Nervi, Marcel Breuer, and B. Zehrfuss was built in reinforced concrete and glass in the shape of a huge 'Y', raised on pilotis. In Milan, Italy, one of the better office blocks in Europe, the Pirelli building (1957–60) by Nervi, Gio Ponti, and Alberto Rosceli owes its slim lines to the plan shaped like an aerofoil for structural reasons. The reinforced-concrete building of Yale University's Department of Art and Architecture, Connecticut, U.S.A. (1961–63), designed by Paul Rudolph (b. 1918), possesses an unmistakable individuality, but is based on the work of masters such as Le Corbusier. Individuality of a different kind is displayed by Juan O'Gorman. He decorated one whole wall of the tower block of his Central Library, University City, Mexico (1951–53) with designs from Pre-Columbian Mexican art carried out in brilliantly coloured mosaics. In the U.S. Chancery building, Grosvenor Square, London (1956–60), Eero Saarinen used precast artificial stone elements for the windows, related to the neo-Georgian windows of the buildings in the square.

The Metropolitan Cathedral of Christ the King, Liverpool (1960–67) is an unusual-looking modern building. Sir Frederick Gibberd's design was the winning entry of 290 in the competition for the cathedral in 1959–60. The building is circular in plan with the high altar in the centre, fulfilling the Archbishop's requirement that the congregation should be as close to it as possible for the celebration of High Mass. The circular nave is ringed with smaller chapels. A concrete-ribbed lantern above the high altar rises dramatically from the round tent-like sloping roof over the nave. The cathedral is built above the crypt of Sir Edwin Lutyens' earlier cathedral, which was interrupted by World War II and never completed.

Alvar Aalto who had turned away from the International style towards his own innovative work in Finland after World War II, used brickwork and timber to great effect, particularly in his village hall, Säynätsalo (1950–51). Louis Kahn (1901–74), Professor of Architecture at Yale University, U.S.A. (1948–

Right
BRAZILIA CATHEDRAL. *c.* 1960.
Architect: Oscar Niemeyer.

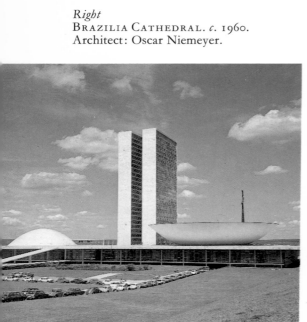

Above
NATIONAL CONGRESS BUILDING,
Brazilia. 1960. Architect: Oscar Niemeyer.

Right
SYDNEY OPERA HOUSE. 1956–73.
Architect: Jørn Utzon. The building has
two concert halls placed side by side, each
with three soaring shells. One hall has
been cut away to show the seating and the
thickness of the reinforced concrete. The
open gable ends of the shell roofs are
fitted with glazing. The superstructure
rests on a platform, below which are
rehearsal rooms, restaurants, and three
smaller halls.

Right
UNITED STATES PAVILION, Expo '67,
Montreal. Architect: R. Buckminster
Fuller.

Below
BRAZILIA CATHEDRAL. *c.* 1960.
Architect: Oscar Niemeyer.

Above
SYDNEY OPERA HOUSE, 1956–73.
Architect: Jørn Utzon.

Opposite
SNYDERMAN HOUSE, Fort Wayne,
Indiana. 1972. East facade.

57), was internationally famous like Aalto. Kahn's use of service towers in clusters with laboratories between in his medical research building, University of Pennsylvania, Philadelphia (1958–60) was new at the time. Hans Scharoun (1893–1972), a little older than Aalto and Kahn, was another innovator whose curiously shaped buildings developed from the plan shapes he pursued with relentless logic. His Philharmonia Concert Hall, Berlin (1956–63) is an outstanding example of his buildings.

Oscar Niemeyer's work after World War II had not changed in character. He was still the superb artist working in smooth reinforced-concrete structures, joyous in form and liberal in glass. During the late sixties he became chief architect for the new capital of Brazil, which began to take shape after Lucio Costa had produced his overall plan for the city in 1967. Brazilia, as the new city was called, was the most ambitious city of the twentieth century to date. More than sixty architects were working for Niemeyer on the designs of the more important buildings for the federal government, the cathedral, a

general hospital, blocks of apartments, schools, theatres, and so on. The presidential Palace of the Dawn was completed earlier. The legislative or congress centre are in front of the city. A senate building shaped like a half sphere, and an assembly building shaped like an inverted sphere lie at the corners of a triangle with a twenty-eight-storey twin-tower block at the apex. The twin towers are joined in the middle with galleries at the eleventh, twelfth, and thirteenth floors. The assembly and senate buildings appear to rest on a platform three storeys high. A reflecting pool surrounds the base of the tower. Niemeyer's imaginative forms are again evident in Brazilia in the undulating curves of the presidential palace, and in the cathedral's graceful structure curving outwards into points at the top, like fingers of supplicating hands.

One of the most remarkable buildings of this period is the Sydney Opera House (1957–73), on a site at Bennelong Point jutting out into Sydney Harbour, Australia. The building has two main concert halls placed side by side, and three smaller halls with dressing rooms, rehearsal rooms, restaurants, bars, kitchens, and so on placed in the base platform on which the superstructure rests. Spread out above the building are great prestressed concrete shells, like the sails of a ship; the openings between the shells are filled with walls of laminated glass in steel and manganese bronze frames. Flatter shell roofs had been used by Eero Saarinen in the flowing lines of his T.W.A. terminal at Kennedy Airport, New York (1956–62). Nothing like Jørn Utzon's imaginative design had been seen before. Utzon, a relatively unknown Danish architect,

won the competition for the Opera House in 1957. It was not only the unusual roof shape which gained acclaim, but Utzon's plan was an ingenious solution to the problems set. However, there were difficulties during the building operations which lasted a long time, while costs spiralled. Utzon resigned in 1966, after the shells and glass walls were completed, and the Australian architects Hall, Todd and Littlemore took over to complete the interior. In 1978 Utzon was honoured for his opera house building, and for his housing work in Denmark, by being awarded

the British Royal Gold Medal for Architecture for that year.

The engineers for the Sydney Opera House, the Ove Arup Partnership, were engineers also for the structure of the Pompidou Centre, Paris, by architects Renzo Piano and Richard Rogers. Certainly, the Pompidou Centre is the most remarkable and most talked-about post World War II building. In 1969, President Pompidou of France had decided there was a need for a major cultural centre in Paris. An international competition was held in 1970–71 for a complex on the site chosen, an area between the

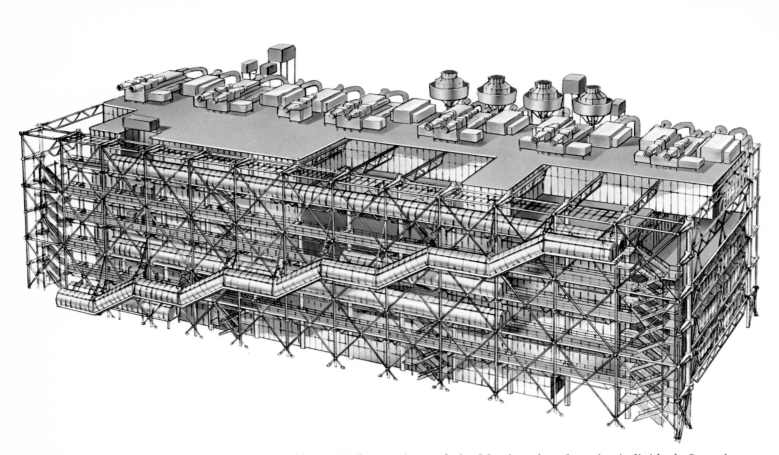

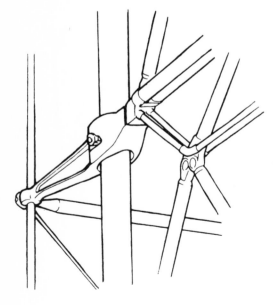

old Les Halles market and the Marais trict near the Ile de la Cité. The design, chosen from 681 entries in the competition, has resulted in a building which is in itself a monument. Half the required accommodation is below the building and under the piazza on the west side, and half above ground. There are five storeys of clear floor space above ground, achieved by placing all the 'guts' of a normal building – structural frame, service pipes, wires, and stairways – on the outside. All the services – water, electricity, and air conditioning – are confined in a space on the east facade, hence the different coloured pipes and giant tubes on that side. On the opposite side, facing the piazza, is the steel and glass covered way with a travelator taking people from the bottom to the top of the building. Floors are supported on exposed steel lattice girders, minutely suspended from the structural frame of solid and hollow steel members, which make up the multiplicity of steel framework seen on the outside of the building. On the inside of the framework the building is clothed in glass. Inside the building, the clear floor spaces, required in the brief for the design, accommodate the Museum of Modern Art, part of the French National Library, exhibitions and many other cultural activities. In the space underground are bus and private car arrival stations and parking, shops, cafés, a cinema, exhibition areas, and so on.

What is at first sight remarkable about this building is its enormous size, dwarfing the individual. It makes an astonishing backcloth to the self-generating activities which have gathered in the piazza – flower stalls, circus shows, entertainers, and all the colour of Paris. The travelators up the side of the building provide an expanding view of Paris. On a clear day all the landmarks stand out, notably the Sacré-Cœur on the hill of Montmartre in miniature. Even the prosaic seventeenth/nineteenth century properties on the other side of the piazza, spic and span in new paint, look refreshing, perhaps in contrast to this incredible building. It says a great deal for the Pompidou Centre that six million people visited it in the first year it opened, just to enjoy themselves apparently. 'Is it architecture?' is a question often asked. It is an extreme expression of megastructure; certainly a great architectural experience. There may be nothing quite like it again. Less demonstratively mechanistic architecture may stem from it. In the post-modern period, there are already examples of what have been called 'High Tec' buildings, in which factory-produced parts, mainly in metal and glass, wires and tubes, predominate. The Pompidou Centre belongs to the mode. There are others completed in America, and the new Sainsbury Art Building, by Foster Associates, completed in 1978, at the University of East Anglia in Britain also belongs. In the future, history may repeat itself in some form or forms of architectural revival, but eventually, a new dawn will break for architecture.

Glossary

Abacus. The top portion of a capital.

Abutment. Masonry which resists the thrust of an arch or vault.

Acanthus. Plant with leaves used in the ornamentation of the Corinthian capital.

Acropolis. The citadel of a Greek city, usually on a hill.

Agora. The central public space of a Greek city.

Aisle. Space parallel with the nave, usually separated from it by columns. Transepts and chancel sometimes have aisles.

A lancettes. Term used to describe Early Gothic (12th century) in France, also called 'Primaire'.

Ambulatory. Space forming an aisle or processional way round the east end of a church, or round the central space of a circular church.

Apadama. The audience hall of the Persian Kings. (Palace of Persepolis)

Arcade. A row of arches on piers or columns.

Architrave. The lowest portion of an entablature in classical architecture.

Arrow loop. Slit in a mediaeval castle wall through which to fire arrows.

Atrium. Courtyard in a Greek or Roman house, or the forecourt of an Early Christian church.

Azulejos. Glazed tiles, brilliantly coloured.

Bailey. Outer fortified area of a mediaeval castle, beyond the keep.

Baldacchino. Canopy supported by columns, usually over an altar.

Balustrade. A horizontal rail supported by miniature pillars, commonly used to top the wall of a Renaissance-style building.

Baroque. A period of Late Renaissance architecture after High Renaissance.

Barrel vault. A continuous semicircular shaped vault, also called a tunnel vault.

Batter. The inward slope of a wall from bottom to top.

Bay. Space between two columns or piers, including the wall and vaulting above, in Romanesque, Gothic or Renaissance buildings, usually churches.

Bema. Space between nave and apse introduced into Early Christian churches, and the forerunner of transepts.

Buttress. Additional masonry added to a wall in order to resist the thrust of a vault or arch (see flying buttress).

Caldarium. The hot room in a Roman Thermae.

Campanile. A free-standing bell tower.

Capital. Terminal part of a column.

Caryatid. A carved female figure used as a pillar.

Cella. Main hall of a classical temple, usually housing a statue of a god.

Cella media. Central hall of a Roman Thermae.

Chac-mool (Mul). An idol used in Toltec-Mayan rights of human sacrifice.

Chaitya Hall. Buddhist hall of worship.

Chancel. Space in a church beyond the nave and crossing, including choir and altar.

Chatras. Succession of umbrella shapes, symbolizing heavens, on a Buddhist stupa mast (*Yasti*).

Chevet. Semicircular east end to a Gothic cathedral, including an ambulatory and apses round the outside perimeter.

Chevron. A zigzag pattern, common in Norman architecture.

Choir. Part of the chancel, but usually placed west of the crossing in Spanish Gothic cathedrals.

Clerestory. The upper window range of a large hall, usually of a church or temple, particularly where the adjacent roofs are below the windows.

Coffering. Sunken panels in ceilings or domes.

Colonnade. Collective term for a row of columns.

Column. A circular pillar used for supporting part of a building, occasionally used as a free standing monument. (Trajan's Column).

Concentric. Walls or defence works in successive rings.

Corbelling. Masonry projected like inverted steps to form a bracket support for an arch or dome.

Corinthian. One of the orders of architecture used by the Greeks and Romans.

Cornice. Top portion of an entablature.

Crenellation. Saw-toothed style parapet wall with solid portions (*merlons*) and gaps (*crenels*) for shooting through.

Crepidoma. Platform of a Greek temple, usually with three steps.

Crossing. The central space of a Greek or Latin cross plan in a church where nave, chancel, and transepts meet.

Crucks. Arched timber beams placed on or near the ground in support of walls and roofs of small timber-framed dwellings.

Curtain wall. Wall of a castle between towers or bastions. In modern steel-framed buildings, the glass and metal cladding.

Dado. Lower part of a wall decorated in a different manner from the remainder.

Dais. A raised platform at the end of a hall, particularly in the mediaeval hall.

Dome. A spherically shaped roof.

Domed groin vault. Groin vault with the vault raised at the groins to form a small dome.

Doric. One of the orders of architecture used by the Greeks and Romans.

Dosseret. A deep block of masonry immediately above the capital, used in Byzantine and Islamic architecture.

Echinus. Lower part of the Doric capital, curved in outline and supporting the abacus above it.

Entablature. Solid masonry above the capital of a Classical order, consisting of architrave, frieze, and cornice.

Entasis. The slightly curved outline given to a column or other element of a building.

Ephebeum (pl. Ephebea). A gymnasium in Roman Thermae.

Exedra. A semicircular or rectangular recess sometimes containing a seat or bench.

Fan vault. Vault with ribs spread out like those of a fan, but in a curve.

Fascia. The vertical face of a portion of the architrave in a Classical order, or a board placed vertically against rafter or joint ends at eaves level.

Finial. The spire-like end of a pinnacle or vertical feature.

Flamboyant. Gothic curved tracery. Also a term applied to French Gothic using curved tracery *c.* fourteenth to *c.* mid-sixteenth centuries.

Fluting. Vertical channels of a column.

Flying buttress. A built-out section of masonry with one or more half arches taken across to the main structure to support upper walls or to take the thrust from arches or vaults. A principal feature of the Gothic style.

Forum. Public open space in a Roman town centre.

Fresco. Painting made on a wall when the plaster is wet. Often used as a general term for wall paintings not done in oils.

Frieze. The middle portion of a classical entablature.

Frigidarium. Cold pool of a Roman Thermae.

Fusuma. Opaque paper-covered interior screens of the Japanese Shoin house.

Garbha-griha. Small shrine of a Hindu temple usually below the great tower – the Sikhara.

Georgian. Term used for late Renaissance architecture in England, particularly houses, *c.* early eighteenth to *c.* mid-nineteenth centuries.

Glacis. A battered stone wall of great strength and thickness at the base of a fortification such as a Mediaeval castle.

Gojunoto. Term for a Japanese pagoda.

Gopuram. A huge gateway tower of the developed Hindu temple.

Gothic. The style developed in Europe between the twelfth and sixteenth centuries from the use of the pointed arch and flying buttress.

Groin vault. Vault formed by two barrel vaults of equal spans meeting at right angles. The groins were formed by the intersections.

Guttae. Small cone-shaped projections under the triglyphs and mutules of the Doric entablature.

Hall church. Church with nave and aisles forming a single large space of about the same height throughout.

Hammer beam roof. Roof with a special form of tied vertical beam.

Hypostile. Term applied to an ancient hall with the roof supported on columns throughout the hall. (Egyptian temple for example.)

Impluvium. Tank sunk in the atrium of Greek and Roman houses to catch rainwater from adjoining roofs.

International style. Name given to the modern movement in architecture in 1932.

Ionic order. An order of architecture used by the Greeks and Romans.

Jamb. The sides of a door frame.

Joists. Horizontal timber beams used for floors and ceilings.

Kalasa. Topmost feature of a Hindu Sikhara.

Keep. Inner citadel of a Mediaeval castle.

Kondo. Hall containing Buddha relics in a Buddhist temple.

Lantern. Turret with windows, surmounting a dome; or a small tower with windows, open from below.

Lierne. Secondary rib of a Gothic vault.

Lintel. Horizontal beam spanning an opening between two supports.

Machiolation. A device, usually with a projecting wall and floor openings, through which to bombard an enemy below.

Mannerism. The name for characteristic architecture in Italy between High Renaissance and Baroque (*c.* 1530–1600).

Mastaba. Early Egyptian tomb, before the pyramids.

Mausoleum. An imposing tomb. Named after the tomb of King Mausolus.

Megaron. The great hall of an Aegean palace or citadel.

Merlon. See Crenellations.

Metope. The space between triglyphs in the Doric order frieze.

Mihrab. Niche in the wall of a mosque, forming the place for the leader of prayers.

Minaret. A slim tower, part of a mosque, from which the *muezzin* called people to pray.

Minbar. A raised dais, sometimes canopied, in a mosque.

Moat. A deep, wide ditch usually filled with water, as defence around town or castle.

Mosque. Muslim meeting place for prayer and assembly.

Mullion. The vertical element dividing a window opening. A number might be used in a wide opening.

Muquarnas. Arabic term for 'stalactite' vaulting by continuous corbelling with the underside elaborately carved: also for arches, squinches, pendentives, and other areas similarly treated.

Mutulis. Projecting masonry in the Greek Doric cornice, derived from rafter ends.

Naos. See Cella.

Narthex. Entrance vestibule across the front of an Early Christian church.

Nave. Church from west end to the crossing or chancel. In Early Christian, Mediaeval, and Renaissance churches, the portion between side aisles.

Neoclassical. Academic Greek and Roman style architecture after Renaissance.

Norman. English form of Romanesque.

Ogee arch. A concave-shaped arch turned into a convex shape at the supports.

Opisthodomus. Rear porch of a Greek temple.

Order. Order of architecture comprising column, base, capital, and entablature devised by the Greeks and Romans.

Parabolic vaulting. Reinforced concrete vaulting with stresses distributed evenly in a shell shaped like the section of a cone.

Pediment. Triangular-shaped masonry, originally the gable end of a Greek temple, later used independently.

Pendentive. The triangular-shaped portion of curved masonry above a corner of a square compartment which completes the circular base needed for a dome.

Peristyle. A row of columns taken round a classic temple or courtyard.

Perpendicular. Term used in England for Late Gothic following the English Decorated period.

Piano nobile. Italian term for principal apartment floor of an Italian palace. Sometimes used in English in connection with Palladian mansions.

Pier. Usually square-shaped free-standing masonry supporting an arch (as opposed to a column supporting an arch).

Pilaster. Square-shaped masonry, like a flat, superimposed column, projecting from the wall and decorated with an order.

Pilotis. Any pillar, post or stanchion raising a building off the ground, leaving the ground floor open.

Pinnacle. A small turret-shaped element used at the top of buttresses, parapet walls, or other projections, sometimes elaborately carved.

Podium. A masonry platform used as a base for a building. In modern architecture often enclosing space for additional accommodation.

Portcullis. Heavy grating, sliding in grooves, and raised or lowered by chains used for defence in gateways, particularly those of mediaeval castles.

Portico. A roofed vestibule with columns on at least one side.

Postern. Small door with zigzag approach used for defence.

Pronaos. Part of a Greek temple in front of the naos, often the same as the portico.

Propylaeum (pl. Propylaea). A monumental entrance way, usually to a sacred enclosure, particularly in classical times.

Purlin. Beams running horizontally at right angles to give support to common rafters.

Pylon. Ancient Egyptian monumental gateway with sloping walled towers, one each side of the entrance way.

Quadripartite vaulting. Vaulting comprising four curved triangular-shaped sections (severies) to the web of each bay.

Quatrefoil. Literally four leaves. A traceried opening in the shape of four rounded leaves.

Rampart. An earthen bank used for defence.

Rayonnant. Term used for French Gothic, second period (*c.* thirteenth century), when circular windows with 'wheel' tracery were favoured.

Refectory. The dining hall of a monastery.

Renaissance. The style reintroducing Classical architecture.

Ridge rib. Non-structural rib between the apexes of rib vaults.

Rococo. Term applied to Late Renaissance detail with persistently rounded forms having no structural basis.

Romanesque. Style in western Europe from *c.* ninth to *c.* twelfth centuries.

Rotunda. A circular-shaped building.

Rubble. Rough stone used for basic walling and infilling.

Rustication. Stonework with recessed joints and roughened surfacing, popular in Renaissance building.

Sanctuary. The holiest place in church or temple.

Säteri roof. Swedish hipped roof with a narrow vertical section just above the middle, sometimes with windows in it.

Severy (pl. Severies). Portion of a vault between ribs making up part of the total shell.

Sexpartite vault. A vault with six severies.

Shinden. Principal building of a mansion in Japanese Heian period. (*Shinden style* was the manner of layout and buildings, including the Shinden.)

Shoji. Translucent paper-covered outer sliding partition to a Japanese house.

Sikhara. Conical tower-like structure of a Hindu temple, erected over the shrines.

Solar. An upper floor apartment in a Mediaeval secular building.

Squinch. An arch built across a corner, used in Mediaeval architecture, to help form the base for a dome above a square or octagonal compartment.

Stoa. A covered space with colonnade, for public use in a Greek city centre.

Stucco. Fine plaster rendering.

Stupa. Buddhist sacred monument.

Stilting. Raising the springing line of an arch by building up the supporting masonry.

Stylobate. The uppermost step of the classical temple's crepidoma on which a colonnade was placed.

Superimposed column or order. An order or column placed against a wall as decoration.

Talud-tablero. Term applied to a treatment of pyramid terraces in Toltec pre-Columbian architecture.

Tatami. Rectangular shaped Japanese rush floor mats. The divisions of the Japanese house were based on its proportions.

Tepidarium. The medium temperature pool of a Roman Thermae.

Thermae. Name for Roman public baths.

Tie beam. Horizontal beam preventing the lower ends of a roof truss from spreading outwards.

Tierceron. Meaning 'third rib'. Additional rib in Gothic vaulting.

Tokonoma. A niche in a Japanese house for exhibiting objects like paintings or flowers.

Torana. Elaborate gateway to a Buddhist Stupa.

Torii. 'Gateway' to a Japenese Shinto shrine.

Tou-kung. Bracket system used in the Chinese roof structure.

Tracery. Elements of the stonework structure holding the glass in Gothic windows.

Transepts. Wings or arms north and south of the crossing of a cruciform-planned church. Hence 'north transept' and 'south transept',

Trefoil. Term applied to Gothic three-leaf tracery.

Triforium. Middle level of a Romanesque or Gothic church between the ground floor arcading and clerestory windows.

Triglyph. Space between metopis of a Greek Doric frieze, decorated with three raised and two sunken vertical strips.

Truss. A wooden framework applied to a roof (roof truss) to support rafters, battens, tiles, or other covering.

Tunnel vault. See Barrel vault.

Tuscan order. Order of architecture added by the Romans.

Tympanum. Triangular space, usually decorated, framed by a Classical pediment.

Undercroft. Chamber below principal rooms of a Mediaeval building.

Volute. Spiral scroll, particularly that of the Ionic capital.

Voussoir. Wedge-shaped pieces of masonry forming an arch.

Yasti. Central mast on a Stupa.

Ziggurat. Stepped pyramid, particularly in Mesopotamia, with a temple on the top.

Bibliography

Fletcher, Sir Banister. *A History of Architecture*. 18th Ed. London, 1975.

Gelder, H. E. van. *Kunstgeschiedents der Nederlan*. Utrecht, 1946.

Hempel, E. *Geschichte der deutschen Bankunt*. Munich, 1949.

Lavedan, P. *L' Architecture Française*. Paris, 1944. London, 1956.

Pevsner, N. *An Outline of European Architecture*. 6th Ed. London, 1960.

Period

Alex, William. *Japanese Architecture*. New York and London, 1963.

Allsop, H. B. *A History of Classical Architecture*. London, 1965.

Anderson, W. J., R. P. Spiers, T. Ashby. *The Architecture of Ancient Rome*. London, 1927.

Basdevant, D. *L' Architecture française*. Paris, 1971.

Blunt, Anthony. *Art and Architecture in France, 1500–1700*. London, 1953.

Boethius, A. and J. B. Ward Perkins. *Etruscan and Roman Architecture*. London, 1970.

Brandon, R. and J. A. *Open Timber Roofs of the Middle Ages.* London, 1849.

Branner, R. *Gothic Architecture.* New York and London, 1961.

Braun, H. *The English Castle.* 3rd Ed. London, 1948.

Braun, H. *Parish Churches.* London, 1970.

Breasted, J. H. *A History of Egypt.* New York, 1905.

Brown, Percy. *Indian Architecture: The Islamic Period.* Bombay, 1942.

Conant, K. J. *Carolingian and Romanesque Architecture 800–1200.* London, 1959.

Cook, G. H. *The English Mediaeval Parish Church.* London, 1954.

Cook, J. Mordaunt. *The Greek Revival.* London, 1972.

Cresswell, K. A. C. *A Short Account of Early Moslem Architecture.* London, 1958.

Dinsmoor, W. B. *The Architecture of Ancient Greece.* 3rd Ed. London, 1950.

Drexler, Arthur. *The Architecture of Japan.* New York, 1955.

Edwards, I. E. S. *The Pyramids of Egypt.* London, 1961.

Frankfurt, H. *The Art and Architecture of the Ancient Orient.* London, 1954.

Frankl, P. *Gothic Architecture.* London, 1962.

Fergusson, J. *The Palaces of Ninevah and Persepolis Restored.* London, 1851.

Gall, E. *Karolingische und Ottonische Kirchen.* Burg, 1930.

Ganay, E. de. *Châteaux de France.* Paris, 1949.

Gerster, G. *Kirchen im Fels.* Stuttgart, 1968. English translation, 1971.

Gropius, Walter. *The New Architecture and the Bauhaus.* London, 1935.

Hitchcock, H. Russell. *Architecture: Nineteenth and Twentieth Centuries.* 3rd Ed. London, 1970.

Hitchcock, H. Russell and P. C. Johnson. *The International Style.* New York, 1932.

Hoag, John D. *Western Islamic Architecture.* New York and London, 1963.

Hubert, J. *L'Architecture religieuse du haut moyen-âge en France.* Paris, 1952.

Hubsch, H. *Monuments de l'architecture chrétienne depuis Constantin jusqu à Charlemagne.* Paris, 1866.

Krautheimer, R. *Early Christian and Byzantine Architecture.* London, 1965.

Kubler, George. *The Art and Architecture of Ancient America.* London, 1962.

Kubler, G. and M. Soria. *Art and Architecture in Spain and Portugal and their American Dominions 1500–1800.* London, 1959.

Kuhnel, Ernst. *Islamic Art and Architecture.* London, 1966.

Lavedan, P. *French Architecture.* London, 1956.

Lawrence, A. W. *Greek Architecture.* 2nd Ed. London, 1967.

Lowry, B. *Renaissance Architecture.* New York and London, 1962.

Martin, R. *Living Architecture: Greek.* London, 1967.

Masuda, T. *Living Architecture: Japan.* London, 1971.

Millon, H. A. *Baroque and Rococo Architecture.* New York and London, 1961.

Picard, G. *Living Architecture: Roman.* Fribourg, 1965.

Pierson, W. H. *American Buildings and their Architects.* Vols. 1 and 2. New York, 1970–73.

Piralozzi- T' Serstevens, M. *Living Architecture: Chinese.* Fribourg and London, 1972.

Richards, J. M. *Guide to Finnish Architecture.* London, 1966.

Rickman, T. *Gothic Architecture.* Oxford and London, 1881.

Robertson, Donald. *Pre-Columbian Architecture.* New York and London, 1963.

Scanton, R. L. *Greek Architecture.* London, 1968.

Smith, E., O. Cook and G. Hutton. *The English Parish Church.* London, 1976.

Stackpole, John. *Colonial Architecture* (in New Zealand). Wellington, Sydney and London, 1976.

Stewart, Cecil. *Early Christian, Byzantine and Romanesque Architecture.* London, 1954.

Viollet-Le-Duc, E. *Dictionnaire raisonné de l'architecture française du XI au XVI Siècles.*

Wheeler, R. E. M. *Roman Art and Architecture.* London, 1964.

Whinney, M. *Renaissance Architecture in England.* London, 1952.

White, J. *Art and Architecture in Italy, 1250–1400.* London, 1966.

Wittkower, R. *Art and Architecture in Italy, 1600–1750.* London, 1958.

Wu, Nelson I. *Chinese and Indian Architecture.* New York and London, 1963.

Acknowledgements

The publishers would like to thank all those organisations and individuals who have provided illustrations for this volume:

p.7: Charles Fowkes; p. 9: Michael Holford; p.11: Spectrum Library, London; p.14: Hirmer Photoarchiv, Munich; 15 *top*: Peter Fraenkel; p. 15 *bottom*: John Bethell Photography (Bernard Cox), St Albans; p. 20: Edwin Smith; p.21: Bildarchiv Foto Marburg; p.22: Tony Stone Associates, London; p.23: Picturepoint Ltd., London; p.27: Zefa; p.28: A. F. Kersting; p.29: Scala, Florence*; p.30: Edwin Smith; p.33: Scala*; p.34: Zefa; p.37: Bildarchiv Foto Marburg; p.38 *top*: John Bethell Photography (Bernard Cox); p.38 *bottom*: Sonia Halliday, London; p.39: Boudot-Lamotte; p.40: Bildarchiv Foto Marburg; p.41: Angelo Hornak Photograph Library, London; p.43: Scala*; p.44: Edwin Smith; p.45: Josephine Powell, Rome; p.47: Zefa; p.49: A. F. Kersting; p.50 *top*: Zefa; p.50 *bottom*: Ronald Sheridan; p.51: John Bethell Photography (Bernard Cox); p.52: Spectrum Colour Library; p.53: Picturepoint Ltd.; p.55: Angelo Hornak; p.57: Wim Swaan, New York; p.58: Wim Swaan; p.59 *top*: Zefa; p.59 *bottom*: John Bethell Photography (Bernard Cox); p.60: John Bethell Photography (Bernard Cox); p.61: J. Allan Cash, London; p.63: Ronald Sheridan; p.64: Tony Stone; p.67 *top*: Douglas Dickins, London; p.67 *bottom*: Douglas Dickins; p.68*; p.69: A. F. Kersting; p.70: Tony Stone Associates; p.72: J. Allen Cash Ltd.; p.75 *top*: Robert Harding Associates, London; p.75 *bottom*: J. Allan Cash; p.76: Sonia Halliday; p.77: Zefa; p.79: Douglas Dickins; p.80: Kokusai Bunka Shinkokai (Society for Cultural Relations), Tokyo; p.81 *top*: M. Sakamoto, Photo Research Laboratory, Tokyo; p.81 *bottom*: Ezra Stoller Associates, Mamaroneck, N.Y.; p.84: Ezra Stoller Associates; p.86: Bildarchiv Foto Marburg; p.87: A. F. Kersting; p.88: A. F. Kersting; p.89 *left*: Jean Roubier; p.89 *right*: Bildarchiv Foto Marburg; p.91 *left*: Salmer; p.91 *right*: Jean Roubier; p.92: John Bethell Photography (Bernard Cox); p.94: Angelo Hornak; p.96: Airviews Ltd., Manchester Airport; p.97: National Trust, London; p.98: Sonia Halliday; p.103: A. F. Kersting; p.104 *left*; p.104 *right*: Jean Roubier; p.105: Michael Holford; p.107 *left*: Erlande Hirmer Foto Archiv, Munich; p.10 *centre*: Jean Roubier; p.107 *bottom*: A. F. Kersting; p.108 *top*: Werner Forman Archive,

London; p.108 *bottom*: Elek (Wim Swaan); p.109: Elek (Wim Swaan); p.112 *left*: Elek (Wim Swaan); p.112 *right*: Camera Press (Wim Swaan), London; p.113 *top*: Camera Press (Wim Swaan); p.113 *bottom*: Bildarchiv Foto Marburg; p.114: John Bethell; p.116: A. F. Kersting; p.117: Michael Holford; p.118: Michael Holford; p.120: A. F. Kersting; p.121: Angelo Hornak; p.123: Angelo Hornak; p.124: Bildarchiv Foto Marburg; p. 125: Bildarchiv Foto Marburg; p.128: Roger-Viollet, Paris; p.129: A. F. Kersting; p.130: Picturepoint; p.132: Bildarchiv Foto Marburg; p. 133: Scala; p.136: Bildarchiv Foto Marburg; p. 137: A. F. Kersting; p.138: Scala; p.139: Tony Stone Associates; p.140: Hirmer Photoarchiv; p.141: Bildarchiv Preussiches Kulturbesitz, Berlin; p.142: John Bethell; p.143: Zefa; p.144: John Bethell; p.145: A. F. Kersting; p.146: Picturepoint; p.147: Foto Archiv Salmer, Barcelona; p.148: John Bethell; p.149 *top*: British Rail, London; p.149 *bottom*: Camera Press (Wim Swaan); p.152: James Austin; p.153: Jean Roubier*; p.154: Tony Stone; p.155: Angelo Hornak; p.156: J. Allan Cash; p.157: Australian Information Services*, London; p.158: Picturepoint; p.159 *top*: Wayne Andrews; p.159 *bottom*: Angelo Hornak; p.161: Bildarchiv Foto Marburg; p.162: D & W Archiv, Berlin*; p.163 Royal Netherlands Embassy, London; p.164: Bildarchiv Foto Marburg; p.165: Photo Boudot-Lamotte; p.167: Keystone Press Agency (Erik Barbesgaard) London; p.168: Building Design; p.69: Bildarchiv Foto Marburg; p.171: Sonia Halliday; p.172: Ezra Stoller; p.173: Architectural Press/Editions du Cerf; p.177: Henk Snoek, London; p.180: A. F. Kersting; p.182 *left*: Picturepoint; p.182 *top right*: Camera Press; p.182 *bottom right*: Picturepoint; p. 183: Robert Harding; p.184: Camera Press; p.185: Michael Graves, New Jersey.
*Photographs of these illustrations are held in the Hamlyn Group Picture Library, Feltham.
Special thanks to Angela Murphy for researching and collecting all of the illustrations. The Publishers would also like to thank all those people who provided reference material for the illustrations, particularly: Dr. Rowland Mainstone for reference prints of Florence Cathedral; the Ancient Monuments Branch for drawings of the Tower of London; Frederick Gibberd and Partners for drawings of the Metropolitan Cathedral of Christ the King, Liverpool; and the staff of the Royal Institute of British Architects (R.I.B.A.) Library and London Library.

Ordinary numbers refer to pages, italic numbers to illustrations.